Reference Material

RESOURCE GUIDE TO
CURRENT SOCIAL ISSUES

This Special Edition of
RESOURCE GUIDE TO CURRENT SOCIAL ISSUES
is dedicated
IN HIS NAME
To Ruby, Janet, Martha, and Frances—my family;
To my parents who have kept religion and the simple ways
of life foremost in their lives;
To my country which continues to lead the world in its stand
for freedom and to provide the strongest hope for se
curing world peace;
To my church, keeper of the light of the world; and
To the Reverend Mack M. Goss, my pastor, and J. Seldon
Osteen, my Sunday school teacher, who together in
spired my financial contribution to help distribute this
book to those engaged in relating the Gospel to the
pressing issues of our day.

FRANK E. STRIDER

Dedicated to

FOY D. VALENTINE

and

JIMMY R. ALLEN

who guided me in my early understanding
of the why and how of
social concern.

PREFACE

This book grew out of a desire to meet definite needs: (1) All persons need information on current issues. (2) Persons involved in dealing with controversial issues need sources to provide insight into the issues. (3) Speakers, writers, teachers, and preachers need a popular-priced book to guide them quickly to excellent, up-to-date resources on current topics. (4) Students need help in researching current issues.

A number of very busy men and organizations gave hours of time in evaluating the manuscript for this book and making valuable suggestions for changes. I am indeed especially deeply indebted to the following specialists on social concerns: The staff of the United States Catholic Conference; Rabbi Solomon Bernards of the Anti-Defamation League of B'nai B'rith; Robert Moon of the General Board of Christian Social Concerns of the Methodist Church; the staff of the National Council of Churches; Jimmy Allen and James Dunn, staff members of the Christian Life Commission of the Baptist General Convention of Texas; Dan McGee, professor of Ethics, Baylor University; C. W. Scudder, professor of Christian Ethics, Southwestern Baptist Seminary; Mrs. Robt. M. Webb, Acting Director, Department of Christian Social Relations, Executive Council, The Episcopal Church; Foy Valentine, Executive-Secretary, Christian Life Commission, Southern Baptist Convention; Huber F. Klemme, Associate Executive Director, Council for Christian Social Action, United Church of Christ; Carl Reuss, Commission on Research and Social Action, American Lutheran Church. Other organizations and persons expressed regret that because of schedule difficulties they could not evaluate the manuscript and I appreciate their interest also. Those who evaluated the manuscript, of course, are not responsible for the material included in the final copy.

Numerous others helped in the undertaking. Among those making suggestions during the planning stage concerning topics and sources were Jimmy Allen, Henlee Barnette, Rabbi Solomon Bernards, Ross Coggins, James Dunn, Bill Dyal, John Howell, T. B. Maston, C. W. Scudder, and James E. Wood, Jr.

Several students in the Graduate School of Southwestern Seminary assisted in research, among them being Gerald Mann, Larry Baker, and Don Hammer. In addition, Don Hammer helped immensely in checking sources and in proofreading. Valerie Wilson, Betty Weisenberger, Mary Dominy, and Mrs. Don Hammer worked efficiently on the project as secretaries. In addition Mrs. Hammer assisted in research, toiled long hours checking details, and typed the final drafts of the manuscript with skill and diligence.

Hundreds of organizations—government, professional, religious, business, labor, civic, educational, and others—cooperated by sending materials for examination and making suggestions of other sources.

The library staff of Southwestern Seminary was gracious in aiding in research on the project. The following made special contributions of time and skill: Wallace Roark, Brooks Wester, and Doug Ezell. Also, Charles Cottle aided in supplying address and ZIP code information.

The staff of the Book Division of Word, Inc. made many helpful suggestions. George Baskin, director of marketing, was patient, encouraging, and creative in all my contacts with him.

A very special word of appreciation is due Foy Valentine. Without his encouragement and the generous assistance of the Christian Life Commission of the Southern Baptist Convention of which he serves as Executive Secretary, the book would have remained only an idea. This man and agency made the book possible.

As always my family was of great strength and help throughout the project. Bobbie supplied the calm home life and wifely warmth to ease jangled nerves; Meredith provided inspiration through a charmingly expanding life; and Allison gave the chuckles and quiet peace which only a baby can supply.

Inclusion of items in this book are in no way endorsements of them by the compiler. The views expressed in recommended material are not necessarily mine. I included items which I felt contributed information or points of view necessary to an adequate understanding of the subject.

Publication plans call for periodic updating and revision of this volume. Please write the author or publisher to make suggestions for additions, deletions, or helpful change, for future editions.

William M. Pinson, Jr.
P. O. Box 22068
Fort Worth, Texas 76122

TABLE OF CONTENTS

HOW TO USE THIS BOOK

This book is designed to help you secure current information on important issues by supplying you with the best resources on those issues. The following comments are intended to guide you in an effective use of these resources.

SCOPE

This resource book deals with over forty topics of wide, current concern. The topics covered are those about which people often need information for public speaking, preaching, writing, counseling, teaching, discussing, or simply carrying on an intelligent conversation.

No effort is made to present an exhaustive list of resources on each topic. Rather, the emphasis is on selectivity. Resources have been selected—often from hundreds of available items—to provide a list of the best up-to-date materials dealing with the most important aspects of each topic. If the topic is controversial, different viewpoints are represented. In the main, the resources are intended to provide information for Americans from the perspective of the United States; a listing of world-wide resources would be impractical.

To further aid you in selecting the very best material, items considered to be of exceptional value are, in most sections, marked with an asterisk (*). If you have only a limited time for research, the items so marked should provide you with basic information and insight.

On many subjects, a great deal of excellent available material is not included in order that the book will be concise and, therefore, more usable. However, in the section entitled *Guide to Further Research* in the *Appendix* directions are given so that you can find quickly and easily more exhaustive lists of resources.

ORGANIZATION

This book is divided into two main sections: (1) a list of resources according to subject and (2) an appendix containing a list of organizations, a list of periodicals, a list of audio-visual sources, an ethics bibliography, and a guide to further research.

SUBJECT GUIDE

Books

Under each subject, the first list of resources includes books. A brief description of each book is included so that you can determine which books will best meet your needs. The books listed have been chosen to represent various points of view, different price ranges, and both hard and paper editions.

Whenever possible, the books listed are still in print and can be purchased through a bookstore. For books in print a price is indicated. (Prices, of course, are subject to change.) Books in print can be ordered for you by a bookstore if the store does not have the books in stock.

Some books are of such significant value that they are included even though they are out of print. These books contain no price but are noted "OP" (out-of-print). They can be borrowed from most public and college libraries or purchased from used book stores. Contact colleges and seminaries in your area about arrangements for borrowing books through the mail or securing books from other libraries through interlibrary loan. Out-of-print books you want to buy often can be located through the columns of the weekly *Antiquarian Bookman*, Box 1100, Newark, New Jersey 07101, a service paper for book dealers, or through a local used-book store. (Note: The *Antiquarian Bookman* does not buy, sell, or trade books nor will the paper accept advertising for book wants from private individuals. It does list books available for many dealers.)

Organizations

Each section contains a list of organizations related to the subject. These organizations are listed with addresses and often with a description of the operation and/or publications of the organization. Often the best, most up-to-date information on a subject can be secured from organizations, rather than books. Don't overlook the organizations as superb sources.

In some sections, the organizations are divided according to their relation to the subject. For example, some are primarily concerned with the subject under consideration while others are only indirectly concerned or have the subject as one of many areas of interest. In some sections, such as communism, economics, extremism, race, war and peace, the organizations are catergorized as to their stand on the subject.

Such categories are set forth on the basis of the organization's description of itself or on the basis of the opinion of numerous informed sources. The labels used in categorizing organizations are not intended to be judgmental but rather descriptive. Obviously, such descriptions are subject to dispute. The categories do not necessarily reflect the opinion of the author about any particular organization.

When writing to an organization for information or materials: (1) Be concise. (2) State clearly what you want to know or what type of materials you need. (3) Enclose a stamped, self-addressed envelope for reply. (4) Be courteous and thoughtful; offer to pay for materials or cover mailing expenses.

Journals and Periodicals

Excellent information can be gained from journals or periodicals specializing in certain fields. Such publications are listed under each subject. For each entry there is subscription information and a brief description of contents.

Under a few subjects the periodicals are categorized as to how they relate to the topic: whether they are exclusively or only indirectly concerned with the topic. In other instances periodicals are listed not because they provide objective information but because they are cited by numerous informed sources as examples of the topic—i.e. communist and extremist periodicals.

If you have an intense or continuing interest in a subject, you will find it helpful to subscribe to one or more of the listed periodicals. Journals and periodicals should be consulted whenever possible in a library as you research a topic.

Printed Materials

Hundreds of pamphlets and booklets from scores of sources are available on most subjects. Under printed materials a select few of these are listed. Each item carries with it a price, description, and source. When the same item is available from several sources, only one is listed for the sake of conciseness. Use this list of materials for selective sources. If you desire a more extensive collection, write all the organizations listed under the subject and request materials.

These materials are helpful not only for your own general information, but also for distributing to others or using as the basis for group studies or discussion. Before ordering in quantity, examine the item you intend to use to determine whether it meets your needs.

Audio Visuals

Moving pictures, filmstrips, slides, records and tape recordings are available on most subjects. Many of these are listed under the Audio-Visuals section of each topic. Each listing indicates whether the audio visual is a 16 mm. moving picture, 35 mm. filmstrip, a record, or a tape recording, how long it takes to present the material, and what the rental or purchase price is. Most rental prices are for one day and do not include mailing charges. For moving pictures, whether they are black and white (B&W) or color is indicated.

A brief description of each listing is included with an address of where the audio visual can be secured. If more than one source supplies the item, usually only one is listed for brevity. Religious organizations will likely want to check with their own denominational audio-visual distributor on the availability of specific audio visuals.

Certain audio-visual sources have locations in different parts of the United States and the location nearest you should be utilized. The addresses for the various locations of the following are found in the Audio-Visual Appendix: Association Films, Baptist Film Centers, Cokesbury.

In securing audio visuals: (1) Write to the source at least a month prior to the scheduled use. (2) State by title and description the visual aid you want to purchase or rent. (3) Indicate the date you wish to use it. (4) Don't enclose payment because (a) prices are subject to change and (b) most sources will bill you.

Audio visuals should be previewed before use to determine whether or not they meet your need.

Other Helps

Extensive bibliographies, resource books, and lists of materials are available on many topics. These are listed for your convenience.

APPENDIX

Religiously-oriented Organizations

Some of the best resources for information on current issues are religiously-oriented, social-concerns organizations. An extensive list of these organizations is provided. Each organization is listed according to its denominational affiliation with a complete address. This list should be especially helpful to clergymen and churchmen in securing resources and materials. Most of these organizations will supply upon request a list of their available materials with prices.

Periodicals and Journals

Many periodicals and journals carry extensive information on current issues. These are listed in this section with subscription information, address, and a brief description.

Audio Visuals

Hundreds of organizations produce and distribute audio-visual aids. This section lists a selected number of denominational and secular sources of such materials. From these sources you can obtain a thorough listing of helpful materials on social issues.

This list also should be used when ordering audio visuals from sources with more than one location. For such sources no addresses are given in the subject section of the book. Simply look up the name of the source in the Audio Visual section of the Appendix and write the location nearest you.

Guide to Further Research

In outline style this section provides guidance for those who wish to go beyond the scope of this book in gathering information on a subject. Practical suggestions on sources and techniques of research are supplied This section is especially designed for students. It assumes the availability of a well-stocked library.

CAUTIONS

The opinion of the author concerning materials may not agree with your opinion. Before ordering large amounts of material for distribution, it would be wise to secure a single copy for your own analysis and approval.

Furthermore, the opinions expressed in or by these suggested resources are not necessarily those of the author.

Also, comments about books, organizations, and materials are intended to be descriptive, not judgmental. Of course, all information contained in this sourcebook is deemed helpful in gaining an understanding of the subject under which it is listed.

Materials are subject to being discontinued and prices are subject to change. Therefore, *when ordering any item listed in this book, it is best not to include payment but rather ask to be billed.*

SUBJECTS WITH RESOURCES

Note

In regard to ordering materials:
(1) Prices are subject to change.
(2) Materials are sometimes no longer available; therefore, send no money but ask that the cost be billed.

SUBJECT GUIDE

ABORTION

(See also Crime, Family, Planned Parenthood)

BOOKS

ABORTION. Lawrence Lader. Bobbs. 1966. $5.95.
Recent insights into the growing controversy over abortion.

*ABORTION AND THE LAW. David Lowe. Pocket Books. 1966. $1.00.
An up-to-date report on the current controversy and proposed changes in regard to law and abortion.

CRIME WITHOUT VICTIMS: DEVIANT BEHAVIOR AND PUBLIC POLICY — ABORTION, HOMOSEXUALITY, DRUG ADDICTION. Edwin M. Schur. Prentice-Hall. 1965. $4.95.
Discussion of abortion in relation to law, crime, and deviant behavior. Helpful information.

CRIMINAL ABORTION. J. E. Bates and E. S. Zawadski. Charles S. Thomas. 1964. $8.50.
A factual and well-documented exposition of the criminal abortion problem. Excellent bibliography.

JUSTIFIABLE ABORTION: MEDICAL AND LEGAL FOUNDATIONS. Eugene Quay. National Catholic Welfare Conference. 1961. $2.50.
An exhaustive survey of medical and legal literature to determine the validity of the usual reasons given to justify abortion. The conclusion is that there are no medical or legal justifications for liberalizing abortion laws. Catholic perspective.

MEDICAL ETHICS. Charles J. McFadden. Davis Co. 1958. $4.75.
Catholic position in general opposition to abortion and contraceptives. Gives pros and cons and reasons for their own position. Good statement.

MORALS AND MEDICINE. Joseph Fletcher. Beacon. 1960. $1.95 paper.
A study from an ethical point of view. Favors abortion under certain conditions.

RELIGION AND BIRTH CONTROL. John Clover Monsma, ed. Doubleday. 1963. OP.
Several chapters by medical doctors from different religious perspectives. Treats abortion as one means of birth control.

*THE SANCTITY OF LIFE AND THE CRIMINAL LAW. Glanville Williams. Alfred Knopf. 1957. $5.00.
Deals with the legal, theological, moral, biological aspects of abortion in two chapters. Excellent material, though somewhat technical for the average reader.

THERAPEUTIC ABORTION. H. Rosen, ed. Julian. 1954. $7.50.
> Medical, psychiatric, legal, anthropological and religious considerations of one aspect of the problem of abortion—therapeutic abortion.

YOUR MARRIAGE AND THE LAW. Harriet F. Pilpel and Theodora Zavin. Collier Books. 1952. OP.
> Chapter on abortion from a legal point of view. Points out reasons behind the laws and possible changes. Relates to abortion in marriage.

ORGANIZATIONS AND SOURCES

The following organizations either deal extensively with abortion or have helpful material:

ASSOCIATION FOR THE STUDY OF ABORTION, INC. Promotes abortion and legal action to ease abortion laws.
> 120 W. 57th St., New York, N. Y. 10019.

*PLANNED PARENTHOOD—WORLD POPULATION. A few pamphlets. Abortion is not considered a desirable form of birth control.
> 515 Madison Ave., New York, N. Y. 10022.

*U.S. CATHOLIC CONFERENCE. Catholic position set forth opposing abortion.
> 1312 Mass. Ave., N. W., Washington, D. C. 20005.

The following organizations can supply material or suggest sources on abortion:

AMERICAN BAR ASSOCIATION.
> 1155 E. 60th St., Chicago, Ill. 60637.

AMERICAN LAW INSTITUTE. Proposes legislation on abortion to liberalize laws.
> 101 N. 33rd St., Philadelphia, Pa. 19104.

*AMERICAN MEDICAL ASSOCIATION. Journals and meetings deal with abortion from both a medical and ethical point of view.
> 535 N. Dearborn St., Chicago, Ill. 60610.

CHRISTIAN MEDICAL SOCIETY. Professional medical organization to encourage Christian witness. Sometimes faces ethical issues such as abortion in publication, *Christian Medical Society Journal.*
> 1122 Westgate, Oak Park, Ill. 60301.

COMMITTEE ON HUMAN DEVELOPMENT. Research on the issue of abortion.
> University of Chicago, Chicago, Ill. 60637.

DEPT. OF MARRIAGE AND FAMILY, NATIONAL COUNCIL OF CHURCHES. Suggestions on sources.
  475 Riverside Dr., New York, N. Y. 10027.

*GENERAL BOARD OF CHRISTIAN SOCIAL CONCERNS, THE METHODIST CHURCH. Limited number of materials analyzing the problem.
  100 Maryland Ave., N. E., Washington, D. C. 20002.

PERIODICALS AND JOURNALS

See appendix for list of journals and other publications dealing with social issues. No generally helpful specialized publication on this subject. See also competent medical journals.

CHRISTIAN MEDICAL SOCIETY JOURNAL. BM $3.00. Occasionally deals with issues such as abortion.
  1122 Westgate, Oak Park, Ill. 60301.

MEDICAL TRIBUNE. 3 times W. $12.50 (without charge to qualified recipient). Editorials and articles deal with abortion issue from time to time.
  120 E. 56th St., New York, N. Y. 10022.

SIECUS NEWSLETTER. Q $2.00. Includes listing of material, some of which relates to abortion.
  SIECUS, 1855 Broadway, New York, N. Y. 10023.

PRINTED MATERIALS

A FOR ABORTION $.10, ABORTION AND THE RIGHT TO LIFE $.05, CRIMINAL ABORTION: A FAILURE OF LAW OR A CHALLENGE TO SOCIETY? $.10. Materials opposed to abortion setting forth the Catholic view.
  Family Life Bureau, U.S. Catholic Conference, 1312 Mass. Ave., N. W., Washington, D. C. 20005.

ABORTION AS A DISEASE OF SOCIETIES. James Newman. An examination of the abortion problem based on a review of the Planned Parenthood Federation of America's Conference on Abortion. $.10.

ABORTION, DISEASE OF SOCIETY. Mary S. Calerone. Facts and figures about abortion in the U.S. and a recommended program for dealing with it. $.10.
  Planned Parenthood—World Population, 515 Madison Ave., New York, N. Y. 10022.

SEXUAL INTEGRITY IN MODERN SOCIETY. A very helpful study guide with a brief section on abortion. $.10.
  Commission on Research and Social Action, The American Lutheran Church, 422 S. 5th St., Minneapolis, Minn. 55415.

AUDIO VISUALS

ABORTION AND THE LAW. 16 mm. B&W. 54 min. $12.50
rental. Focuses on the legal, moral, social and psychological
aspects of abortion in the U.S. Presents clergymen, lawyers and
physicians who hold diametrically opposed views on suggestion
that the present laws against abortion need amending. Graphic
evidence of the dangerous and serious consequences of illegal
abortions.

> Office for Audio Visuals, United Church of Christ, 1720 Chouteau
> Ave., St. Louis, Mo. 63103.

AGING

(See also Family, Mental Health)

BOOKS

*THE CHURCH AND THE OLDER PERSON. Robert M. Gray
and David O. Moberg. Eerdmans 1962. $1.95.
> Provides helpful analyses and numerous practical suggestions for
> church leaders.

*GROWING OLD GRACEFULLY. Paul H. Lorhan. Vantage. 1965.
$2.75.
> Practical suggestions in an up-to-date setting and inexpensive form
> for meeting creatively the problems of aging.

THE NATURE OF RETIREMENT. Elon H. Moore. Macmillan.
1959. OP
> A handbook for retired persons and a guide to preparing for retire-
> ment. Financial, physical, and social aspects. Secular.

OLDER MEMBERS IN THE CONGREGATION. Arthur Ris-
miller. Augsburg. 1964. $1.95 paper.
> An indication of the increasing number of older persons in churches
> and suggestions on their role in the church and the church's
> ministry to them.

THE OLDER PEOPLE IN YOUR LIFE. Justus J. Schifferes. Washington Square. 1962. $2.95.
> Offers understanding counsel and practical information for those grown-up and married daughters who struggle in the middle of a three-generation family.

SOCIAL AND PSYCHOLOGICAL ASPECTS OF AGING. Clark Tibbitts, ed. 1962. $20.00.

SOCIAL WELFARE OF THE AGING. Jerome Kaplan, ed. 1962. $8.00.

BIOLOGICAL ASPECTS OF AGING. Nathan W. Shock, ed. 1962. $7.50.

MEDICAL AND CLINICAL ASPECTS OF AGING. Herman T. Blumenthal, ed. 1961-62. $12.00.
> A series of excellent, technical books on aging by Columbia University Press.

SOCIAL CHANGE AND AGING IN THE TWENTIETH CENTURY. Daniel E. Alleger. U. of Florida Press. 1964. $3.75 paper.
> A sociological study of aging. Introductory to problems.

YOU AND YOUR AGING PARENTS. Edith Stern and Mabele Ross. Harper. 1965. Rev. ed. $3.95.
> A book of instructions with practical suggestions to the child of elderly parents who need care.

ORGANIZATIONS AND SOURCES

Organizations devoted primarily to problems of the aging:

*ADMINISTRATION ON AGING, U.S. DEPT. OF HEALTH, EDUCATION, AND WELFARE. Ask for list of publications and materials. Listing of films and other audio-visual aids available. Reprints and fact sheets on aging available.
> Washington, D. C. 20201.

AMERICAN ASSOCIATION OF RETIRED PERSONS. Publications and conferences for the older citizen. Many services and programs.
> 419 Dupont Circle Bldg., Washington, D. C. 20036.

AMERICAN GERIATRICS SOCIETY. One of several professional organizations for those working with the aging. Publishes a monthly journal. Encourages research.
> 10 Columbus Circle, New York, N. Y. 10019.

BROWN UNIVERSITY CENTER FOR AGING RESEARCH. Research programs in the nature and effects of aging on individuals and on society.
> Brown University, Providence, R.I. 02912.

*NATIONAL COUNCIL ON THE AGING. List of publications;
  can provide a great deal of information.
  315 Park Ave., S., New York, N. Y. 10010.

NATIONAL INSTITUTE OF MENTAL HEALTH. Mental aspect
  of the aging process studied and reported on.
  Bethesda, Maryland 20014.

SENIOR CITIZENS OF AMERICA. Nonprofit scientific, educational, philanthropic organization whose activities include scientific research, personal counsel, correspondence, *Senior Citizen,*
  and other publications.
  1424—16th St., N. W., Washington, D. C. 20036.

Organizations only indirectly related but with helpful material:

CONCORDIA TRACT MISSION, Box 201, St. Louis, Mo. 63166.

DEPT. OF SOCIAL WELFARE, NATIONAL COUNCIL OF
  CHURCHES, 475 Riverside Dr., New York, N. Y. 10027.

INSTITUTE OF LIFE INSURANCE, 488 Madison Ave., New
  York, N. Y. 10022.

JOHN HANCOCK MUTUAL LIFE INSURANCE CO., HEALTH
  EDUCATION SERVICE, 200 Berkeley St., Boston, Mass.
  02117.

METROPOLITAN LIFE INSURANCE CO., One Madison Ave.,
  New York, N. Y. 10010.

PUBLIC AFFAIRS PAMPHLETS, 381 Park Ave., S., New York,
  N. Y. 10016.

SERVICE DEPT., GENERAL BOARD OF CHRISTIAN SOCIAL
  CONCERNS, THE METHODIST CHURCH, 100 Maryland
  Ave., N.E., Washington, D. C. 20002.

PERIODICALS AND JOURNALS

*AGING. M $1.00, $.10 for single copies. Newsmagazine of Adminis-
  tration on Aging, U.S. Dept. of Health, Education, and Welfare,
  Washington, D.C. 20201. Subscriptions should be addressed to:
  Superintendent of Documents, Washington, D. C. 20402.

DYNAMIC MATURITY. BM $2.00.

MODERN MATURITY. BM $2.00 (includes BM AARP News-
  letter). Published by American Association of Retired Persons.
  Subscription Dept., 408 E. Grand Ave., Ojai, Cal. 93023.

HARVEST YEARS. M $4.50, $.40 per copy. For people above 50 who wish to plan a balanced and fruitful retirement. Covers money, housing, activities, food, etc.
> 681 Market St., San Francisco, Cal. 94105.

THE MATURE YEARS. Q $1.50, $.30 per copy. Published by the Methodist Church.
> General Board of Education to the Editorial Div., 201—8th Ave., S., Nashville, Tenn. 37203.

SENIOR CITIZEN. M $5.00 to nonmembers, $1.00 per single copy, life membership $100.00.
> Senior Citizens of America, 1424—16th St., N.W., Washington, D. C. 20036.

PRINTED MATERIALS

THE CHRISTIAN FAMILY AND ITS AGED MEMBERS. A pamphlet discussing ways families should respond to aged members. Brief but helpful. $.02.
> Christian Life Commission, 206 Baptist Bldg., Dallas, Tex. 75201.

THE CHURCH AND THE AGING. Foy Valentine. Brotherhood Seminar Series. Constructive insights and information. $.20.
> The Brotherhood Commission, Southern Baptist Convention, 1548 Poplar Ave., Memphis, Tenn. 38104.

*CHURCHES AND THE AGING. A statement on church responsibility. Issue of *Social Action*. $.25. Study packet, $1.00.
> The Council for Christian Social Action, United Church of Christ, 289 Park Ave., S., New York, N. Y. 10010.

*CHURCHES AND THEIR SENIOR CITIZENS. A practical outline of constructive suggestions. Selected bibliography. Listing of films, film strips, and other materials. $.50.
> Institute of Gerontology, State Univ. of Iowa, Iowa City, Iowa 52240.

THE CONGREGATION SERVES OLDER PEOPLE. Practical suggestions for program planners at the local church level. $3.75 per 100.
> Dept. of Social Welfare, National Council of Churches, 475 Riverside Dr., New York, N. Y. 10027.

A FULL LIFE AFTER 65. Speaks cheerfully to the older person of the rich opportunities which are his for making life meaningful. $.25.

MAKING THE MOST OF YOUR YEARS. A simple, practical discussion addressed directly to the aging person of a great variety of important matters involved in growing old. $.25.
> Public Affairs Pamphlets, 381 Park Ave., S., New York, N. Y. 10016.

LOOKING FORWARD TO THE LATER YEARS. An instructional and inspirational message, directed to the aging person. $.15.
> Public Health Service, U.S. Dept. of Health, Education, and Welfare, Washington, D. C. 20201.

PROBLEMS OF AGING. C. M. Lambright. A very helpful introduction to the various problems associated with aging. $.05.
> Service Dept., Methodist Church, 100 Maryland Ave., N. E., Washington, D. C. 20002.

*REPORTS AND GUIDELINES FROM THE WHITE HOUSE CONFERENCE ON AGING. A series of booklets on many different phases of aging. $3.75.
> U.S. Dept. of Health, Education, and Welfare, Special Staff on Aging, Washington, D. C. 20201.

RESOURCES FOR THE AGING: AN ACTION HANDBOOK. A catalogue of national resources which can provide financial or other assistance to community programs for the aging. *Limited distribution;* no charge.
> National Council on the Aging, 315 Park Ave., S., New York, N. Y. 10010.

THE YEARS OF OUR LIFE. Lutheran Forum Series. Booklet for study and information. $.07.
> Commission on Research and Social Action, The American Lutheran Church, 422 S. 5th St., Minneapolis, Minn. 55415.

AUDIO VISUALS

An extensive listing of films can be obtained from:
  (1) Jewish Federation of Film Library, 101 No. 20 St., Omaha, Neb. 68102.
  (2) "Selected References on Aging: Films on Aging," OA No. 303, Adm. on Aging, U.S. Dept. of HEW, Washington, D. C. 20201.

AGING IN THE MODERN WORLD—AN INTRODUCTORY DISCUSSION. One 10″ 33-⅓ rpm record. $2.00 purchase. Emphasizes the need for citizens to consider the topic of aging. An introduction to the problems. May be used in conjunction with the text AGING IN TODAY'S SOCIETY, published by Prentice-Hall, Inc.
> Audio Visual Center, Indiana University, Bloomington, Ind. 47405.

*CHRISTIANS FACE THE SENIOR YEARS. Filmstrip series, guide, 33-⅓ rpm record, 40 and 41 frames. Each filmstrip with guide $6.50, with record and guide $10.00, both with record and guide $16.50. (1) MIDDLE AGE—MAKING THE MOST OF IT. Some typical problems that men and women have to face in the middle years of life. Christian resources for meeting them and making middle age a time for continuing growth and satisfaction. (2) PLANNING AHEAD FOR RETIREMENT. The importance of planning ahead in order to enjoy retirement. How Christian faith and the church fellowship can help in finding happiness and satisfaction in the retirement.

OUR SENIOR YEARS. 16mm. B&W 30 min. $10.00 rental. An active worker is retired at 65. Without preparation for his senior years, he quickly becomes bored and bewildered. Through a series of events, he is helped by his faithful wife, grandson and Christian friends to find a new adventure in living by serving God.

> Cokesbury.

A PLACE TO LIVE. 16 mm. B&W 25 min. $8.00 rental. This film sensitively examines the needs of any dignified human being who reaches an age that society classifies as old age. He needs, most of all, something to do and a place to live. An artistic and meaningful study which places special emphasis on standards of care in homes for older people.

> Visual Education Service, Church of the Brethren, 1451 Dundee Ave., Elgin, Ill. 60120.

PREPARATION FOR THE LATER YEARS: FINANCIAL PLANNING. 16 mm. B&W 30 mn. $12.50 rental. Aids people in their middle years to think and plan for their later years.

> Dynamic Films, Inc., 405 Park Ave., New York, N. Y. 10022.

RETIRE TO LIFE. 16 mm. B&W 23 min. $2.00 service charge. Depicts problems of retirement and indicates how many of them can be avoided by adequate preparation.

THE GOLDEN AGE. 16 mm. B&W 20 min. 1958. $3.00 rental. Depicts three different responses to retirement and stresses importance of early preparation for retirement.

> Canadian Film Institute, 1762 Carling Ave., Ottawa, Ontario, Canada.

WHERE LIFE STILL MEANS LIVING. 16 mm. Color. 24 min. $15.00 rental. Explores the inner emotional world of an aged couple frightened by chronic illness and mental confusion. Dramatic scenes unfold their feelings of rejection by their children, their helplessness, and their ultimate admission to a progressive home for the aged where they find life still has meaning. Recommended by U. S. Administration on Aging.

> Edward Feil Productions, 1514 Prospect Ave., Cleveland, Ohio 44115.

OTHER HELPS

FEDERAL PUBLICATIONS ON AGING. Bibliography, annotated. By Federal Council on Aging.

SELECTED REFERENCES ON AGING. Listing of helpful government publications. $.50.

> Supt. of Documents, U.S. Government Printing Office, Washington, D. C. 20402.

ALCOHOL—ALCOHOLISM

(See also Mental Health, Narcotics)

BOOKS

ALCOHOL EDUCATION FOR CLASSROOM AND COMMUNITY: A SOURCE BOOK FOR EDUCATORS. Raymond McCarthy, ed. McGraw-Hill. 1964. $7.95.

> Designed as basic source book for high school and college classes. Excellent materials.

ALCOHOL IN AND OUT OF THE CHURCH. Wayne E. Oates. Broadman. 1966. $3.95.

> A psychological look at the drinking problem with a special emphasis on the role of the church.

*BASIC INFORMATION ON ALCOHOL. Albion Roy King. Cornell College Press. 1953, rev. 4th ed. $2.50 paper. Order from Narcotics Education Inc., Box 4390, Washington, D. C. 20012.

> As reviewed in the *Quarterly Journal of Studies on Alcohol,* "It is the most scholarly and factual exposition of knowledge about alcohol ever published by an adherent of the cause of abstinence."

THE CUP OF FURY. Upton Sinclair. Channel Press. 1956. $3.00. Revell. $.60 paper.

Accounts the role played by alcohol in the degeneration of a number of leading authors.

THE DISEASE CONCEPT OF ALCOHOLISM. E. M. Jellinek. Hillhouse. 1960. $6.00.

A significant study of the development of the disease concept of alcoholism related to attitudes around the world as well as the United States. Extensive bibliography.

DRINKING AMONG TEEN-AGERS. George L. Maddox and Bevode C. McCall. Rutgers Center of Alcohol Studies. 1964. $6.00.

From a social science perspective this is an authoritative book.

*HELPING THE ALCOHOLIC AND HIS FAMILY. Thomas J. Shipp. Prentice-Hall. 1963. $2.95.

Written by a pastor with extensive personal experience in ministering to alcoholics. A practical book designed to help those who are working with alcoholics.

*THE MANY FACES OF ETHYL. William S. Garmon. Broadman. 1966. $1.50.

A readable book with extensive information on alcohol and alcoholism. Contains a helpful bibliography.

UNDERSTANDING AND COUNSELING THE ALCOHOLIC. Howard Clinebell, Jr. Abingdon. 1965. $3.75.

A discussion of possible causes and cures of alcoholism with a special emphasis on prevention and the role of the pastor.

ORGANIZATIONS AND SOURCES

Organizations devoted to study of alcohol and alcoholism with extensive material:

AL-ANON FAMILY GROUP HEADQUARTERS, INC. Books, monthly newsletter, leaflets and pamphlets available. Write for price list. Helps families of alcoholics.

Box 182 Madison Square Station, New York, N. Y. 10010.

THE AMERICAN BUSINESS MEN'S RESEARCH FOUNDATION. Much helpful information. Statistical resources available on request. Publishes *Report on Man's Use of Alcohol*. BM $2.00.

431 S. Dearborn, Chicago, Ill. 60605.

AMERICAN COUNCIL ON ALCOHOL PROBLEMS, INC. List of films, several pamphlets and monthly papers available.

119 Constitution Ave., N. E., Washington, D. C. 20002.

AMERICAN TEMPERANCE SOCIETY. Pamphlets, films, and *Listen* magazine.

6840 Eastern Ave., N. W., Washington, D. C. 20012.

COMMITTEE ON ALCOHOLISM, COUNCIL ON MENTAL HEALTH, AMERICAN MEDICAL ASSOCIATION. Materials available from a medical viewpoint.
535 N. Dearborn St., Chicago, Ill. 60610.

*DIVISION OF TEMPERANCE AND GENERAL WELFARE, GENERAL BOARD OF CHRISTIAN SOCIAL CONCERNS, THE METHODIST CHURCH. Many leaflets, pamphlets, and audio-visuals. Excellent source book available.
100 Maryland Ave., N. E., Washington, D. C. 20002.

GENERAL SERVICE OFFICE OF ALCOHOLICS ANONYMOUS. Pamphlets and tapes available. Primarily concerned with helping and rehabilitating the alcoholic. Information concerning AA groups in particular areas.
Box 459 Grand Central Station, New York, N. Y. 10017.

NATIONAL CENTER FOR THE CONTROL AND PREVENTION OF ALCOHOLISM. Research and reports.
Bethesda, Md. 20014.

*THE NATIONAL COUNCIL ON ALCOHOLISM, INC. "Catalogue of Publications" available upon request. They also have books and alcoholism information kits. Emphasis on effect of alcohol on business and industry.
2 E. 103rd St., New York, N. Y. 10029.

NATIONAL WOMAN'S CHRISTIAN TEMPERANCE UNION. Catalogue available with complete list of materials.
1730 Chicago Ave., Evanston, Ill. 60201.

*PUBLICATIONS DIVISION, RUTGERS CENTER OF ALCOHOL STUDIES. Catalogue available listing books, pamphlets, and reprints on all aspects of alcohol problems. Films available for loan. A superb source of information.
Box 566, Rutgers, New Brunswick, N. J. 08903.

Organizations with helpful material:

CHRISTIAN LIFE COMMISSION, SOUTHERN BAPTIST CONVENTION.
460 James Robertson Parkway, Nashville, Tenn. 37219.

COMMISSION ON RESEARCH AND SOCIAL ACTION, THE AMERICAN LUTHERAN CHURCH.
422 S. 5th St., Minneapolis, Minn. 55415.

CONCORDIA TRACT MISSION.
Box 201, St. Louis, Mo. 63166.

OFFICE OF PUBLICATION AND DISTRIBUTION, NATION-

AL COUNCIL OF CHURCHES.
475 Riverside Dr., New York, N. Y. 10027.

U. S. GOVERNMENT PRINTING OFFICE. Many pamphlets and booklets on alcohol and alcoholism. Write for listing.
Supt. of Documents, U.S. Government Printing Office, Washington, D. C. 20402.

Refer also to various state and city commissions and councils on alcoholism.

PERIODICALS AND JOURNALS

AMERICAN BUSINESS MEN'S RESEARCH FOUNDATION REPORT. BM $2.00. Collected items of interest on alcohol problems.
431 S. Dearborn St., Chicago, Ill. 60605.

AMERICAN ISSUE. M $1.00. Report on activities of the Council and information on alcohol problems.
American Council on Alcohol Problems, 119 Constitution Ave., N.E., Washington, D. C. 20002.

FAMILY GROUP FORUM. M $1.50. Information to help the families of alcoholics.
Al-Anon Family Group Headquarters, Inc., Box 182, Madison Square Station, New York, N. Y. 10010.

*LISTEN. BM $3.00. Problems of drug addiction and alcoholism for popularized reading and study purposes.
Pacific Press Publishing Assoc., American Temperance Society, 6840 Eastern Ave., N. W., Washington, D. C. 20012.

*QUARTERLY JOURNAL OF STUDIES ON ALCOHOL. Q $10.00. Research on all aspects of alcohol problems, including alcoholism, from all disciplines and professions. The world's scientific literature is covered by bibliography and informative abstracts and is subject-indexed. Excellent source of information.
Box 560, Rutgers Univ., New Brunswick, N. J. 08903.

PRINTED MATERIALS

*ALCOHOL: ISSUE AND ANSWER SERIES ($.05), I MAKE MY COMMITMENT, SHOULD LIQUOR ADVERTISING BE PROHIBITED? WHAT LIQUOR IS DOING TO THE HOME, and WHY NOT GET THE REVENUE? Brief pamphlets dealing with important phases of the alcohol problem. Single copies free; $.02 each in quantity except the first.

Christian Life Commission, S.B.C., 460 James Robertson Parkway, Nashville, Tenn. 37219.

THE CASE FOR TOTAL ABSTINENCE. Well-written, reasonable pamphlet. Sample free, $.03 each, $2.00 per 100.

Div. of Christian Action, Board of Christian Education, Presbyterian Church, U. S., Box 1176, Richmond, Va. 23209.

A CHRISTIAN APPROACH TO THE ALCOHOLIC BEVERAGE QUESTION. Examines several alternate views of Christians. Available on request.

Commission on Research and Social Action, American Lutheran Church, 422 S. 5th St., Minneapolis, Minn. 55415.

DECIDING ABOUT DRINKING and WE PREFER NOT TO DRINK. Written primarily for young people. $.02 each.

Christian Life Commission, 206 Baptist Bldg., Dallas, Tex. 75201.

DRINKING PROBLEMS. Roger Burgess and Thomas E. Price. Comprehensive listing of facts and statistics about alcohol problems. $.50.

*FAMILY PACKET ON ALCOHOLISM ($1.75), PARENTS' PACKET ON ALCOHOLISM ($.25), PASTOR'S PACKET ON ALCOHOLISM ($1.75). Each contains selected resource material.

WHAT THE BIBLE SAYS. A brief pamphlet setting forth Bible interpretation on the problem of alcohol. $.02.

Service Dept. The Methodist Church, 100 Maryland Ave., N. E., Washington, D. C. 20002.

HELP FOR THE ALCOHOLIC'S FAMILY. Positive suggestions for family help. $.15.

Family Life Bureau, U. S. Catholic Conference, 1312 Mass. Ave., N. W., Washington, D. C. 20005.

THE PROBLEM: ALCOHOL-NARCOTICS. A 95-page booklet filled with statistics and factual information. $1.00.

TANE Press, 2814 Oak Lawn Ave., Dallas, Tex. 75219.

AUDIO VISUALS

Extensive listing of films available from:

The Rutgers Center of Alcohol Studies, Box 566, Rutgers, New Brunswick, N. J. 08903.

Division of Alcohol Problems and General Welfare, General Board of Christian Social Concerns of the Methodist Church, 100 Maryland Ave., N. E., Washington, D. C. 20002.

ALCOHOL AND THE HUMAN BODY. 16 mm. Sound. B&W.

14 min. $3.65 rental. Illustrates different types of alcoholic beverage and effect on human body.

ALCOHOLISM. 16 mm. Sound. B&W. 23 min. $4.15 rental. Presents in detail the case history of an alcoholic.

> Audio-Visual Center, Div. of University Extension, Indiana University, Bloomington, Ind. 47405.

ALCOHOL AND YOUR HEALTH. 35 mm. color filmstrip with record and guide. 44 frames. 15 min. $9.50 purchase. Alcohol as a depressant; immediate and cumulative physical effects; and alcohol as a national health problem.

> Society for Visual Education, Inc., 1345 Diversey Parkway, Chicago, Ill. 60614.

*BASIC INFORMATION ABOUT ALCOHOL. Set of four 35 mm. B&W filmstrips with two 33-1/3 rpm records. 55 to 75 frames each. $6.00 each or $20.00 for set of four, purchase. Produced for Methodism's Division of Alcohol Problems and General Welfare. Subjects: ALCOHOL AND THE HUMAN BODY, ALCOHOL AND PERSONALITY, ALCOHOL AND SOCIAL PROBLEMS, ALCOHOL AND THE CHRISTIAN FAITH. Suitable for adults and older young people.

> Service Dept., 100 Maryland Ave., N. E., Washington, D. C. 20002.

*A NEW LOOK AT THE OLD SAUCE. 35 mm. color filmstrip with record and guide. 17 min. $10.00 purchase. Cartoon approach on alcohol for young people. Excellent and appealing.

> Texas Commission on Alcoholism, 803 Sam Houston State Office Bldg., Austin, Tex. 78701.

THEOBALD FACES THE FACTS. 16 mm. Sound. Color. 13-1/2 min. $7.00 rental. Produced for the National Woman's Christian Temperance Union by Cal Dunn Studios. A cartoon film answering some commonly misunderstood questions about the use of alcoholic beverages. To use with children and junior high students.

> National Woman's Christian Temperance Union, 1730 Chicago Ave., Evanston, Ill. 60201.

VERDICT AT 1:32. 16 mm. Sound. Color. 22 min. $7.50 daily rental. Effects of alcohol on the brain dramatically demonstrated.

> Association Films, Inc.

OTHER HELPS

*ALCOHOL PROBLEMS AND GENERAL WELFARE. Comprehensive resource list. $.25.

BOOKS, PAMPHLETS, AUDIOVISUALS. Selected list of resources in alcohol problems and general welfare. Free.

RESOURCE LISTS OF TEMPERANCE MATERIALS. Listing
of books, dramas, pamphlets and leaflets. Free. These are
excellent source materials.

Service Dept., The Methodist Bldg., 100 Maryland Ave., N. E., Washington, D. C. 20002.

INTERNATIONAL BIBLIOGRAPHY OF STUDIES ON AL-
COHOL. Mark Keller, ed. Vol. 1 References 1901-1950; Vol.
II Indexes, 1901-1950. This is the most thorough bibliography
available. $55.00.

SELECTED STATISTICAL TABLES ON THE CONSUMP-
TION OF ALCOHOL, 1850-1962, AND ON ALCOHOLISM,
1930-1960. Vera Elron and Mark Keller. 1963. OP. Essential
information for the careful study of the problems related to
alcohol in the U.S. Primary usefulness in regard to history
and trends.

Publication Div., Rutgers Center of Alcohol Studies, New Brunswick,
N. J. 08903.

ANTI-SEMITISM

(See also Extremism, Mental Health, Race)

BOOKS

*ANTI-SEMITISM: A CASE STUDY IN PREJUDICE AND
DISCRIMINATION. J. Milton Yinger. Anti-Defamation
League of B'nai B'rith. $1.25.

An analysis of the history of anti-Semitism from its inception to
the present.

ANTI-SEMITISM. James Parkes. Quadrangle. 1964. $5.00.

A concise world history of anti-Semitism. Discusses the psychology of prejudice, Christian roots of anti-Semitism, and the onslaughts on Jews in the modern world.

BARRIERS: PATTERNS OF DISCRIMINATION AGAINST JEWS. N. C. Belth, ed. Anti-Defamation League of B'nai B'rith. 1958. $1.50.

A thorough examination of discrimination in education, housing, and employment, as well as social and resort discrimination; and an analysis by Gordon W. Allport of "Why People Scapegoat." Concludes with a report on the present status of Jews in the U. S. Discussion guide.

*CHRISTIAN BELIEFS AND ANTI-SEMITISM. Charles Y. Glock and R. Stark. Harper. 1966. $8.50.

The controversial report of a sociological study of the relation of Christian teaching and doctrine to anti-Semitism. Rates the degree of anti-Semitism in various Christian groups in America.

CHRISTIANITY AND ANTI-SEMITISM. Nicholas Berdyaev. Philosophical Library. 1954. $1.95.

The author urges a condemnation of all anti-Semitism by the Christians both in formal edicts and their personal lives. All are to realize that the real struggle in life is inward not in the lives of others. In many ways this essay is a confession of sin by every Christian.

CROSS-CURRENTS. Arnold Forster and Benjamin R. Epstein. Anti-Defamation League of B'nai B'rith. $2.50.

Documented and often shocking expose of international and domestic anti-Semitism.

JEWS IN THE MIND OF AMERICA. Charles Herbert Stember and others. Basic Books, Inc. 1966. $12.50.

Contains the results of surveys of over a quarter of a century to determine exactly how the Jews appeared in the mind of America. Dr. Stember, professor of sociology at Rutgers, is a well-known figure in the field of survey research.

SOME OF MY BEST FRIENDS. Benjamin R. Epstein and Arnold Forster. Farrar, Straus and Giroux. 1962. $4.50.

An account and analysis of the nature and extent of American anti-Semitism as evidenced by social discrimination and discrimination in housing, higher education, and employment.

THE TEACHING OF CONTEMPT: CHRISTIAN ROOTS OF ANTI-SEMITISM. Jules Isaac. Holt, Rinehart and Winston 1964. $4.00, $2.15 paper.

Effort to bring Christians to a deeper examination of the roots of ancient prejudice. Concludes that an important cause of anti-Semitism can be found in certain elements of the doctrines of Christianity which portray the Jewish people negatively.

ORGANIZATIONS AND SOURCES

Organizations which have extensive material on anti-Semitism:

AMERICAN JEWISH CONGRESS. Bibliography available of publications and other resources. Strives to preserve Jewish identity.

     15 E. 84th St., New York, N. Y. 10028.

*ANTI-DEFAMATION LEAGUE OF B'NAI B'RITH. Catalog of publications and catalog of audio-visual materials available. Basic source.

     315 Lexington Ave., New York, N. Y. 10016.

INSTITUTE OF HUMAN RELATIONS. An agency of the American Jewish Committee devoted to combat prejudice in all forms including anti-Semitism.

     165 E. 56th St., New York, N. Y. 10022.

*THE NATIONAL CONFERENCE OF CHRISTIANS AND JEWS. Price list available on reprints, articles, books, pamphlets, scripts, films, filmstrips.

     43 W. 57th St., New York, N. Y. 10019.

Examples of Organizations and papers often cited as Anti-Semetic:

AMERICAN NAZI PARTY.

     P.O. Box 5505 Arlington, Va. 22205.

THE CHURCH TIMES. An anti-Semitic mimeographed paper published infrequently.

     P. O. Box 2, Oak Hill, West Va. 25901.

NATIONAL CHRISTIAN NEWS. M $3.00. Strongly anti-Jewish paper.

     P. O. Box 10924, St. Petersburg, Fla. 33733.

NATIONAL CHRISTIAN PUBLISHERS. Produces tapes, pamphlets, and a newspaper, *National Christian News,* denouncing Jews and Communism as a Jewish conspiracy.

     Box 412, Ocala, Fla. 32670.

NATIONAL STATES RIGHTS PARTY. Publishes *Thunderbolt* each month.

     Box 783, Birmingham, Ala. 35201.

PERIODICALS AND JOURNALS

THE CHRISTIAN FRIENDS BULLETIN. Published especially for Christian clergymen and educators to help improve intergroup understanding.

*RIGHTS. Attempts to counter anti-Semitic material. Periodic.
    Anti-Demafation League of B'nai B'rith, 315 Lexington Ave., New
    York, N. Y. 10016.

COMMENTARY. M $7.00. Public affairs information. Helpful
    insight into one aspect of Jewish thought.
    American Jewish Committee, 165 E. 56th St., New York, N. Y.
    10022.

CONGRESS BI-WEEKLY. BW $4.00.

JUDAISM. Q $4.50, $1.25 per copy. Strives to preserve Jewish
    identity. Helpful insight into Jewish belief and practices.
    American Jewish Congress, 15 E. 84th St., New York, N. Y. 10028.

PRINTED MATERIALS

The Anti-Defamation League of B'nai B'rith, 315 Lexington Ave.·
New York, N. Y. 10016, has many pamphlets and booklets available, including the following six listings:

AMERICAN JEWS: THEIR STORY. Oscar Handlin. A brief
    illustrated history of Jewish life in America from 1654 to the
    present. $.35.

*ANTI-SEMITISM IN AMERICA. Melvin M. Tumin. A study
    of the attitudes and motivations behind anti-Semitism. $.25.

DANGER IN DISCORD. Oscar and Mary Handlin. A history
    of the origins and causes of anti-Semitism in the U. S. $.50

THE JEWISH FAMILY. Topics discussed include the relation-
    ship between the Jewish religion and the Jewish home, the
    Jewish attitude toward marriage, divorce, juvenile delinquency
    and alcoholism. $.20.

JEWS IN AMERICAN LIFE. A list of books and pamphlets
    currently in print and available from publishers which shed
    light on the influence of Judaism on democracy and American
    society. Over 60 titles. Free.

**THE SIN OF ANTI-SEMITISM: STATEMENTS BY CHRIS-
    TIAN CHURCHES.** Contains the full text of the Vatican
    Council's "Declaration on the Relations of the Church to non-
    Christian Religions" plus statements by Protestant bodies.

*ANTI-SEMITISM. Booklet from a Christian point of view. Nov.,
    1960 issue of *Social Action* magazine. $.25.
    Council for Christian Social Action, United Church of Christ, 289
    Park Ave., S., New York, N. Y. 10010.

THE CHRISTIAN AND HIS JEWISH NEIGHBOR. A booklet setting forth history of Christian-Jewish relations and ways better relations can be established. $.25.

    The Episcopal Church, 815 2nd Ave., New York, N. Y. 10017.

AUDIO VISUALS

Anti-Defamation League of B'nai B'rith, 315 Lexington Ave., New York, N. Y. 10016, has many films and filmstrips available, all listed in a free catalog. The following are selected items:

*AN AMERICAN GIRL. 16 mm. B&W 29-½ min. $3.00 rental. Tells the story of an American teen-ager who is mistakenly believed to be Jewish by her friends and neighbors. Shows the harm and stupidity of prejudice.

*THE CHOSEN PEOPLE. 16 mm. B&W. 27 min. $3.00 rental. Dramatization of the problems of anti-Semitism in America, originally presented on NBC-TV by the National Council of Catholic Men.

NO EASY ANSWER. 16 mm. B&W. 17 min. $3.00 rental. Designed to aid Jewish parents in dealing with the effects of anti-Semitism on their children.

THE NATURE OF ANTI-SEMITISM. 16 mm. B&W. 29 min. $3.00 rental. A kinescope in the NBC "Open Mind" series. Panel discuss various aspects of anti-Semitism. Adult and secondary school levels.

OTHER HELPS

BIBLIOGRAPHY OF PUBLICATIONS AND OTHER RESOURCES OF COMMISSION ON JEWISH AFFAIRS. Free on request.

    American Jewish Congress, 15 E. 84th St., New York, N. Y. 10028.

BIBLIOGRAPHY ON JUDAISM AND JEWISH-CHRISTIAN RELATIONS. An annotated bibliography of several hundred basic publications on Judaism and Jewish-Christian relations. An invaluable tool for libraries, theological seminaries, religious schools and all those interested in this field. $1.00.

    Anti-Defamation League of B'nai B'rith, 315 Lexington Ave., New York, N. Y. 10016.

ARTIFICIAL INSEMINATION
(See also Family, Planned Parenthood, Sex)

BOOKS

ARTIFICIAL INSEMINATION IN THE HUMAN. A Schellen. Elsevier Publishing Co., 1957. $17.50.
> An exhaustive study from physiological, psychological, legal, and religious points of view. Good index. Excellent source.

LAW AND MORALS. Norman St. John-Stevas. Hawthorn. 1964. $3.50.
> A chapter considers the theological and legal aspects. Presents Catholic opinion.

*MORALS AND MEDICINE. Joseph Fletcher. Beacon. 1960. $1.95 paper.
> Extensive chapter discusses religious, moral, psychological, medical, and legal aspects. Generally favors the practice under certain circumstances.

NEW PROBLEMS IN MEDICAL ETHICS. D. Peter Flood, ed. 2 Vols. Newman. 1954. $4.50 each.
> Contains a series of articles on various aspects of artificial insemination: legal, moral, medical.

NEWER ETHICAL PROBLEMS IN MEDICINE AND SURGERY. Bernard J. Ficarra. Newman. 1951. OP.
> Roman Catholic discussion. Sets forth various aspects of each issue, the pros and cons, and takes a stand. Generally conservative.

PLANNING YOUR FAMILY. Alan F. Guttmacher. Macmillan. 1963. $5.95.
> Discusses artificial insemination as a possible means of overcoming childlessness.

*THE SANCTITY OF LIFE AND THE CRIMINAL LAW. Glanville Williams. Alfred Knopf. 1957. $5.00.
> One chapter deals with the legal, theological, medical, moral, and biological aspects of artificial insemination.

SEXUAL MORALITY. Ronald Atkinson. Harcourt, Brace & World. 1966. $4.50.
> Analyzes in one section the arguments usually advanced for and against artificial insemination.

YOUR MARRIAGE AND THE LAW. Harriet F. Pilpel and Theodora Zavin. Rinehart & Co. 1952. OP.
> A chapter to help married couples decide about artificial insemination. Considered mainly from legal and psychological perspective.

ORGANIZATIONS AND SOURCES

Information on current legal and medical developments may be obtained from:

AMERICAN BAR ASSOCIATION.
1155 E. 60th St., Chicago, Ill. 60637.

AMERICAN MEDICAL ASSOCIATION.
535 N. Dearborn St., Chicago, Ill. 60610.

PERIODICALS AND JOURNALS

None devoted exclusively to the subject. See medical, sociological, and ethical journals for possible articles.

❧   PRINTED MATERIALS

SEXUAL INTERGRITY IN MODERN SOCIETY. A study booklet with a brief section on artificial insemination. $.10.
Commission on Research and Social Action, The American Lutheran Church, 422 S. 5th St., Minneapolis, Minn. 55415.

AUDIO VISUALS

None for general use.

CAPITAL PUNISHMENT
(See also Crime)

BOOKS

CAPITAL PUNISHMENT. J. T. Sellin. Harpers. 1967. $3.50 paper.
A recent work of arguments and trends.

CAPITAL PUNISHMENT: A WORLD VIEW. James Avery
Joyce. Thomas Nelson & Sons. 1961. $5.00.
> An excellent study of capital punishment throughout the world.

CAPITAL PUNISHMENT AS A DETERRENT AND THE
ALTERNATIVE. Gerald Gardiner. Camelot Press Ltd. 1956.
OP.
> Explores and refutes each argument in favor of capital punishment.

CRIME IN AMERICA. Herbert A. Bloch, ed. Philosophical Library. 1961. $6.00.
> Two chapters with extensive statistics by experts in the field of
> criminology.

CRISES IN MORALITY. C. W. Scudder, ed. Chapter 6. Broadman. 1964. $3.50.
> A chapter listing the pro and con arguments and dealing with the
> biblical material on capital punishment.

THE DEATH PENALTY IN AMERICA (An Anthology). Hugo
Adam Bedau, ed. Anchor Books, Doubleday. 1964. $1.95 paper.
> An exhaustive study of capital punishment by competent authorities.
> This is a basic source of study on the subject.

DEATH ROW CHAPLAIN. Byron E. Eshelman. Prentice Hall.
1962. OP.
> The chaplain at San Quintin penitentiary writes movingly about
> the human side of the death penalty.

ESSAYS ON THE DEATH PENALTY. T. Robert Ingram, ed.
St. Thomas Press. 1963. $1.95.
> Essays favoring capital punishment. Biblical and social studies.
> Excellent source from this perspective.

A HISTORY OF CAPITAL PUNISHMENT. John Laurence
Pritchard. Citadel. 1960. OP.
> History of the forms and extent of capital punishment. Interesting
> background.

THE POWER OF LIFE OR DEATH. Michael DiSalle and Lawrence G. Blochman. Random House. 1965. $4.95.
> Recommended by the National Council on Crime and Delinquency
> as a study on capital punishment. The former governor of Ohio
> speaks out against capital punishment.

ORGANIZATIONS AND SOURCES

The following organizations deal extensively with capital punishment:

AMERICAN LEAGUE TO ABOLISH CAPITAL PUNISH-
MENT. Publishes *Journal News-Notes* and special bulletins.
Reprints and leaflets.
> 14 Pearl St., Brookline, Mass. 02146.

THE OKLAHOMA SOCIETY FOR THE ABOLITION OF
CAPITAL PUNISHMENT. Some leaflets available.
912 N. W. 57th, Oklahoma City, Okla. 73118.

PENNSYLVANIA COUNCIL TO ABOLISH THE PENALTY
OF DEATH. Several inexpensive pamphlets, booklets· re-
prints, books and some free material.
Room 300, 311 Juniper St., Philadelphia, Pa. 19107.

Organizations and sources having helpful information:

BOARD OF SOCIAL MINISTRY, LUTHERAN CHURCH IN
AMERICA.
231 Madison Ave., New York, N. Y. 10016.

*CHRISTIAN LIFE COMMISSION, BAPTIST GENERAL
CONVENTION OF TEXAS.
206 Baptist Bldg., Dallas, Tex. 75201.

CHRISTIAN LIFE COMMISSION, SOUTHERN BAPTIST
CONVENTION.
460 James Robertson Parkway, Nashville, Tenn. 37219.

COUNCIL FOR CHRISTIAN SOCIAL ACTION, UNITED
CHURCH OF CHRIST.
289 Park Ave., S., New York, N. Y. 10010.

DEPT. OF CHRISTIAN SOCIAL RELATIONS, EXECUTIVE
COUNCIL, EPISCOPAL CHURCH.
815 2nd Ave., New York, N. Y. 10017.

DIVISION OF CHRISTIAN SOCIAL CONCERN, AMERICAN
BAPTIST CONVENTION.
Valley Forge, Pennsylvania 19481.

FRIENDS COMMITTEE ON LEGISLATION.
245—2nd St., N. E., Washington, D. C. 20002.

*GENERAL BOARD OF CHRISTIAN SOCIAL CONCERNS
OF THE METHODIST CHURCH.
100 Maryland Ave., N. E., Washington, D. C. 20002.

NATIONAL COUNCIL OF CHURCHES.
475 Riverside Dr., New York, N. Y. 10027.

PERIODICALS AND JOURNALS

None specifically devoted to subject. For general area of crime and
punishment see section on Crime.

PRINTED MATERIALS

CAPITAL PUNISHMENT. Includes questions and answers on the
subject and a discussion of the problem. $.10.

Board of Christian Education, Presbyterian Church in the U.S., Box 1176, Richmond, Va. 23209.

CAPITAL PUNISHMENT. A staff report by the Board of Social Ministry of the Lutheran Church in America. $.10.
231 Madison Ave., New York, N. Y. 10016.

CAPITAL PUNISHMENT. Study document on U.S.A. use of death penalty. $.25.
Social Justice Dept., National Council of Churches, 475 Riverside Dr., New York, N. Y. 10027.

CAPITAL PUNISHMENT. Richard M. Werkheiser and Arthur C. Barnhart. A 1961 statement. $.35.
Executive Council of the Episcopal Church, 815 2nd Ave., New York, N. Y. 10017.

CAPITAL PUNISHMENT. Presentation of a case against capital punishment with a discussion which challenges the presentation. $.25.
Center for the Study of Democratic Institutions, Box 4068, Santa Barbara, Cal. 93103.

THE CHRISTIAN AND CAPITAL PUNISHMENT. John H. Yoder. A 24-page booklet with a theological orientation from the Institute of Mennonite Studies. $.50.
Mennonite Publishing House, Herald Press, Scottsdale, Pa. 15683.

CONCERNS FOR CHRISTIAN CITIZENS, Sept., 1965. The entire issue was devoted to a study of capital punishment. $.25.
Div. of Christian Social Concern of the American Baptist Convention, Valley Forge, Pa. 19481.

THE DEATH PENALTY AND CIVIL LIBERTIES. A case against capital punishment from a legal point of view. $.10.
American Civil Liberties Union, 156 Fifth Ave., New York, N. Y. 10010.

THE DEATH PENALTY AND THE STATE OF OKLAHOMA A brief pamphlet dealing with the 14 most asked questions about capital punishment. Single copy free on request.
The Oklahoma Society for the Abolition of Capital Punishment, 912 N. W. 57th St., Oklahoma City, Okla. 73118.

THE METHODIST CHURCH AND REHABILITATION OF THE CRIMINAL. Contains article and list of sources. $.50.

TENNESSEE VS. WASH JONES: THE CLOSING ARGU-MENT FOR THE DEFENSE. A closing statement by a lawyer pleading for the end to the death penalty. $2.00 per 100.

WHAT DO THE CHURCHES SAY ON CAPITAL PUNISH-MENT? Statements from various church groups. $.25.
General Board of Social Concerns of the Methodist Church, 100 Maryland Ave., N. E., Washington, D. C. 20002.

MAN'S RIGHT TO LIFE. Ruth Leigh. 1959. A 56-page paperback booklet with study questions, charts, and bibliography. $.35.

    Commission on Social Action of Reform Judaism, Union of American Hebrew Congregations, 838 Fifth Ave., New York, N. Y. 10021.

MURDER AND THE PENALTY OF DEATH. Thorsten Sellin ed. The Nov. 1952 issue of *The Annals* of the American Academy of Political and Social Science. A major source piece $2.00.

    3937 Chestnut St., Philadelphia, Pa. 19104.

*A STUDY OF ARGUMENTS FOR AND AGAINST CAPITAL PUNISHMENT. An 8-page pamphlet setting forth the issues from a biblical and secular perspective. $.10.

    Christian Life Commission, Baptist General Convention of Texas, 206 Baptist Bldg., Dallas, Tex. 75201.

*THIS LIFE WE TAKE. A strong case against capital punishment from a Christian viewpoint. 34 pages. Statistics and summary of world trends. $.25.

    Friends Committee on Legislation, 245—2nd St., N. E., Washington, D. C. 20002.

AUDIO VISUALS

THE DOOMED. 22 min. motion picture. B&W. $5.00 rental. A young man has killed another and must pay for his crime with his life. In his last hour, he tries to discuss his sentence with the guards, but they can give him only the "pat" answers of society. A minister appears, but his words too are ineffectual. The viewer sees the reactions of the prisoner as he is strapped into the chair and the gas applied.

    University of Southern California, Film Distribution Div., University Park, Los Angeles, Cal. 90007.

WE ARE MURDERERS. B&W. 113 min. Rental with no admission charge $45.00, with admission charge $60.00. Andre Cayatte (director) and Charles Spaak (screenwriter), both former lawyers, have made a relentless attack on the institution of capital punishment. French dialog with English subtitles.

    Brandon Films, Inc., 200 W. 57th St., New York, N. Y. 10019.

CHURCH AND STATE

(See also Citizenship and Political Action)

BOOKS

AMERICA'S WAY IN CHURCH, STATE, AND SOCIETY. Joseph M. Dawson. Macmillan. 1953. OP

> A forthright declaration for complete separation of church and state.

*CHURCH, STATE, AND FREEDOM. Leo Pfeffer. Beacon. 1953, Rev. Ed. $15.00.

> The best single volume on the historical and legal aspects of church and state in the U. S.

CHURCH AND STATE IN AMERICAN HISTORY. John F. Wilson. D. C. Heath & Co. 1965. OP

> Helpful in setting the background for current issues in the church-state field.

CHURCH AND STATE IN SCRIPTURE, HISTORY, AND CONSTITUTIONAL LAW. James E. Wood, Jr., E. Bruce Thompson, and Robert T. Miller. Baylor Univ. Press. 1958. $3.00. $1.75 paper.

> An excellent introductory volume on the important aspects of the church-state issue. The chapter on law is dated but still provides helpful insight. Order from Baylor Book Store, P. O. Box 6325, Waco, Texas 76706. Add $.25 handling charge.

CHURCH AND STATE IN THE UNITED STATES. Anson Phelps Stokes. 3 vol. Harper. 1950. $12.50.

> The definitive treatment of church and state in America; contains a fairly comprehensive annotated bibliography.

*CHURCH AND STATE IN THE UNITED STATES. Anson Phelps Stokes and Leo Pfeffer. Harper. 1964. $12.50.

> A one-volume, condensed revised edition.

CHURCH AND STATE IN YOUR OWN COMMUNITY. Elwyn A. Smith. Westminster. 1963. $1.25.

> Useful in study groups. Provides background information on different positions regarding church-state relations and deals with concrete issues on the community level.

CHURCH AND STATE UNDER GOD. Albert G. Huegli. Concordia. 1964. $8.00.

> A re-evaluation of church-state relations with special reference to emerging trends in political and social life. A symposium by competent Lutheran scholars.

*JOHN COURTNEY MURRAY: CONTEMPORARY CHURCH-STATE THEORY. Thomas T. Love. Doubleday. 1965. $4.95.

> A critique of the progressive Roman Catholic concept of church-state relations especially as found in the U. S.

*PROTESTANT CONCEPTS OF CHURCH AND STATE.
Thomas Sanders. Doubleday. 1965. $1.45.
    A recent survey of major non-Catholic opinions of the relation of
    church and state. Demonstrates that a variety of beliefs have been
    held on this subject.

RELIGIOUS LIBERTY: AN INQUIRY. M. Searle Bates. Harper. 1945. OP.
    The best book on the subject of religious liberty around the world;
    excellent case studies of various nations of the world. Dated.

THE STATE IN THE NEW TESTAMENT. Oscar Cullman.
Charles Scribner's Sons. 1966. $3.95, $1.45 paper.
    The best single volume on the subject. Helpful insight into the
    relation of Jesus to the state and why he took the position he did.

ORGANIZATIONS AND SOURCES

The following organizations are devoted to church and state or have
extensive material:

*AMERICANS UNITED FOR SEPARATION OF CHURCH
AND STATE. Many pamphlets, booklets, films, tapes, and
records. Publish monthly *Church and State*. List of materials
available. Has available the largest stock of materials on church
and state in the U. S. Favors strong separation of church and
state.
    1633 Mass. Ave., N. W., Washington, D. C. 20036.

BAPTIST JOINT COMMITTEE ON PUBLIC AFFAIRS. Staff
reports, pamphlets, booklets. Publish *Report from the Capital*.
Sponsor annual conferences. List of materials available.
    200 Maryland Ave., N. E., Washington, D. C. 20002.

INSTITUTE OF CHURCH AND STATE OF VILLANOVA
UNIVERSITY SCHOOL OF LAW. Publishes an annual review of church and state and of religion, law, and society
entitled *Religion and the Public Order*.
    Villanova University School of Law, Villanova, Pa. 19085.

J. M. DAWSON STUDIES IN CHURCH AND STATE. An
academic program of research, graduate courses, and publishing. Emphasis on entire field of religious liberty and church-
state relations both in the United States and abroad.
    Baylor University, Waco, Tex. 76703.

RELIGIOUS FREEDOM AND PUBLIC AFFAIRS OF THE
NATIONAL CONFERENCE OF CHRISTIANS AND
JEWS. Study papers and pamphlets available particularly in
regard to Sunday closing laws.
    43 W. 57th St., New York, N. Y. 10019.

*RELIGIOUS LIBERTY, DEPT. OF SOCIAL JUSTICE, NA-
TIONAL COUNCIL OF CHURCHES. Booklets, study papers
materials from the 1964 conference on church and state, and
bibliographies available.
475 Riverside Dr., New York, N. Y. 10027.

The following organizations have helpful materials:

AMERICAN CIVIL LIBERTIES UNION. Vast amounts of
material available, particularly related to laws or practices
violating civil liberty.
156 Fifth Ave., New York, N. Y. 10010.

AMERICAN JEWISH COMMITTEE. Seriously written material on religious liberty.
165 E. 56th St., New York, N. Y. 10022.

AMERICAN JEWISH CONGRESS. Helpful to gain a Jewish
perspective.
15 E. 84th St., New York, N. Y. 10028.

*THE ANTI-DEFAMATION LEAGUE OF B'NAI B'RITH.
Church-state issues examined from a Jewish perspective.
315 Lexington Ave., New York, N. Y. 10016.

BOARD OF SOCIAL MINISTRY, LUTHERAN CHURCH IN
AMERICA.
231 Madison Ave., New York, N. Y. 10016.

CENTER FOR THE STUDY OF DEMOCRATIC INSTITU-
TIONS. Material on church-state relations and on religion in
the free society.
Box 4068, Santa Barbara, Cal. 93103.

COMMISSION ON RESEARCH & SOCIAL ACTION, THE
AMERICAN LUTHERAN CHURCH.
422 S. 5th St., Minneapolis, Minn. 55415.

GENERAL BOARD OF CHRISTIAN SOCIAL CONCERNS.
The Methodist Bldg., 100 Maryland Ave., N. E., Washington, D. C.
20002.

NATIONAL ASSOCIATION OF EVANGELICALS. Material
and information from the conservative Protestant position.
1405 G St., N. W., Washington, D. C. 20005.

*U. S. CATHOLIC CONFERENCE. Information on Catholic
position on church and state, generally favoring an increase
of tax support for church-related institutions.
1312 Mass. Ave., N. W., Washington, D. C. 20005.

PERIODICALS AND JOURNALS

CHURCH AND STATE: A MONTHLY REVIEW. M (except Aug.) Minimum membership contribution of $5.00 includes $3.00 for 1 yr. subscription, single copies $.35. Published by Americans United for Separation of Church and State.
> 1633 Mass. Ave., N. W., Washington, D. C. 20036.

A JOURNAL OF CHURCH AND STATE. 3 times a yr. $3.50. $1.50 for single copy. Published by J. M. Dawson Studies in Church and State of Baylor University.
> Box 258, Baylor University, Waco, Tex. 76703.

LIBERTY. BM $1.25. Published for the Religious Liberty Association of America. A Seventh-Day Adventist publication for church-state separation and religious freedom.
> Review and Herald Publishing Assoc., 6840 Eastern Ave., N. W., Washington, D. C. 20012.

REPORT FROM THE CAPITAL. 10 times a yr. $1.50. Bulletin to set forth information and interpretation about public affairs that are relevant to Baptist principles.
> Baptist Joint Committee on Public Affairs, 200 Maryland Ave., N. E., Washington, D. C. 20002.

PRINTED MATERIALS

*BASES FOR SEPARATION OF CHURCH AND STATE. A 16-page booklet outlining the biblical, historical, and constitutional grounds for the separation of church and state. $.10.

*CHRISTIANITY AND RELIGIOUS LIBERTY. A compilation of speeches by authorities in the field of religious liberty. $1.00.
> Christian Life Commission, 206 Baptist Bldg., Dallas, Tex. 75201.

BASIC DOCUMENTS RELATING TO THE RELIGIOUS CLAUSES OF THE FIRST AMENDMENT. A booklet listing significant documents from American history which aid in interpreting the religious clauses of the First Amendment to the Constitution. $1.00.

THE CURRENT CHALLENGE TO CHURCH-STATE SEPARATION. A discussion of trends and forces which are reshaping the relation of church and state in the U. S. $1.00.

STUDIES IN CHURCH-STATE RELATIONS: THE AMERICAN WAY. A booklet outlining a separation position for church-state relations in the U. S. and pointing out that Catholics are a serious threat to this position. $1.00.
> American United, 1633 Mass. Ave., N.W., Washington, D.C., 20036.

WE HOLD THESE TRUTHS. A compilation of speeches by competent spokesmen in the field of church-state relations. $1.00.

> Americans United, 1633 Mass. Ave., N. W., Washington, D. C. 20036.

CHURCH, STATE, AND PUBLIC SCHOOL FOR CITIZENS. A helpful booklet for insight into a Jewish position on religion in public schools. $.35.

> Institute of Human Relations Press, American Jewish Committee, 165 E. 56th St., New York, N. Y. 10022.

CHURCH AND STATE. A booklet prepared by the J. M. Dawson Studies in Church and State, Baylor University, setting forth the historical and contemporary materials needed to comprehend present church-state tensions. $.15.

> The Supreme Council, 33°, Ancient and Accepted Scottish Rite of Freemasonry, Southern Jurisdiction, U.S.A., 1733—16th St., N. W., Washington, D. C. 20009.

CHURCH AND STATE A LUTHERAN PERSPECTIVE. A booklet setting forth a Lutheran position on church-state issues. $.35.

> Board of Social Ministry, Lutheran Church in America, 231 Madison Ave., New York, N. Y. 10016.

*THE MEANING OF RELIGIOUS LIBERTY. A concise statement on religious liberty, its meaning, implications for the U.S., and relation to church-state separation. Single copy free on request.

PAPERS FROM THE ANNUAL STUDY CONFERENCE OF THE BAPTIST JOINT COMMITTEE ON PUBLIC AFFAIRS. Comprehensive treatment of various phases of the church-state issue in the U. S. by competent authorities. Write for a complete list of topics covered and prices.

SUPREME COURT PACKET. Pamphlets outlining recent Supreme Court decisions related to religious liberty and church-state separation. $1.00.

> Baptist Joint Committee on Public Affairs, 200 Maryland Ave., N. E., Washington, D. C. 20002.

*PAPERS FROM THE NATIONAL STUDY CONFERENCE ON CHURCH AND STATE. Preparatory papers and reports from the National Study Conference on Church and State with much valuable information.

> Religious Liberty Dept., National Council of Churches, 475 Riverside Dr., New York, N. Y. 10027.

*RELIGIOUS FREEDOM PACKET. Selected materials on religious liberty, church-state, civil liberty, and civil rights. $3.00.

> Church of the Brethren, Elgin, Ill. 60120.

AUDIO VISUALS

BOYCOTT. 16 mm. B&W 30 min. $10.00 rental. Film on how a man who stood alone against church-state violations in his community was forced to suffer for his convictions.

THE CHALLENGE TO CHURCH-STATE SEPARATION. A speech by E. S. James, former editor, *Baptist Standard,* on record and tape. $2.00.

SEPARATION AND FREEDOM. A speech by Gerald H. Kennedy, Bishop of the Methodist Church, on record and tape. $2.00.

> Americans United, 1633 Mass. Ave., N. W., Washington, D. C. 20036.

CAPTURED. 16 mm. B&W 40 min. $10.00 rental. Semi-documentary drama on a public school controlled by Catholics. Points up a problem in church-state relations.

MAGNIFICENT HERITAGE. 16 mm. Color. 60 min. $24.00 rental. The story behind the Bill of Rights, its conception and eventual passage by the newly formed Congress, revolves about one key figure—John Leland—a courageous Baptist minister who dedicated himself to the concept of "freedom of religion for all men." His story is recreated here, depicting Baptist participation in the struggle for religious freedom.

THE PRICE OF FREEDOM. 16 mm. B&W 8 min. $3.00 rental. Develops the religious struggle of early Baptists and shows how their fight has given us the freedom we enjoy today.

> Southern Baptist Film Centers.

OTHER HELPS

A SELECTED BIBLIOGRAPHY for Graduate Seminar on Church and State, J. M. Dawson Studies in Church and State, Baylor University. A helpful selected, annotated bibliography prepared for distribution to graduate students. Not for general distribution but available for examination.

> J. M. Dawson Studies in Church and State, Baylor University, Waco, Tex. 76703.

SELECTED RECENT BIBLIOGRAPHY ON RELIGIOUS LIBERTY (1958-1965) assembled by A. F. Carrillo de Albornoz for the Secretariat on Religious Liberty of the World Council of Churches, 1965. Contains both books and articles. Worldwide in scope. Lacks annotation.

> Secretariat on Religious Liberty, World Council of Churches, 150 Route de Ferney, Geneva, Switzerland.

CITIZENSHIP AND POLITICAL ACTION

(See also Economics, Extremism, International Relations, United Nations, War-Peace)

BOOKS

*THE CHRISTIAN ENCOUNTERS POLITICS AND GOVERNMENT. P. G. Elbrecht. Concordia. 1965. $1.00 paper.

> A direct and easy-to-follow presentation of the American political system. The author, a political officeholder, calls Christians to service within the American political system.

CHRISTIANITY AND DEMOCRACY. Jacques Maritain. Hillary. N.D. $1.50.

> A Catholic viewpoint on politics in a democratic setting by a leading scholar.

CHRISTIANITY AND POLITICAL RESPONSIBILITY. Alden D. Kelley. Westminster. 1961. $5.00.

> Discusses the relation between religion and culture, the meaning of communication, nature of political philosophy and the historical church in society. From this basis he maps the lines of Christian political responsibility today.

CHRISTIANS AND POWER POLITICS. Alan Booth. Association. 1961. $3.00.

> As the Secretary of the Commission of the Churches on International Affairs in Great Britain—the body which keeps in touch with politics on behalf of the World Council of Churches—the author seeks to ascertain the relevance of the Christian gospel to the conflicts in international relations.

CHRISTIANS AND THE STATE. John Bennett. Scribners. 1958. $4.50.

> Discusses the theological basis of the state itself, the state's nature and function, and problems of political ethics. Last sections consider current church-state issues.

*CHRISTIANS ARE CITIZENS. Malcom Calhoun, ed. John Knox. 1957. $1.25.

> Presbyterians discuss the role of the responsible Christian citizen in our era of political upheaval. A practical appeal to and guideline for Christians in political action.

*CITIZENSHIP FOR CHRISTIANS. Foy Valentine. Broadman. 1965. $1.50.

> A book of approximately 100 pages which deals with citizenship from a biblical, historical, and contemporary perspective. Offers practical suggestions for Christian involvement in politics and action as citizens.

POLITICS AND EVANGELISM. Philippe Maury. Doubleday. 1960. OP.

> By a Frenchman, this little book explores a seldom-treated subject

in an exciting way. It shows that political action and evangelism are closely related.

*POLITICS FOR CHRISTIANS. William Muehl. Association. 1956. $3.00.

> An interesting, readable book on political involvement and action by one who has been in politics. Practical and helpful for developing better citizenship.

THE PROTESTANT AND POLITICS. William Lee Miller. Westminster. 1958. $1.00.

> Criticizes Protestants for lack of effective political action and shows how the Christian faith can raise the level of political activity in the U. S.

ORGANIZATIONS AND SOURCES

Political Parties:

DEMOCRATIC NATIONAL COMMITTEE.
> 1730 K St., N. W., Washington, D. C. 20006.

REPUBLICAN NATIONAL COMMITTEE.
> 1625 I St., N. W., Washington, D. C. 20006.

Examples of organizations generally considered conservative directly concerned with political action:

AMERICANS FOR CONSTITUTIONAL ACTION.
> 20 E. St., N. W., Washington, D. C. 20001.

AMERICA'S FUTURE, INC.
> 542 Main St., New Rochelle, N. Y. 10801.

AMERICAN SECURITY COUNCIL.
> 123 N. Wacker Dr., Chicago, Ill. 60606.

Examples of organizations generally considered liberal directly concerned with political action:

AFL-CIO.
> 815 16th St., N. W., Washington, D. C. 20006.

AMERICAN CIVIL LIBERTIES UNION.
> 156 Fifth Ave., New York, N. Y. 10010.

AMERICANS FOR DEMOCRATIC ACTION.
> 1223 Connecticut Ave., N. W., Washington, D. C. 20036.

Organizations not directly involved in political action with materials on citizenship concerns:

BROOKINGS INSTITUTION.
> 1775 Mass. Ave., N. W., Washington, D. C. 20036.

CENTER FOR INFORMATION ON AMERICA.
Washington, Conn. 06793.

CENTER FOR THE STUDY OF DEMOCRATIC INSTITU-
TIONS.
Box 4068, Santa Barbara, Cal. 93103.

THE CHAMBER OF COMMERCE OF THE U. S.
1615 H St., N. W., Washington, D. C. 20006.

THE LEAGUE OF WOMEN VOTERS EDUCATION FUND.
1026—17th St., N. W., Washington, D. C. 20036.

Religiously-affiliated organizations with materials on citizenship concerns:

BACK TO GOD TRACT COMMITTEE.
2850 Kalamazoo Ave., S. E., Grand Rapids, Mich. 49508.

CHRISTIAN LIFE COMMISSION OF THE BAPTIST GEN-
ERAL CONVENTION OF TEXAS.
206 Baptist Bldg., Dallas, Tex. 75201.

CHRISTIAN LIFE COMMISSION OF THE SOUTHERN
BAPTIST CONVENTION.
460 James Robertson Parkway, Nashville, Tenn. 37219.

COUNCIL FOR CHRISTIAN SOCIAL ACTION, UNITED
CHURCH OF CHRIST.
289 Park Ave. S., New York, N. Y. 10010.

DIVISION OF CHRISTIAN ACTION, BOARD OF CHRIS-
TIAN EDUCATION, PRESBYTERIAN CHURCH, U. S.
Box 1176, Richmond, Va. 23209.

DIVISION OF CHRISTIAN CITIZENSHIP, EXECUTIVE
COUNCIL, EPISCOPAL CHURCH.
815 2nd Ave., New York, N. Y. 10017.

THE DIVISION OF CHRISTIAN RELATIONS OF THE
BOARD OF CHURCH EXTENSION FOR THE PRES-
BYTERIAN CHURCH OF THE U.S.
341 Ponce de Leon Ave., N. E., Atlanta, Ga. 30305.

GENERAL BOARD OF CHRISTIAN SOCIAL CONCERNS,
METHODIST CHURCH.
100 Maryland Ave., N. E., Washington, D. C. 20002.

NATIONAL COMMISSION ON CITIZENSHIP AND CIVIC
AFFAIRS OF THE ANTI-DEFAMATION LEAGUE OF
B'NAI B'RITH (Jewish).
315 Lexington Ave., New York, N. Y. 10016.

NATIONAL COUNCIL OF CHURCHES.
> 475 Riverside Dr., New York, N. Y. 10027.

RELIGIOUS ACTION CENTER OF THE UNION OF AMERICAN HEBREW CONGREGATIONS.
> 2027 Mass. Ave., N. W., Washington, D. C. 20036.

U. S. CATHOLIC CONFERENCE.
> 1312 Mass. Ave., N. W., Washington, D. C. 20005.
> See also Appendix, Religiously-Oriented Organizations.

Examples of religiously-affiliated organizations with an active concern in national legislation:

BAPTIST JOINT COMMITTEE ON PUBLIC AFFAIRS.
> 200 Maryland Ave., N. E., Washington, D. C. 20002.

FRIENDS COMMITTEE ON NATIONAL LEGISLATION.
> 245—2nd St., N. E., Washington, D. C. 20002.

U. S. CATHOLIC CONFERENCE.
> 1312 Mass. Ave., N. W., Washington, D. C. 20005.

PERIODICALS AND JOURNALS

(See also list of periodicals in appendix, many of which relate to politics.)

ADA WORLD. M except July, Aug. $5.00. Gives liberal slant on national and international issues.
> Americans for Democratic Action, 1223 Connecticut Ave., N. W., Washington, D. C. 20036.

AMERICAN POLITICAL SCIENCE REVIEW. Q $15.00, $3.75 per copy. Offers essays, studies, bibliographies, and news and notes on contemporary political developments.
> American Political Science Assn., 1726 Mass. Ave., N. W., Washington, D. C. 20036.

*THE ANNALS OF THE AMERICAN ACADEMY OF POLITICAL AND SOCIAL SCIENCE. BM $8.00. Factual, scholarly, readable articles on issues of concern to citizens. Book reviews.
> 3937 Chestnut St., Philadelphia, Pa. 19104.

BETWEEN THE LINES. SM $2.50. Newsletter dealing with affairs in the news with Wells' own interpretation. He is generally pacifist in viewpoint.
> Charles Wells, 7 Patton Ave., Box 143, Princeton, N. J. 08540, or Newtown, Pa. 18940.

FOREIGN AFFAIRS. Q $6.00, $1.50 per copy. A non-partisan review of current ideas and policies affecting U. S. relations in all parts of the world, including international political, commercial, and cultural relations. Majority of contributors are from academic, government, and business communities.

> Council on Foreign Relations, Inc., 58 E. 68th St., New York, N. Y. 10021.

HUMAN EVENTS. W $12.50. An extremely conservative publication. News and interpretation on domestic and international affairs, politics and economics.

> 410 First St., S. E., Washington, D. C. 20003.

*NATIONAL VOTER. 10 times a yr. $1.00. Non-partisan factual information on political action and issues.

> League of Women Voters of the U. S., 1026—17th St., N. W., Washington, D. C. 20036.

THE NEW REPUBLIC. W $9.00. Articles, editorials, and news. Written from a liberal, secular perspective.

> 1244—19th St., Washington, D. C. 20036.

POLITICAL SCIENCE QUARTERLY. Q $6.00, $1.50 per copy. Non-partisan periodical in the fields of political science and economics. Of interest to scholars and laymen.

> Academy of Political Science, Fayerweather Hall, Columbia University, New York, N. Y. 10027.

PRINTED MATERIALS

ACTION COURSE IN PRACTICAL POLITICS. An education course explaining the mechanics of politics in 8 pamphlets. $3.00.

> The Chamber of Commerce of the U. S., 1615 H St., N. W., Washington, D. C. 20006.

BELIEFS INTO ACTION. A 14-page guide to political involvement and action. $.15.

HOW-TO-WRITE YOUR CONGRESSMAN AND THE PRESIDENT, HOW-TO-WORK IN POLITICS, HOW-TO-VISIT YOUR CONGRESSMAN, and HOW-TO-WRITE A LETTER TO THE EDITOR. A series of brief helpful pamphlets on political action. $.05 each.

REGISTER CHRISTIAN OPINION. A guide to political action. Practical and to the point. Includes addresses of government offices and a Congressional Directory. $.15.

> Friends Committee on National Legislation, 245—2nd St., N. E., Washington, D. C. 20002.

THE BIBLE SPEAKS ON CITIZENSHIP and CHRISTIAN PRINCIPLES APPLIED TO CITIZENSHIP. Two brief pamphlets setting forth biblical teachings related to citizenship and urging Christians to function as effective citizens. $.02 each.

*CHRISTIANITY AND POLITICAL ACTION. Collection of addresses on Christian involvement in government and political action. $1.00.

> Christian Life Commission, 206 Baptist Bldg., Dallas, Tex. 75201.

*THE CITIZEN AND POLITICAL PARTIES. History, organization, and function of political parties locally, in the states, and in the nation. Urges participation. $.35.

*LOBBYING. A step-by-step objective analysis of the process of lobbying in modern government. $.35.

*PUBLIC OFFICES AT THE LOCAL LEVEL. Answers the questions "Who should try? How does one get elected?" $.35.

*WHO, ME A POLITICIAN?!? A 15-page booklet telling why and how citizens should become involved in political action. $.35. (These four are part of an excellent series GRASS ROOTS GUIDE. Write for full listing.)

> Center for Information on America, Washington, Conn. 06793.

*CITIZENSHIP AND POLITICAL LIFE PACKET. Materials on the Christian and politics, the church and state, and political action. $3.00.

> Church of the Brethren, Elgin, Ill. 60120.

HOW A BILL BECOMES A LAW. An illustrated guide for national legislation.

> National Commission on Citizenship and Civic Affairs, B'nai B'rith, 1701 K St., N. W., Washington, D. C. 20006.

HOW TO GET BETTER GOVERNMENT. Well-written pamphlet on practical steps to better government. $.25.

*MAN AND HIS GOVERNMENT. Explains the theory of government and philosophies of the governing of men. $.60.

> Public Affairs Pamphlets, 381 Park Ave. S., New York, N. Y. 10016.

LEGISLATORS AND LOBBYISTS. Description of the way lobbyists operate, indications of lobby spending, and specific examples of lobby efforts. $2.50.

POLITICS IN AMERICA: 1945-1964. A 128-page chronological report on the issues and decisions in American politics. $2.50.

> Congressional Quarterly, Inc., 1735 K St., N. W., Washington, D. C. 20006.

THE MAZES OF MODERN GOVERNMENT: THE STATES, THE LEGISLATURE, THE BUREAUCRACY, THE COURTS. Leading figures in government discuss the nature and inter-relation of various aspects of government in America. $.35.

> Center for the Study of Democratic Institutions, Box 4068, Santa Barbara, Cal. 93103.

UNITED STATES GOVERNMENT ORGANIZATION MANUAL. A complete guide to the various departments which compose the government of the U.S. Published annually. $1.75 Official Congressional Directory also available.

> Supt. of Documents, U. S. Government Printing Office, Washington, D. C. 20402.

AUDIO VISUALS

BUILDING POLITICAL LEADERSHIP: GETTING INTO POLITICS. 16 mm. Sound. B&W 16 min. $3.90 rental. Discusses means whereby the private citizen may get into politics. Indicates the key approaches such as registering to vote, keeping informed on key issues, becoming active in political organizations, and seeking elective or appointive office.

*BUILDING POLITICAL LEADERSHIP: HOW OUR TWO-PARTY SYSTEM OPERATES. 16 mm. B&W Sound 21 min. $3.90 rental. Pictures the growth of political parties in America, describes the structure of the major parties, and outlines laws controlling the organization and activities of political parties. Discusses the growth of the two-party system, pointing out its strengths and weaknesses; indicates the lack of difference in parties; and emphasizes the fact that parties are only as good as the active citizens composing them.

> Audio Visual Center, Indiana University, Bloomington, Ind. 47405.

CHRISTIAN CONCERN IN POLITICS. 16 mm. B&W 13 min. Guide. $6.00 rental. An active Christian is asked to spearhead a clean-up movement in his community by seeking election to membership on the city council. He pleads that he is not qualified and does not want to "dirty his hands" by active participation in politics. A panel of three men discuss the pros and cons of the situation and suggest alternatives open to the man as a Christian citizen.

> Southern Baptist Film Centers.

*A CHRISTIAN IN POLITICS. 16 mm. B&W 30 min. $9.00 rental. An intriguing story of a man asked to run for political office and some timely words of wisdom from his pastor about Christian obligation. Highly recommended.

> Office for Audio Visuals, United Church of Christ, 1720 Chouteau Ave., St. Louis, Mo. 63103.

GOVERNMENT IN ACTION. Filmstrip series No. 7460. Color. 55 frames each. $6.00 each purchase. Series of 8 boxed $48.00. The intricate organizations of local, state, and federal governments are clearly illustrated by this series of original drawings which points out the sources of power and responsibilities of each segment of government. Titles: THE PRESIDENT, THE CONGRESS, THE FEDERAL COURTS, EXECUTIVE DEPARTMENTS AND AGENCIES, STATE GOVERNMENT, LOCAL GOVERNMENT, MUNICIPAL GOVERNMENT, THE UNITED NATIONS.

> Encyclopaedia Britannica Films Inc., 1150 Wilmette Ave., Wilmette, Ill. 60091.

HOW A BILL BECOMES A LAW. 16 mm. B&W Sound. 15 min. $3.25 rental. Defines and illustrates each step in the creation of new laws. Discusses laws, as created by the legislative body, administered by the executive body, and applied by the judicial body from their origin to their final emergence as laws of the land. Demonstrates numerous ways of creating new laws.

POLITICS AND ELECTIONS. 16 mm. B&W Sound. 19 min. $3.75 rental. Shows the methods of elections, the need for good government, and how to secure it. Shows how to evaluate a candidate.

> The University of Texas, Visual Instruction Bureau, Austin, Tex. 78712.

*WHO CARES? 16 mm. Color. Sound. 21 min. Free. The story of the birth of American Democracy—rule by the people, of the long struggle to resolve disagreements by ballots instead of bullets, and of a course of action to overcome a growing apathy to political affairs.

> "Who Cares?", Hughes Aircraft Co., Culver City, Cal. 90230.

YOU CAN WIN ELECTIONS. 16 mm. 25 min. $3.00 rental. While somewhat dated (1954) this film shows step-by-step procedure to win elections which is still workable.

> AFL-CIO Film Div., 815—16th St., N. W., Washington, D. C. 20006.

COMMUNISM

(See also Extremism, International Affairs, War-Peace)

BOOKS

CHRISTIANITY AND WORLD ISSUES. T. B. Maston. Macmillan. 1957. $5.95.

> Two chapters outline Communist beliefs and a Christian response to Communism. Brief introduction to Communism and how to evaluate it.

CHRISTIANS CONFRONT COMMUNISM. Paul Geren. Convention Press. 1962. $.75.

> This brief introduction discusses and evaluates the Communist view of God, history, man, ethics, science, church and state, and economics.

*COMMUNISM AND THE CHRISTIAN FAITH. Lester De Koster. Eerdmans. 1956. Rev. 1962. $3.50.

> A very readable volume providing insight into Communist belief particularly as related to basic Christian concepts. The use of word illustrations helps immensely in understanding what Communists really believe.

COMMUNISM AND THE CHURCHES. Ralph Lord Roy. Harcourt. 1960. $7.50.

> A lengthy account of the relation of Communism to Christian groups, primarily the Soviet Union and the United States. Discusses the reactions of churches to communism and the efforts of Communists to use the churches.

COMMUNISM OF MAO TSE-TUNG. Arthur A. Cohen. University of Chicago. 1964. $5.00, $1.75 paper.

> A recent view of the brand of Communism advocated by the Chinese Communist leader. Readable and reliable.

COMMUNISM: WHO? WHAT? WHY? Henlee H. Barnette. Broadman. 1962. $.95 paper.

> A brief booklet setting forth in simple terms the basic facts about Communism in a question-answer format. Helpful introduction.

DOCUMENTARY HISTORY OF COMMUNISM. Robert V. Daniels, ed. Random. 1960. 2 vol. $1.65 each, paper.

> Using the basic documents related to Communism this book traces the development of Communist thought and organization.

*STUDY OF COMMUNISM. J. Edgar Hoover. Holt, Rinehart, and Winston. 1963. $1.96 paper.

> A practical book on the idea, practices, and goals of Communists. Comes with a teacher's manual and answer book, $.72.

*THE THEORY AND PRACTICE OF COMMUNISM. R. N. Carew Hunt. Macmillan. 5th ed. 1957. $5.50, $1.25 paper (Penguin).

> Provides understanding in basic Communist philosophy and organiza-

tion. Technical rather than popular in approach. Emphasis on theory rather than current events.

TODAY'S ISMS: COMMUNISM, FACISM, SOCIALISM, CAPITALISM. W. Ebenstein. Prentice Hall. 4th ed. 1966. $4.65 paper.
> A popularly written comparison and contrast of the four leading economic-political theories of the modern world.

VOCABULARY OF COMMUNISM. Lester De Koster. Eerdmans. 1963. $3.50.
> A very helpful tool in understanding writings by or about Communists. Essentially a dictionary of Communist terms, phrases, and concepts.

WHAT WE MUST KNOW ABOUT COMMUNISM. Harry and Bonaro Overstreet. W. W. Norton and Co. 1958. $4.95, $.75 paper (Pocket Books).
> A clear presentation of the beliefs and plans of the Communists. Gives historical perspective.

*THE WORLD OF COMMUNISM. Rodger Swearingen. Houghton Mifflin. 1962. $3.75.
> A textbook on Communism. Comprehensive and scholarly. Recommended by Research Institute on Communist Strategy and Propaganda of the University of Southern California.

Primary source books:

CAPITAL. Karl Marx. Modern Library. $2.95.

COMMUNIST MANIFESTO. Karl Marx and Friedrich Engels, ed. by Samuel H. Beer. Appleton. $.50 paper.

QUOTATIONS FROM CHAIRMAN MAO TSE-TUNG. Peking: Foreign Language Press. 1966.

Books about Communist countries: Books describing conditions in Communist countries are dated almost as soon as they are written. Ask your librarian or bookdealer about the latest· best books on the subject. An excellent volume in this category is *House Without a Roof*, Maurice Hindus. Doubleday. 1960. $6.95. About Russia.

ORGANIZATIONS AND SOURCES

The following are sources of Communist material:

COMMUNIST PARTY, U.S.A. Pamphlets and information about the party. Publish newspaper twice weekly *The Worker*. Booklet *New Program of the Communist Party (U.S.A.)* $.95.
> 23 W. 26th St., New York, N. Y. 10010.

EMBASSY, UNION OF THE SOVIET SOCIALIST REPUBLICS (RUSSIA). Information on the Soviet Union.
1125 16th St., Washington, D. C. 20036.

POLITICAL AFFAIRS PUBLISHERS
23 W. 26th St., New York, N. Y. 10010.

The following organizations are devoted to a study of Communism:

THE HOUSE COMMITTEE ON UN-AMERICAN ACTIVITIES. "Guide to Subversive Organizations and Publications" and copies of hearings and testimony before the committee are available.
Secure list of publications from: The Supt. of Documents, U. S. Government Printing Office, Washington, D. C. 20402.

THE RESEARCH INSTITUTE ON COMMUNIST AFFAIRS. List of publications available, most of which are reprints of articles written by the Fellows of the Institute for various periodicals.
Columbia University, 435 W. 116th St., New York, N. Y. 10027.

RESEARCH INSTITUTE ON COMMUNIST STRATEGY AND PROPAGANDA. Maintains lecture series, summer institute on Communism, produces documentary TV-film series, publishes bi-monthly journal *Communist Affairs,* research reports and monographs, translates periodical literature from the Communist world and maintains a specialized library of historic materials dealing with Communism. Several extensive bibliographies are available from them.
School of International Relations, University of Southern California, Los Angeles, Cal. 90007.

The following have been classified as "professional anti-Communist organizations": (See also Extremism, Anti-Communist Organizations.)

CARDINAL MINDSZENTY FOUNDATION. Offers educational information on the evils of Communism. Pamphlets suitable for church racks, monthly publication *The Mindszenty Report,* and a "Guide for . . . Teachers, Parents, Students" for instruction on Communism listing books, films, publications, and pamphlets for various grades. ($.03 each).
Box 321, Clayton Branch, St. Louis, Mo. 63105.

CHRISTIAN ANTI-COMMUNISM CRUSADE. Booklets, tracts, manuals, tapes, records, and films. Lists of materials free. C.A.C.C. newsletter free to individuals, churches and schools.
124 E. 1st St., Long Beach, Cal. 90801.

CHRISTIAN CRUSADE. Magazine, tapes, books, booklets available. Holds conferences and schools throughout the U. S.
Box 977, Tulsa, Okla. 74102.

The following very conservative religious organizations have extensive material on Communism:

THE AMERICAN COUNCIL OF CHRISTIAN CHURCHES.
15 Park Row, New York, N. Y. 10038.

CHURCH LEAGUE OF AMERICA. Publishes monthly documented summary of current subversive activity *News and Views* and special detailed documented reports on organizations, individuals, publications and movements. Catalog of Publications and Training Aids is available. It includes reports, pamphlets, booklets, books, tapes, films, and film strips.
422 N. Prospect, Wheaton, Ill. 60187.

The following have materials on Communism though this is not their exclusive interest:

CENTER FOR STUDY OF DEMOCRATIC INSTITUTIONS.
Box 4068, Santa Barbara, Cal. 93103.

CHRISTIAN LIFE COMMISSION OF THE BAPTIST GENERAL CONVENTION OF TEXAS.
206 Baptist Bldg., Dallas, Tex. 75201.

CHRISTIAN LIFE COMMISSION OF THE SOUTHERN BAPTIST CONVENTION.
460 James Robertson Parkway, Nashville, Tenn. 37219.

COMMISSION ON RESEARCH AND SOCIAL ACTION, THE AMERICAN LUTHERAN CHURCH.
57 E. Main St., Columbus, Ohio 43215.

CONCORDIA TRACT MISSION.
Box 201, St. Louis, Mo. 63166.

THE COUNCIL FOR CHRISTIAN SOCIAL ACTION OF THE UNITED CHURCH OF CHRIST.
289 Park Ave., S., New York, N. Y. 10010.

GENERAL BOARD OF CHRISTIAN SOCIAL CONCERNS OF THE METHODIST CHURCH.
100 Maryland Ave., N. E., Washington, D. C. 20002.

THE NATIONAL COUNCIL OF CHURCHES.
475 Riverside Dr., New York, N. Y. 10027.

U. S. CATHOLIC CONFERENCE.
1312 Mass. Ave., N. W., Washington, D. C. 20005.

PERIODICALS AND JOURNALS

Study journals on Communism:

*COMMUNIST AFFAIRS. BM $5.00. Review of documentary materials.

> Research Institute on Communist Strategy and Propaganda, University of Southern Cal., University Park, Los Angeles, Cal. 90007.

CURRENT DIGEST OF THE SOVIET PRESS. W $150.00, $3.00 per copy. Basic source material (in English) on Soviet affairs from some 60 Soviet newspapers and magazines. Listings of contents of *Pravda* and *Izvestia* each week with translations of about ⅓ of the content.

> Edwards Brothers, Inc., W. 117th St., New York, N. Y. 10027.

*THE PROBLEMS OF COMMUNISM. BM $2.50, $.50 per copy. Publication of the U. S. Information Agency. Available to residents of the U. S. Discusses weaknesses and happenings of the Communist world.

> Supt. of Documents, U. S. Government Printing Office, Washington, D. C. 20402.

RELIGION IN COMMUNIST DOMINATED AREAS. BM $10. Reports on state of religious life in Communist areas.

> Dept. of International Affairs, National Council of Churches, 475 Riverside Dr., New York, N. Y. 10027.

Publications often classified as "Anti-Communist":

THE CHRISTIAN ANTI-COMMUNISM CRUSADE NEWSLETTER. Irregular. Rates on request. Dr. Fred Schwartz, editor.

> Box 890, Long Beach, Cal. 90801.

CHRISTIAN CRUSADE. M $2.00. Publication with a strong conservative slant on economics, politics, religion, and the U. N.

> Box 977, Tulsa, Okla. 74102.

NATIONAL CHRISTIAN NEWS. M $2.00.

> Box 10924, St. Petersburg, Fla. 33733.

THE TRUTH ABOUT COMMUNISM. Ultra-conservative paper, 6 issues $2.00.

> The Truth, Inc., 3400 W. Michigan, Milwaukee, Wis. 53208.

Communist publications:

CHINA PICTORIAL. M $2.50. A propaganda picture magazine selling Communism as practiced in China. Example of Communist propaganda.

> Guozi Shudian, P. O. Box 399, Hsitan Bldg., Peking, China.

POLITICAL AFFAIRS. M $5.00, students $4.00. Publication of Communist viewpoint, theoretical magazine.

> 799 Broadway, New York, N. Y. 10003.

SOVIET LIFE, M $3.50. The only magazine circulated in the U.S.A. by reciprocal agreement between the governments of the U.S.A. and U.S.S.R. Highly illustrated.
1706—18th St., N. W., Washington, D. C. 20009.

THE WORKER. SW $7.00, students $4.00. Paper whose editorial policy reflects the Communist viewpoint.
Communist Party, U.S.A., 23 W. 26th St., New York, N. Y. 10010.

PRINTED MATERIALS

COMMUNISM'S CHALLENGE TO AMERICA AND AMERICAN CHURCHES. An excellent booklet for use in churches with study groups. $.07.
Commission on Research and Social Action, The American Lutheran Church, 422 S. Fifth St., Minneapolis, Minn. 55415.

COMMUNISM: CHALLENGE TO CHRISTIANITY and COMMUNISM: CHALLENGE TO CHRISTIANS. Two brief pamphlets describing Communism and its relations to churches and individual Christians. $.02 each.
Christian Life Commission of the Southern Baptist Convention, 460 James Robertson Parkway, Nashville, Tenn. 37219.

COMMUNISM IN FERMENT: A REVIEW OF SOME RECENT LITERATURE. *Information Service,* Sept. 25, 1965. $.20. Bibliographic information and description of recent helpful materials.
National Council of Churches, 475 Riverside Dr., New York, N. Y. 10027.

*GUIDE TO SUBVERSIVE ORGANIZATIONS AND PUBLICATIONS. Listings of government-declared subversive organizations and publications in the U. S. Contains names of Communist front organizations. $.70.

LIST OF PUBLICATIONS. Relating to Communism issued by congressional committees, departments, and agencies of the U. S. Free.
Supt. of Documents, U. S. Government Printing Office, Washington, D. C. 20402.

HOW TO COMBAT COMMUNISM. A 24-page guide for study and action. $.20.
Council for Christian Social Action, United Church of Christ, 289 Park Ave., S., New York, N. Y. 10010.

*THE PROFILE OF COMMUNISM. A presentation of basic information about Communism which analyzes Communist programs, economy, inconsistencies, empire-building, and totalitarianism. 160 pp. $.95.

Anti-Defamation League, 315 Lexington Ave., New York, N. Y. 10016.

TWELVE WAYS TO COMBAT COMMUNISM. A brief booklet outlining practical sane action to thwart Communism. Prepared in co-operation with Lions International. Free.

All-American Conference to Combat Communism, 516 LaSalle Bldg., 1028 Conn. Ave., N. W., Washington, D. C. 20036.

*WHAT CHRISTIANS SHOULD KNOW ABOUT COMMU-NISM, WHY CHRISTIANS SHOULD OPPOSE COMMU-NISM, and WHAT CHRISTIANS SHOULD DO ABOUT COMMUNISM. Three brief pamphlets clearly setting forth Communist beliefs and practices and suggested responses by Christians. $.02 each.

Christian Life Commission, 206 Baptist Bldg., Dallas, Tex. 75201.

AUDIO VISUALS

COMMUNIST TARGET—YOUTH. 16 mm. B&W Sound 33 min. $4.25 rental. Explains techniques and methods used by Commu-nists to gain and wield control over young people of the world. Techniques used to indoctrinate youth of the USSR, Red China, and satellite nations in the concept of materialism are described. The Communist in action is reviewed in uncommitted countries, in areas of unrest, and in the U. S.

The University of Texas, Visual Instruction Bureau, Austin, Tex. 78712.

THE COMMUNIST THREAT. 16 mm. B&W 30 min. $9.00 rental. Story of an escape of small group of Christians from East Berlin. Tells story of Communist beliefs, practices, and expansion.

*CONCEPT OF GOD. 16 mm. B&W 15 min. $6.00 rental. Three concepts of God are discussed: God and His creation, God and His love, and God and His work in the Holy Spirit. Contrast is made between Christian concepts and the Communist point of view. The comparison is placed in a court room situation.

*CONCEPT OF LIFE. 16 mm. B&W 15 min. $6.00 rental. In a mock court situation, a Christian and a member of the Com-munist party are questioned about their philosophies of life.

*CONCEPT OF MAN. 16 mm. B&W 15 min. $6.00 rental. Two men, one representing Christianity and one representing Com-munism, debate the concept of man before a jury representing the nations of the world. A moderator periodically clarifies and summarizes the discussions and arguments of the two men.

Southern Baptist Film Centers.

*DOCUMENTARY TV-FILM SERIES ON COMMUNISM. "Communism: Myth vs. Reality." 16 mm. B&W Sound 30 min. 38 films. Description and price of each available in booklet form. Interesting and factual.

*FILMS RELATING TO COMMUNISM. Annotated survey of 1,000 motion pictures.

> Research Institute on Communist Strategy and Propaganda, School of International Relations, University of Southern California, Los Angeles, Cal. 90007.

LIVING IN CHINA TODAY. Color filmstrips, 20 min. each, each filmstrip with teacher's guide $6.50; record for two filmstrips $3.50; set of 4 filmstrips with 2 records, guides $29.75.
AGRICULTURE AND RURAL LIFE 288-1
CITIES AND CITY LIFE 288-2
RESOURCES, INDUSTRIES, TRANSPORTATION, AND COMMUNICATION 288-3
LAND OF CHANGE AND GROWTH 288-4

LIVING IN THE SOVIET UNION TODAY. Color, captioned filmstrips, approximately 55 frames each. Each $6.50; set of 7 filmstrips with teacher's guide $39.75.
HOUSING AND HOME LIFE 295-1, SCHOOLS AND PIONEER ACTIVITIES 295-2, AGRICULTURE 295-3, FOODS, MARKETS, AND STORES 295-4, TRANSPORTATION AND COMMUNICATION 295-5, FOUR CITIES 295-6, NATURAL RESOURCES 295-7.

> Society for Visual Education, Inc., 1345 Diversey Parkway, Chicago, Ill. 60614.

PROFILE OF COMMUNISM: PART I, THE GROWTH OF COMMUNISM. 35 mm. filmstrip. 61 frames. Color. $6.00 purchase. Surveys beginnings of Communism and progress to WW II.

PROFILE OF COMMUNISM: PART II, THE U.S.S.R. TODAY. 35 mm. filmstrip. 60 frames. Color. $6.00 purchase. Life in the Soviet Union in regard to education, religion, arts, legal process, public information.

STUDY KIT. The above two filmstrips plus three study books. $11.00 purchase.

> Anti-Defamation League, 315 Lexington Ave., New York, N. Y. 10016.

THE RED TRAP. 16 mm. B&W 30 min. $9.00 rental. A young law student is tempted to become a Communist. The film portrays the efforts of his father, a chaplain, an FBI agent, and others to show him the errors of Communism.

> Cokesbury.

*WHO GOES THERE? A PRIMER ON COMMUNISM. 16 mm.
B&W 55 min. $10.80 rental. Attempts to arrive at a definition
of Communism. Reviews the history of its leaders—Marx, with
his ideology; Lenin, with his revolution; Stalin, with his totalitarianism; and Khrushchev, with his imperialism. Traces the
evolution of Communist thought and actions from the ideal
communities of Fourier to Communism as it is practiced in
Russia today. Appraises the advances and setbacks of Communism as they appeared in 1963. Mounted on two reels.
> Visual Aids Service, Division University Extension, University of
> Illinois, Champaign, Ill. 61820.

OTHER HELPS

COMMUNISM: A SELECTED AND ANNOTATED BIBLIOG-
RAPHY. Most comprehensive available from a Christian point
of view. $.40.
> National Council of Churches, 475 Riverside Dr., New York, N. Y.
> 10027.

BIBLIOGRAPHY ON THE WORLD COMMUNIST MOVE-
MENT. Reprint of speech in *Congressional Record* Jan. 25,
1962, by Hon. Donald C. Bruce in the House of Representatives.
> All-American Conference to Combat Communism, 1028 Conn. Ave.,
> N. W., Washington, D. C. 20036.

BOOKS ON COMMUNISM. R. N. Carew Hunt. Ampersand Ltd.
1959. OP. A superb bibliography of over 300 pages of many
aspects of Communism. Annotated.

BOOKS ON COMMUNISM. Walter Kolarz. Oxford University
Press. 1964. $4.80. An extensive, annotated bibliography of
books on all phases of Communism.

CHRISTIANITY IN THE SOVIET UNION: AN ANNOTATED
BIBLIOGRAPHY AND LIST OF ARTICLES (works in
English) $1.25.

FILMS RELATING TO COMMUNISM. An annotated survey
of 1000 films of interest to public affairs specialists, historians,
teachers, and scholars examining Communist affairs. $4.00 (dis-
count $2.50 to teachers, students, and bookdealers).

RECENT PUBLICATIONS ON COMMUNISM: A BIBLIOG-
RAPHY OF NON-PERIODICAL LITERATURE, 1957-1962.
Basic bibliography of 1,000 books in English on Communism.
$2.00.

Research Institute on Communist Strategy and Propaganda, School of International Relations, University of Southern California, Los Angeles, Cal. 90007.

CRIME

(See also Capital Punishment, Citizenship, Juvenile Delinquency)

BOOKS

BROTHERHOOD OF EVIL; THE MAFIA. Frederick Sondern, Jr. Farrar, Straus, and Cudahy. 1959. $3.95.

> A fascinating story of the "inner core" of organized crime—the Mafia. The author is qualified to tell this story, having been in many battles against this group.

THE CHURCH AND THE CRIMINAL. J. Arthur Hoyles. Epworth. 1965. $2.50.

> One of the few books treating the church's relation to the criminal. Deals with the relation of theology and crime and contains helpful suggestions for the minister. English point of view.

CRIME AND JUVENILE DELINQUENCY: A RATIONAL APPROACH TO PAROLE PROBLEMS. Sol Rubin. Oceana. 2nd Ed. 1961. $5.00.

> Published for National Council on Crime and Delinquency. Secular insights into the problem of crime and suggestions for reforms.

CRIME IN AMERICA. Herbert A. Bloch ed. Philosophical Library. 1961. $6.00.

> Articles by authorities on many phases of crime in America. A frank appraisal of modern penology's problems and approaches to the study of crime and delinquency.

*CRIME IN THE UNITED STATES. J. Edgar Hoover. Beacon. 1965. $1.45.

> A well-written overview of the crime picture in the U. S. by one who is considered by many the best authority on the subject. Nontechnical.

*ETHICS, CRIME AND REDEMPTION. Stanley Rowland. Westminister. 1963. $1.25 paper.

> One of a series of books designed to help laymen think theologically about current issues. Provides insight into how Christians can minister to those involved in crime and what the Christian's responsibility is to curtail crime.

THE EXPLANATION OF CRIMINALITY. Gordon Trasler. Humanities Press. 1962. $4.00.

> An attempt to help formulate a systematic theory of criminality adequate for the needs of social scientists and clinicians whose work is with offenders. Urges a standardization of procedures in evaluating an offender.

ORGANIZED CRIME IN AMERICA: A BOOK OF READINGS. Gus Tyler. University of Michigan Press. 1962. $7.50.

> One of America's foremost commentators on criminal activity in America has drawn together testimony to prove his thesis that organized crime is a product and reflection of our national culture. It would make excellent illustrative material for the minister.

PRACTICE AND THEORY OF PROBATION AND PAROLE. David Dressler. Columbia. 1959. $7.50.

> A textbook on probation and parole beginning with their origins and stating the present policies. Helpful for church leaders who work in this area.

PRINCIPLES OF CRIMINOLOGY. Donald R. Cressey and Edwin H. Sutherland. Lippincott. 1960. $9.95, $7.50 text ed.

> An authoritative, standard text with extensive bibliography.

THE ROOTS OF EVIL: A SOCIAL HISTORY OF CRIME AND PUNISHMENT. Christopher Hibbet. Little, Brown. 1963. $6.95.

> Historical tracing of crime from the Age of Chivalry to the present. Contains an excellent bibliography. Brings some current problems of crime and punishment into perspective.

SECRET RULERS: CRIMINAL SYNDICATES AND HOW THEY CONTROL THE U. S. UNDERWORLD. Fred J. Cook. Meredith. 1966. $6.95.

> A popular reporter writes about the power and influence of the elements of organized crime. Readable and informative.

ORGANIZATIONS AND SOURCES

AMERICAN ASSOCIATION OF CRIMINOLOGY. An association of professional persons in the study and active prevention of crime.

> Box 3014, University Station, Eugene, Ore. 97402.

AMERICAN BAR ASSOCIATION. Professional association of lawyers. Deals with relation of crime to law and the courts.

> 1155 E. 60th St., Chicago, Ill. 60637.

AMERICAN SOCIAL HEALTH ASSOCIATION. Research and publication on social problems, including crime.
1790 Broadway, New York, N. Y. 10019.

GENERAL BOARD OF CHRISTIAN SOCIAL CONCERNS OF THE METHODIST CHURCH. Lists of available materials on crime and punishment sent upon request.
100 Maryland Ave., N. E., Washington, D. C. 2000?.

*NATIONAL COUNCIL ON CRIME AND DELINQUENCY. Publishes a journal, booklets, pamphlets. Write for list of resources. Library has extensive collection of materials most of which is available for loan. Library provides information service by mail and telephone.
44 E. 23rd St., New York, N. Y. 10010.

*UNITED STATES DEPT. OF JUSTICE. Mimeographed papers and reprints available. They publish the Uniform Crime Report giving statistical information on crime in the U. S.
Federal Bureau of Investigation, Washington, D. C. 20535.

PERIODICALS AND JOURNALS

*CRIME AND DELINQUENCY. Q $4.50. A competent journal presenting many facets of the national crime picture.
CURRENT PROJECTS IN THE PREVENTION, CONTROL, AND TREATMENT OF CRIME AND DELINQUENCY. SA Available free to workers in the field. Compiled by the Information Center on Crime and Delinquency.
INTERNATIONAL BIBLIOGRAPHY ON CRIME AND DELINQUENCY. BM Free.
JOURNAL OF RESEARCH IN CRIME AND DELINQUENCY. SA $4.50. $2.50 single copy. Research reports and projects.
NCCD NEWS. 5 issues a year. $1.50. News of the Council.
National Council on Crime and Delinquency, 44 E. 23rd St., New York, N. Y. 10010.

*FEDERAL PROBATION. Q Free to persons actively engaged in correctional work or to students majoring in the study of crime and penology. Covers all phases of preventive and correctional activities in crime.
U. S. Dept. of Justice, Washington, D. C. 20530.

PRINTED MATERIALS

*THE CHALLENGE OF CRIME IN A FREE SOCIETY. The report of the President's Commission on Law Enforcement and

Administration of Justice discusses the problems of crime in America today and recommends ways to reduce crime and improve the fairness and effectiveness of police, courts, and correctional agencies. The result of 18 months' work by several hundred of the Nation's leading experts in crime prevention. Deals with trends of crime, its costs, its impact, the relationship of social conditions to crime and juvenile delinquency, organized crime, narcotics and drug abuse, the handling of drunkenness offenders, and the potentials of science and technology in crime control. $2.25.

Supt. of Documents, U. S. Government Printing Office, Washington, D. C. 20402.

THE CRIME PROBLEM. An outline of the extent, course, and suggested cure of crime in America.

*CRIME IN THE UNITED STATES: UNIFORM CRIME REPORTS. Annual summary of information on crime. Single copy free.

FEDERAL PRISON SYSTEM. Illustrated brochure describing the Federal Prison System with data on prisoners.

THE INSIDE STORY OF ORGANIZED CRIME AND HOW YOU CAN HELP SMASH IT. The organization and operation of organized crime by J. Edgar Hoover.

U. S. Dept. of Justice, Washington, D. C. 20530.

COMBATING ORGANIZED CRIME. *Annals,* 1963, edited by Gus Tyler. Information on organized crime in America and what to do about it. $3.00, $2.00 paper.

CRIME AND THE AMERICAN PENAL SYSTEM. *Annals,* 1962, a study by competent authors of crime and punishment in the U. S. $2.00.

American Academy of Political and Social Science, 3937 Chestnut St., Philadelphia, Pa. 19104.

*CRIME AND PUNISHMENT. A background paper by Harvey Seifert dealing with Christian attitudes toward crime and punishment. $.05.

CRIME AND REHABILITATION. Special issue of *Concern*. $.35.

THE METHODIST CHURCH AND REHABILITATION OF THE CRIMINAL. A booklet with guidelines for church action. Valuable to others than Methodists. $.50.

General Board of Christian Social Concerns of the Methodist Church, 100 Maryland Ave., N. E., Washington, D. C. 20002.

AUDIO VISUALS

CRIME AND DELINQUENCY. 16 mm. B&W 29 min. NET-2033.

$5.40 rental. Discusses the rise in violence and deviant behavior in America. Dr. Margaret Mead and Dr. Bertram Beck are questioned on the causes of delinquency and what can be done about the rise in crime. Includes emphasis on the new problem of suburban delinquency.

*THE CRIMINAL MAN SERIES. 16 mm. B&W 30 min. each. Series of 20 films. $5.40 rental each. Presents a definitive study of the cause, prevention, and treatment of crime. Uses dramatic re-enactments and film clips to illustrate important points. Defines crime and criminals. Discusses myths, folk lore, and common superstition surrounding crime. Analyzes the true causes of crime. Looks at current penal policies and their weaknesses regarding rehabilitation:

THE CRIMINAL	SICK MINDS AND CRIME
THE BORN CRIMINAL	BRAKES AND MISBEHAVIOR
THE ANTHROPOMORPHIC CRIMINAL	NARCISSUS, OEDIPUS, AND CRIME
THE ETHNOLOGICAL CRIMINAL	THE ROOTS OF CRIMINALITY
LEFT HANDS, RED HAIR, AND CRIME	THE TRUE CRIMINAL
	SEXUALITY AND CRIME
WEATHER MAPS, CALENDARS, & CRIME	CRIME UNDER TWENTY-ONE
CULTURE AND CRIME	EMOTIONS AND CRIME
THE ALCOHOLIC CRIMINAL	THE CRIMINAL AND PUNISHMENT
TEA, HORSE, AND CRIME	THE CRIMINAL AND HOW
I.Q. AND CRIME	TO NEUTRALIZE HIM

Audio Visual Center, Indiana University, Bloomington, Ind. 47405.

CRIME IN THE CITIES. 16 mm. B&W Sound 30 min. Approximately $5.50 rental. Provides insight into the problem of crime in the U. S. today. Poses the question: Does the volume of crime warrant the crisis atmosphere that exists in our nation today?
Bureau of Audiovisual Services, The University of Arizona, Tucson, Arizona 85721.

TYPES OF INMATES. 16 mm. B&W 30 min. 46 sec. 1965. $8.00 rental. Illustrates the basic types of criminal personality an officer is likely to encounter and shows how each type is likely to react to custody.
Contemporary Films, Inc., 267 W. 25th St., New York, N. Y. 10001.

OTHER HELPS

BIBLIOGRAPHICAL MANUAL FOR THE STUDENT OF CRIMINOLOGY. Thorsten Sellin and Leonard D. Savitz. 3rd ed. rev. 1965. 104 pp. $1.00.

SELECTED READING LIST IN DELINQUENCY AND CRIME. A 38-page booklet of up-to-date listings of books and other sources. Free.

> National Council on Crime and Delinquency, 44 E. 23rd St., New York, N. Y. 10010.

THE METHODIST CHURCH AND REHABILITATION OF THE CRIMINAL. Excellent bibliography of crime, juvenile delinquency, and capital punishment in booklet form. $.50.

> The Methodist Bldg., 100 Maryland Ave., N. E., Washington, D. C. 20002.

DAILY WORK

(See also Economics, Labor, Leisure, Poverty)

BOOKS

*ALL YE WHO LABOR. Wade H. Boggs. John Knox. 1961. $1.50 paper.

> The theme of God's command to subdue the earth is traced through the Bible and applied to work, worship, and leisure in modern life.

THE BIBLICAL DOCTRINE OF WORK. Alan Richardson. Allenson. 1958. $1.50 paper.

> A brief statement of the biblical view of work and vocation.

THE CHRISTIAN AS A BUSINESSMAN. Harold L. Johnson. Association. 1964. $3.75.

> This volume seeks to bridge the gulf between theory as heard from the pulpit and the realities encountered in the world of business in terms of Christian vocation.

CHRISTIAN CALLING AND VOCATION. Henlee H. Barnette. Baker. 1965. $1.50 paper.

> Biblical, historical, and contemporary study of work, vocation, and the concept of calling.

CHRISTIAN FAITH AND MY JOB. Alexander Miller. Association. 1959. $.75 paper.

> Insights into the relation of the faith of a Christian and his job. Practical and helpful in discussions.

THEOLOGY OF WORK. Edwin G. Kaiser. Newman. 1966. $8.75.

> A Catholic book that traces the history of work to current problems. Central portion of the work delves into the "theological values" in work. Concludes with a special area of Papal teaching on work. Good definitive study on the Catholic concept of work.

THE THEOLOGY OF WORK. M. D. Chenu. Henry Regnery Co. 1966. $1.25 paper.

> The writer explores work not as the means by which man accumulates material values but rather as one of the means by which man puts the stamp of his original and social personality on creation.

*WORK AND VOCATION—A CHRISTIAN DISCUSSION. John Oliver Nelson, ed. Harper and Brothers. 1954. $2.75. OP

> A superb study from biblical, historical, and contemporary perspectives on Christian concepts of work and vocation. Excellent bibliography, though now dated, for current affairs.

YOUR OTHER VOCATION. Elton Trueblood. Harper and Brothers. 1952. $2.50.

> A call for Christians to live under the lordship of Christ in work as well as in all of life.

ORGANIZATIONS AND SOURCES

AFL-CIO RESEARCH DEPT. Many pamphlets and booklets related to work, leisure, and automation.

> 815—16th St., N. W., Washington, D. C. 20006.

AMERICAN VOCATIONAL ASSOCIATION, INC. Publication list available, material on vocational education.

> 1025—15th St., N. W., Washington, D. C. 20005.

B'NAI B'RITH VOCATIONAL SERVICE. Publish *Counselor's Information Service*, a quarterly bibliography; other publications are listed in their catalogue.

> 1640 Rhode Island Ave., N. W., Washington, D. C. 20036.

BOARD OF CHRISTIAN EDUCATION, Presbyterian Church, U. S.

> Box 1176, Richmond, Va. 23209.

CHRISTIAN LIFE COMMISSION, BAPTIST GENERAL CONVENTION OF TEXAS.
206 Baptist Bldg., Dallas, Tex. 75201.

CHRISTIAN LIFE COMMISSION, SOUTHERN BAPTIST CONVENTION.
460 James Robertson Parkway, Nashville, Tenn. 37219.

DETROIT INDUSTRIAL MISSION. Designed to help men relate faith to work. Publish paper and pamphlets.
8646 Puritan, Detroit, Mich. 48238.

DEPT. OF CHRISTIAN ACTION IN COMMUNITY SERVICE OF THE UNITED CHRISTIAN MISSIONARY SOCIETY.
Missions Bldg., Indianapolis, Ind. 46207.

CHURCH AND CULTURE DEPT. AND SOCIAL JUSTICE DEPT. NATIONAL COUNCIL OF CHURCHES. Publications and literature related mainly to church-related vocations.
*DEPT. OF CHURCH AND ECONOMIC LIFE. A volume of material on daily work.
475 Riverside Dr., New York, N. Y. 10027.

DIVISION OF CHRISTIAN SOCIAL CONCERN, AMERICAN BAPTIST CONVENTION.
Valley Forge, Pa. 19481.

*DIVISION OF HUMAN RELATIONS AND ECONOMIC AFFAIRS, GENERAL BOARD OF CHRISTIAN SOCIAL CONCERNS OF THE METHODIST CHURCH. Pamphlets and resource materials.
100 Maryland Ave., N. E., Washington, D. C. 20002.

*ECONOMICS-ETHICAL STUDIES. Publish *Management Ethics Guide*, $1.50, and the following free materials: *Economic Ethics Bibliography, Relationale for Management Ethics Guide, Ethical Perspectives in Marketing Decisions.*
South Dakota State University, Brookings, S. D. 57006.

PUBLIC AFFAIRS PAMPHLETS. Write for a current list of practical, brief pamphlets, most for $.25.
381 Park Ave. S., New York, N. Y. 10016.

VOCATIONAL GUIDANCE DEPT. OF THE SUNDAY SCHOOL BOARD OF THE SOUTHERN BAPTIST CONVENTION. Pamphlets and publications primarily related to church and church-related vocations.
127 Ninth Ave., N., Nashville, Tenn. 37203.

PERIODICALS AND JOURNALS

AMERICAN VOCATIONAL JOURNAL. M (Sept. to May) $3.00.
Exclusive coverage of vocational and industrial arts education.
American Vocational Association, 1010 Vermont Ave., N. W., Washington, D. C. 20005.

COUNSELOR'S INFORMATION SERVICE. Q $7.00. Annotated
bibliography of current literature on educational and vocational
guidance.
B'nai B'rith Vocational Service, 1640 Rhode Island Ave., N. W.,
Washington, D. C. 20036.

DEVELOPMENTS. 3 or 4 times a year. $1.00. A publication largely
devoted to news about church-related vocations.
National Council of Churches, 475 Riverside Dr., New York, N. Y.
10027.

*MONTHLY LABOR REVIEW. M $7.50. $.75 per copy. Cat.
#L2.6. The Labor Dept.'s report on trends of employment and
payrolls, hourly and weekly earnings, weekly working hours,
collective agreements, industrial accidents, industrial disputes,
etc. Subscribers receive an annual statistic supplement.
Supt. of Documents, Washington, D. C. 20402.

NATION'S BUSINESS. M $6.75. Business leaderships, national
affairs, and government activities.
Chamber of Commerce of USA, 1615 H St., N. W., Washington,
D. C. 20006.

PRINTED MATERIALS

APPLYING CHRISTIANITY IN THE DAY'S WORK. Viewpoints of laymen and clergy. $.35.

*THE CHRISTIAN AND HIS DAILY WORK. A booklet by Cameron P. Hall on the Christian meaning of work for today with
questions for self-examination and group study. $.35.

CHRISTIANITY AND WORK. A booklet by Benson Y. Landis
and James Myers. $.25.

ON THE JOB ETHICS. Analysis by men engaged in six occupations. $1.65.

RELATING FAITH TO DECISION. A theologian and two Christian laymen discuss ethical compromise. $.50.

YOU, YOUR CHURCH, AND YOUR JOB. A study guide affirming that the churches should seek to develop among their members the idea that there is Christian vocation in all constructive
work. $.35.
The Dept. of Church and Economic Life, National Council of the
Churches of Christ, 475 Riverside Dr., New York, N. Y. 10027.

*BIBLE SPEAKS ON ECONOMICS, CHRISTIAN PRINCIPLES APPLIED TO DAILY WORK, WORKING WIVES AND MOTHERS. Concise helpful pamphlets for helping deal with issues. $.02 each.

*CHRISTIANITY AND THE WORKADAY WORLD. A series of speeches on daily work and leisure by leading authorities. Much helpful material. $1.00.

> Christian Life Commission, 206 Baptist Bldg., Dallas, Tex. 75201.

*CHRISTIAN DAILY WORK PACKET. Selected materials on Christian decision-making on the job and the ministry of laity in the world of work. $3.00.

> Church of the Brethren, Elgin, Ill. 60120.

CYBERCULTURE. Automation and its effect on life. $.10.

CYBERNATION AND HUMAN RIGHTS. Analysis of trends. $.20.

TECHNOLOGICAL SOCIETY. A book on the dehumanizing effect of the technological revolution.

TOWARD A MORAL ECONOMY. Discusses the moral aspect of the new technology. $.10.

> Fellowship Publications, Box 271, Nyack, N. Y. 10970.

*DECISION MAKING IN BUSINESS. A 48-page booklet by Cameron Hall on how complex business decisions are made and how a Christian should take part in them. $.50.

> Service Dept. Methodist Church, 100 Maryland Ave., N. E., Washington, D. C. 20002.

THE NATURE OF AUTOMATION. An issue of the *Annals* of the American Academy of Political and Social Science, March, 1962, devoted to the nature and impact of automation. $2.00.

> 3937 Chestnut St., Philadelphia, Pa. 19104.

AUDIO VISUALS

AUTOMATION: THE NEXT REVOLUTION. 16 mm. B&W 29 min. $3.00 rental. Documentary which examines the impact of automation on workers and the problems it creates for society.

THE LIVING MACHINE. 16 mm. B&W 29 min. $7.50 rental. Shows progress in electronics technology. Main purpose is to provoke discussion about human values in a machine age.

THE SEARCH. 16 mm. 25 min. $3.00 rental. Research specialists from Massachusetts Institute of Technology demonstrate and explain various types of automation.

> AFL-CIO Dept. of Education, 815—16th St., N. W., Washington, D. C. 20006.

BEING CHRISTIAN IN BUSINESS. 35 mm. Color filmstrip. 42

frames. $6.50. With record and script $10.00. Discusses ways of making a living that conflict with Christian principles and parallels these to Jesus' temptations.

Cokesbury.

THE BIGGEST THING IN MIDDLEVILLE. 83-frame color cartoon filmstrip with recording and script. $12.50 purchase. A story of how decisions in business lead to a new understanding of the social responsibility of Christians in their daily work.

The Dept. of Church and Economic Life, National Council of Churches, 475 Riverside Dr., New York, N. Y. 10027.

THE FORGOTTEN FACTOR. 16 mm. Color. 90 min. $15.00 rental. A dramatic clash between two men and their families in the midst of a work situation. Insight into better human relations in respect to work.

RAM Productions, 833 S. Flower St., Los Angeles, Cal. 90017.

LIVING RIGHT AT OUR WORK KIT. Set of five filmstrips. B&W. 33-⅓ rpm records, 10 min. each. Scripts, guides. $3.50 rental each. Complete kit $49.00 purchase. Discussional filmstrips on the theme of "living right." Designed to get people to talk, think, live Christian principles on the job. Should be used in five consecutive meetings. Titles: RIGHT CHOICE, 68 frames; RIGHT ATTITUDE, 59 frames; RIGHT COUNSEL, 70 frames; RIGHT OUTLOOK, 67 frames; RIGHT LEADERSHIP, 66 frames.

Office for Audio Visuals, United Church of Christ, 1720 Chouteau Ave., St. Louis, Mo. 63103.

*THE OTHER SIX DAYS. 16 mm. Color. 30 min. $15.00 rental. Documents the problems of business ethics and Christian living.

Family Films, 5823 Santa Monica Blvd., Hollywood, Cal. 90038.

*OUTSIDE THE DOORS. 22 min. color filmstrip. Guide. 33-⅓ rpm recording. $9.00 purchase. Decisions and actions related to daily work are visible witnesses to God at work in the world. This theme is presented in story form. Highly recommended for discussion and motivation with young people through adults. 1960.

American Baptist Films, Valley Forge, Pa. 19481.

OTHER HELPS

ECONOMIC ETHICS BIBLIOGRAPHY. An annotated bibliography of recent and classic publications. Very useful. Free

Ethical Studies, South Dakota State University, Brookings, South Dakota 57006.

SELECTED BIBLIOGRAPHY OF RESOURCE MATERIALS

ON CHRISTIAN VOCATIONS. General information on source for vocational guidance.

Dept. of Christian Vocations, Board of Christian Education, Presbyterian Church U. S., Box 1176, Richmond, Va. 23209.

DECISION MAKING ON MORAL ISSUES

BOOKS

CONSCIENCE ON CAMPUS. Waldo Beach. Association. 1958. $2.50, $1.00 paper.

Practical, helpful book on moral issues and how to deal with them from a Christian point of view. Directed to the college student.

*DEEDS AND RULES IN CHRISTIAN ETHICS. Paul Ramsey. Scribners. 1967. $5.95.

Guide in an approach to decision making. Critical of situation ethics from an informed position.

*GOD'S WILL AND YOUR LIFE. T. B. Maston. Broadman. 1964. $1.95.

A discussion of Christian decision making as it relates to finding the will of God. Emphasis on youth but helpful for all ages.

MAKING ETHICAL DECISIONS. Howard C. Kee. Westminster. 1957. $1.00 paper.

A brief book setting forth an approach to decision making within a religious context. Specific areas of life, such as family, are used to illustrate the approach.

RIGHT OR WRONG? T. B. Maston. Broadman. 1955. $2.00.

Principles for making moral decisions are set forth and then applied to specific decisions such as drinking, petting, honesty, and smoking. Very helpful for young adolescents.

*THE STRUCTURE OF CHRISTIAN ETHICS. Joseph Sittler. Louisiana State U. Press. 1958.

Deals with methodology of ethical decisions and the problems involved.

*THE WAY IN THE WORLD. Roy P. Adelberg. Friendship. 1965.
    $1.75 paper.
>   Seven stories focusing on adults and teen-agers in the midst of
>   making important decisions. Reflected in their struggle is their atti-
>   tude toward Jesus Christ. Contains questions to stimulate thought
>   and discussion.

The following books set forth the so-called New Morality (from a
religious perspective) or situation ethics in decision making:

CHRISTIAN MORALS TODAY. John A. T. Robinson. West-
    minster. 1964. $.65 paper.

MORAL RESPONSIBILITY. Joseph Fletcher. Westminster. 1967
    $1.95 paper.

NO NEW MORALITY. Douglas Rhymes. The Bobbs-Merrill Co.
    Inc. 1964. $3.50.

SITUATION ETHICS: THE NEW MORALITY. Joseph Fletch-
    er. Westminster. 1966. $3.95, $1.95 paper.

A TIME FOR CHRISTIAN CANDOR. James A. Pike. Harper
    & Row. 1965. $3.50.

ORGANIZATIONS AND SOURCES

The religiously-oriented organizations listed in the appendix are concerned with decision making on moral issues.

SCIENCE RESEARCH ASSOCIATES, INC. Booklets and ma-
    terials on moral values available.
        259 E. Erie St., Chicago, Ill. 60611.

PERIODICALS AND JOURNALS

The publications listed in the appendix deal in varying degree
with decision making on moral and social issues.

PRINTED MATERIALS

DECISION-MAKING IN BUSINESS. An incisive look into how
    complex business decisions are made and what the Christian's
    role ought to be. By Cameron P. Hall. 48-page booklet, $.50.
    Leaflets, $4.00 per 100.
*DECISION-MAKING IN PERSONAL LIFE. Focuses on how in-
    dividual Christians can know right from wrong—and can do the
    right. 48-page booklet, $.50. Leaflets, $4.00 per 100.

DECISION-MAKING IN WORLD AFFAIRS. How to evaluate and influence world affairs. By Harvey Seifert. 48-page booklet, $.50. Leaflets, $4.00 per 100.

SOURCES OF CHRISTIAN MORALITY. Orlo Strunk, Jr. Presents study of responsible behavior. 48-page booklet, $.50. Leaflets, $4.00 per 100.

> Service Dept. Methodist Church, 100 Maryland Ave., N. E., Washington, D. C. 20002.

HELPING CHILDREN DEVELOP MORAL VALUES. Ashley Montague. Educational approach to moral decision-making ability. $.84.

> Science Research Associates, Inc., 259 E. Erie St., Chicago, Ill. 60611.

*ISSUES AND ANSWERS SERIES. A series of pamphlets on current issues designed to help in decision-making and Christian action. $.05 each.

> Christian Life Commission, Southern Baptist Convention, 460 James Robertson Parkway, Nashville, Tenn. 37219.

MAKING ETHICAL JUDGMENT IN A CHANGING WORLD. Offers criteria for responsible Christian decision-making in a world that won't stand still. $.15.

> Commission on Research and Social Action, American Lutheran Church, 422 S. 5th St., Minneapolis, Minn. 55415.

AUDIO VISUALS

FACE TO FACE. 35 mm. Color filmstrip with 33-⅓ rpm recording. 88 frames. 18 min. $10.00 purchase. An analysis of modern young adult life and the search for meaningful existence.

> Audio-Visual Center, P.O. Box 871, Nashville, Tenn. 37202.

HOW FREE ARE YOU? 35 mm. Color filmstrip. 75 frames. 33-⅓ rpm record. $7.50 purchase. Shows four ways men often reject responsibility and lose their freedom through drinking, gambling, narcotics, and obscene literature.

*THE PROFESSOR AND THE ANGEL. 35 mm. 15 min. Color. Script. Guides. 33-⅓ rpm recording. $10.00 purchase. A novel 71-frame filmstrip which depicts in cartoon form an angel doing research on why people act as they do.

> Service Dept., The Methodist Church, 100 Maryland Ave., N. E., Washington, D.C. 20002.

*HOW TO SAY NO. 16 mm. B&W Sound 10 min. $3.00 rental. In situations involving social pressures, some practical help is given teen-agers on how to say "no"—smoking, drinking, love-making.

WHAT YOU OUGHT TO WANT. 16 mm. B&W Sound. 14 min.
$5.00 rental. Lecture presentation of the basic facets which
can be used to measure the effect of choices one makes.
    Cokesbury.

I NEVER LOOKED AT IT THAT WAY BEFORE. 35 mm. 2
full color filmstrips, 2 12″ lp records. Part I, 68 frames, 16 min.
Part II, 76 frames, 15 min. $29.95 purchase. This 2-part sound
filmstrip raises some very pertinent questions about the pressure to conform that is generated by a youngster's peer group.
The material also probes the teen-ager's concept of status, and
suggests that one's own self-image may be much more important
than the image held by those around him.

VALUES FOR TEENAGERS: THE CHOICE IS YOURS. Two
35 mm. color filmstrips with records. Part I, 18 min. Part II,
13-½ min. $29.95 purchase. For young people 13-18 to be shown
on separate occasions. Current. Some may not aprove of
frankness. Shows young people as they question values about
them and face decisions. Non-directive. Main value is for
stimulating discussion. Secular.
    Guidance Associates, Pleasantville, N. Y. 10570.

MAKING YOUR OWN DECISIONS. B&W 11 min. $2.25 rental.
Presents questions which should precede a decision—and illustrates how the decision, action based on it, and responsibility
for it can follow the answers to these questions. Secular point
of view.
    Visual Instruction Bureau, University of Texas, Austin, Tex. 78712.

MAKING A DECISION. B&W 6 min. 22 sec. 1957. $5.00 rental.
Teen-agers resent being told what they ought to do, but have
they the resources for making their own decisions? Suggestions
for providing teen-agers with decision-making ability.
    Contemporary Films, Inc., 267 W. 25th St., New York, N. Y. 10001.

MAKING CHRISTIAN CHOICES. Two-part filmstrip kit. Each
filmstrip with guide, $6.50 purchase. Filmstrip with record and
guide $10.00. Kit of both filmstrips in full color with 12″ 33-⅓
rpm record and leader's guides $16.50. To give guidance to
young teens (12-14) in the very important—but very difficult—
area of making right choices and decisions. Designed to help
them look at all choices in the light of their Christian com-
mitment, and seek God's will in making decisions.
CHRISTIAN STANDARDS OF RIGHT AND WRONG
(78A)
CHRISTIAN CHOICES IN ACTION (78B)

Lutheran Church Supply Stores, 2900 Queen Lane, Philadelphia, Pa. 19129.

RIGHT OR WRONG? (MAKING MORAL DECISIONS).

B&W 11 min. $2.35 rental. A gang of 13-year-olds throws rocks at a warehouse window. As a result, the night watchman, the warehouse owner, a parent, a police sergeant, and a member of the gang must make important decisions that affect others. Uses live action and dialogue to present an unsolved problem for discussion.

Visual Aids Service, Div. University Extension, University of Illinois, Champaign, Ill. 61822.

DIVORCE

(See also Family)

BOOKS

*DIVORCE, THE CHURCH, AND REMARRIAGE. James G. Emerson, Jr. Westminster. 1961. $3.95.

One of the few books dealing openly, frankly with the church's role in regard to divorce and remarriage. Analyzes problems and offers suggested solutions.

THE FAMILY IN CHRISTIAN PERSPECTIVE. C. W. Scudder. Broadman. 1962. $3.50.

While the entire book is not devoted to divorce, it contains a lengthy discussion on the subject. An example of a view opposing divorce and remarriage.

*MARRIAGE AND THE BIBLE. Earnest White. Broadman. 1965. $3.50.

Biblical teachings on marriage and divorce. Sets forth various interpretations of biblical material on divorce.

PASTORAL COUNSELING IN SOCIAL PROBLEMS. Wayne
Oates. Westminster. 1966. $.75 paper.
> Information on several subjects including sex and divorce. Valuable
> reference book.

THE WORLD OF THE FORMERLY MARRIED. Morton M.
Hunt. McGraw-Hill. 1966. $5.95.
> A study of the divorced and separated in the American middle
> class. A descriptive rather than a prescriptive book, it offers no
> guidelines for either lessening the number of "formerly married" nor
> improving their emotional lot. Emphasis on sex and emotional ad-
> justments.

ORGANIZATIONS AND SOURCES

AMERICAN ASSOCIATION OF MARRIAGE COUNSELORS,
INC. No material or publications available to general public
except the annual *Directory of Members* to be used for referral
purposes, $2.00.
> 27 Woodcliff Dr., Madison, N. J. 07940.

CHILDREN'S BUREAU, U.S. DEPT. OF HEALTH, EDUCA-
TION, AND WELFARE. Send for list of available materials
related to child care and welfare.
> Washington, D. C. 20201.

FAMILY LIFE BUREAU, U.S. CATHOLIC CONFERENCE.
Reprints, pamphlets, and bimonthly bulletin *Catholic Family
Leader.* Guidance for Catholic families; helpful insight for
all into many aspects of family life.
> 1312 Mass. Ave., N. W., Washington, D. C. 20005.

*PARENTS WITHOUT PARTNERS, INC. An international, non-
profit, non-sectarian, educational organization devoted to the
interests and welfare of single parents and their children. They
publish *The Single Parent* magazine, chapter newsletters, manuals, and pamphlets of organization instructions. A number of
regional chapters exist.
> 80 Fifth Ave., New York, N. Y. 10011.

PERIODICALS AND JOURNALS

FROM THE STATE CAPITALS. 14 or more issues per yr. $21.00.
Covers state and local action throughout the nation dealing
with divorce and other family issues.
> Bethune Jones, 321 Sunset Ave., Asbury Park, N. J. 07712.

*THE SINGLE PARENT. M $5.00. Journal devoted to welfare
and interests of single parents and their children.
> Parents Without Partners, Inc., 80 Fifth Ave., New York, N. Y.
> 10011.

SOCIAL WELFARE COURT DIGEST. M $10.00. Summary of recent court decisions most of which are related to family life. 1860 Broadway, New York, N. Y. 10023.

PRINTED MATERIALS

*CHRISTIAN ANSWERS TO FAMILY PROBLEMS: DIVORCE. One of a series of 15 pamphlets on family life. Concise, colorful, helpful. $.02 each.

> Christian Life Commission, Southern Baptist Convention, 460 James Robertson Parkway, Nashville, Tenn. 37203.

DIRECTOR OF MEMBERS, AMERICAN ASSOCIATION OF MARRIAGE COUNSELORS, INC. A list, by states and alphabetically, of marriage counselors who are members of the American Association of Marriage Counselors, Inc. Helpful in locating competent persons for help with family counseling. $2.00.

> 27 Woodcliff Dr., Madison, N. J. 07940.

*THE ONE PARENT FAMILY. A brief pamphlet for any single parent, applicable to the divorcée with children. Suggestions and guidance. $.25.

*SAVING YOUR MARRIAGE. For those considering divorce. Practical suggestions from a secular point of view on how to avoid divorce. $.25.

> Public Affairs Pamphlets, 381 Park Ave., S., New York, N. Y. 10016.

TEACHINGS AND PRACTICE ON MARRIAGE AND DIVORCE. A statement commended by the American Lutheran Church. Presents pros and cons of divorce and remarriage and guides in thinking through the problem. $.05.

> Commission on Research and Social Action, The American Lutheran Church, 422 S. 5th St., Minneapolis, Minn. 55415.

AUDIO VISUALS

*CHRISTIANS AND DIVORCE. Color filmstrip. 42 frames. 10 min. $2.50 rental, $10.00 purchase. A frank examination of divorce and its effects on the persons involved and a study of Jesus' teachings about divorce.

*MARRIAGE AND DIVORCE. Film. 15 min. $4.00 rental. This picture frankly surveys the problems of broken homes and offers the opinions of experts as to what should be done.

> Visual Education Service, Church of the Brethren, 1451 Dundee Ave., Elgin, Ill. 60120.

MARRIAGE IS FOR KEEPS. B&W 30 min. $10.00 rental. Color $15.00. Points out ways to keep marriage strong even in face of crisis.

    Family Films, 5823 Santa Monica Blvd., Hollywood, Cal. 90038.

ECONOMICS

(See also Communism, Daily Work, Labor, Leisure)

BOOKS

THE AMERICAN ECONOMY—ATTITUDES AND OPINIONS. A. Dudley Ward, et. al. Harper. 1955. OP.

AMERICAN INCOME AND ITS USE. Elizabeth E. Hoyt, et. al. Harper. 1954. OP.

CHRISTIAN VALUES AND ECONOMIC LIFE. John C. Bennett, et. al. Harper. 1954. OP.

*ETHICS FOR AN INDUSTRIAL AGE: A CHRISTIAN INQUIRY. Victor Obenhaus. Harper. 1965. $4.75.

GOALS OF ECONOMIC LIFE. A Dudley Ward, ed. Harper. 1953. OP.

THE ORGANIZATIONAL REVOLUTION. Kenneth E. Boulding. Harper. 1953. OP.

RESPONSIBILITY IN MASS COMMUNICATION. Wilbur Schramm. Harper. 1957. $5.50.

SOCIAL RESPONSIBILITIES OF THE BUSINESSMAN. Howard R. Bowen. Harper. 1953. OP

> A series of books "Ethics and Economics of Society" produced under the direction of a study committee authorized by the Federal Council (now National Council) of Churches. These books represent the most ambitious attempt yet made to relate the Christian faith and ethic to economic life.

TODAY'S ISMS: COMMUNISM, FACISM, SOCIALISM,

CAPITALISM. W. Ebenstein. Prentice Hall. 4th ed. $4.65, $3.50 paper.

> A readable, concise explanation of the main features of the four leading economic theories practiced in today's world. Secular approach.

*THE CHRISTIAN ENCOUNTERS THE WORLD OF ECONOMICS. Paul T. Heyne. Concordia. 1965. $1.00 paper.

> A brief work written to introduce Christians to their responsibility in the economic order. Practical and inspirational.

CHRISTIAN RESPONSIBILITY IN ECONOMIC LIFE. Albert Rasmussen. Westminster. 1965. $1.25 paper.

> A discussion of the relation of ethics to economics. Historical as well as contemporary.

CHRISTIANS IN A TECHNOLOGICAL ERA. Hugh C. White, Jr., ed. Seabury. 1964. $3.50.

> Ethical implications of new technology, cybernetics, and the technician mentality. An ecumenical discussion.

THE CHURCH AND ECONOMICS. Christopher Hollis. Burns and Oates. 1961. $1.50.

> A brief discussion (110 pages) of the teachings and actions of the Catholic Church in regard to economics with a special emphasis on the nineteenth and twentieth centuries.

THE CHURCH AND THE WORKINGMAN. John F. Cronin and Harry W. Flannery. Hawthorn. 1965. $3.50.

> A brief but excellent presentation of the Catholic teachings on many phases of economics, especially topics related to the laboring man —wages, unions, employment and social legislation.

*CONTEMPORARY ECONOMIC SYSTEMS. Carl Landauer. Lippincott. 1964. $7.00.

> An excellent comparison and contrast of capitalism, socialism, communism, and other economic systems. Factual, objective, and readable.

DICTIONARY OF ECONOMICS. Harold S. Sloan and Arnold J. Zurcher. Barnes & Noble. 1961. $1.95 paper.

> A useful dictionary in the specialized area of economics. Understandable for the non-professional but thoroughly respectable.

GOD, GOLD, AND GOVERNMENT. Howard E. Kershner. Prentice-Hall. 1957. $2.95 paper.

> An outspoken plea for capitalism and free enterprise based on the author's religious convictions. Highly critical of government actions in the economic arena. An example of an ultra-conservative approach to economics from a religious perspective.

HISTORY OF ECONOMIC THOUGHT. K. William and Lore L. Kapp, ed. Barnes & Nobles. 1963. $2.50 paper.

> Thirty-seven generously proportioned selections from the writings

of great political economists with a section on twentieth-century economics planning. Selections on pre-capitalism, capitalism, socialism, and communism. Helpful introduction to primary sources.

THE PROTESTANT ETHIC AND THE SPIRIT OF CAPITALISM. Max Weber. Scribner. $1.45 paper.

Contends that Puritanism was a mighty stimulus to the rise of capitalism. A classic in the study of the relation of religion and economics.

PROTESTANTISM AND CAPITALISM. Robert W. Green, ed. Heath. 1959. $1.60 paper.

A setting forth of Weber's thesis on the close relation of Calvinism and capitalism and the chief criticisms of the theory.

RELIGION AND ECONOMIC RESPONSIBILITY. Walter G. Muelder. Charles Scribner's Sons. 1953. OP

Touches on almost every aspect of economic life. While dated, still an excellent discussion from a Christian perspective.

RELIGION AND THE RISE OF CAPITALISM. R. H. Tawney. New American Library. $.75 paper.

A classic work on the inter-relation of religion and economics. Stresses especially the affinities between Calvinism and capitalism in general support of Weber's thesis.

ORGANIZATIONS AND SOURCES

Organizations with general information on economics:

AFL-CIO. Information on economics from perspective of labor with a generally liberal slant. Compare materials for contrast with Chamber of Commerce and National Association of Manufacturers.

815—16th St., N. W., Washington, D. C. 20006.

BROOKINGS INSTITUTION. Nonpartisan organization devoted to research, education, and publication in economics and government.

1775 Mass. Ave., N. W., Washington, D. C. 20036.

CHAMBER OF COMMERCE OF THE UNITED STATES. Publishes a number of pamphlets on various phases of economics from a generally conservative perspective. Write for Publications Directory.

1615 H St., N. W., Washington, D. C. 20006.

COMMITTEE FOR ECONOMIC DEVELOPMENT. Research and policy material reflect a less conservative slant than Chamber of Commerce.

711 5th Ave., New York, N. Y. 10022.

*DEPT. OF CHURCH AND ECONOMIC LIFE, NATIONAL COUNCIL OF CHURCHES. Pamphlets, booklets, audio-visuals on economics from a religious perspective.
475 Riverside Dr., New York, N. Y. 10027.

DIVISION OF HUMAN RELATIONS AND ECONOMIC AFFAIRS, GENERAL BOARD OF CHRISTIAN SOCIAL CONCERNS OF THE METHODIST CHURCH. Pamphlets and resource material.
100 Maryland Ave., N. E., Washington, D. C. 20002.

*ECONOMICS-ETHICAL STUDIES. Bibliographies and guides for the study of ethics in business.
South Dakota State University, Brookings, S. D. 57006.

*JOINT COUNCIL ON ECONOMIC EDUCATION. List of materials and filmstrips available, all annotated. Newsletter published 3 times a year informs of new materials. Materials prepared mainly for use in schools in the teaching of economics.
1212 Ave. of the Americas, New York, N. Y. 10036.

NATIONAL ASSOCIATION OF MANUFACTURERS, CLERGY-INDUSTRY RELATIONS DEPT. Organization to present industry's point-of-view to the clergy and people of America's churches and synagogues on economic and social questions. Conservative slant.
277 Park Ave., New York, N. Y. 10017.

THE TWENTIETH CENTURY FUND. Nonprofit foundation specializing in research and public education on the vital issues of the day, with an emphasis on economic and social questions.
41 E. 70th St., New York, N. Y. 10021.

Organizations generally considered advocates of a very "liberal" economic position:

AMERICANS FOR DEMOCRATIC ACTION. A political organization which advocates and works for liberal economic legislation. Publishes the *ADA World* which presents the organization's views on current issues.
1223 Connecticut Ave., N. W., Washington, D. C. 20036.

LEAGUE FOR INDUSTRIAL DEMOCRACY. Education for increasing democracy in our economic, political and cultural life. Favors planned economy, strong labor unions, and government controls in economy. Openly favors many aspects of socialism.
112 E. 19th St., New York, N. Y. 10003.

Organizations generally considered advocates of a very "conservative" economic position:

CHRISTIAN FREEDOM FOUNDATION, INC. Devoted to advancing the free enterprise system and curtailing socialism. Publishes a number of booklets and a fortnightly paper *Christian Economics*.

> 3030 W. 6th St., Los Angeles, Cal. 90005.

THE FOUNDATION FOR ECONOMIC EDUCATION, INC. Catalogue of books and miscellaneous releases available. "A Literature of Freedom," catalogue of materials, available on request. Advocates free market, criticizes government controls.

> 30 S. Broadway, Irvington-on-Hudson, N. Y. 10533.

NATIONAL ECONOMIC COUNCIL, INC. Organization to stimulate and develop the economic life of the U.S., to prevent increase in government spending, to arouse opposition to unilateral disarmament, and to reduce government bureaucracy, labor power, and inflation.

> 156 Fifth Ave., Suite 1100, New York, N. Y. 10010.

PERIODICALS AND JOURNALS

AFL-CIO AMERICAN FEDERATIONIST. M $2. Discusses in depth many problems most related to economics, from labor's point of view.

> AFL-CIO, 815 16th St., N. W., Washington, D. C. 20006.

AMERICAN ECONOMIC REVIEW. Q $8.00, $2.00 per copy. Contains several lead articles on economic subjects, occasional review articles, records of special investigations by individuals and public commissions, book reviews, and lists of new books and articles appearing in other periodicals, classified according to subject-matter fields.

> American Economic Association, Northwestern University, Evanston, Ill. 60201.

AMERICAN JOURNAL OF ECONOMICS AND SOCIOLOGY. Q $3.00, $1.00 per copy. Valuable contributions by distinguished scholars. Keeps the reader abreast of the many meaningful developments that are now taking place in economics, sociology, psychology and philosophy.

> 50 E. 69th St., New York, N. Y. 10021.

BUSINESS WEEK. W $7.00, $.50 per copy. Reports and interprets the week's news about all phases of business—production, labor, finance, marketing, research, economics, exports, transportation, labor relations, and new products.

McGraw-Hill, Inc., 330 W. 42nd St., New York, N. Y. 10036.

CHRISTIAN ECONOMICS. BW No charge. Voluntary contributions solicited. Advocates conservative approach, free enterprise, reduction of government control in economics, and gold standard.

Christian Freedom Foundation, 3030 W. 6th St., Los Angeles, Cal. 90005.

LID NEWS BULLETIN. An example of liberal publication. Irregular. No charge.

League of Industrial Democracy, Inc. 112 E. 19th St., New York, N. Y. 10003.

*QUARTERLY JOURNAL OF ECONOMICS. Q $6.00, $1.75 per copy. Articles on prices, money and credit, international economic problems, public finance and taxes, monopolies, agriculture, industry, trade unions, and labor problems. Directed primarily to economists and serious students of economics.

Harvard University Press, Cambridge, Mass. 01922.

*STATISTICAL YEARBOOK. A $10.00 per copy. Annual statistical data for more than 250 countries and territories covering a wide range of economic and social subjects. English and French.

Publication Service, United Nations, New York, N. Y. 10017.

PRINTED MATERIALS

AMERICAN AND SOVIET ECONOMIES, A CONTRAST AND COMPARISON. 1962. 15 pp. Factual information and bibliographical material. $.50.

*HOW THE AMERICAN ECONOMY IS ORGANIZED. 1961. 34 pp. A primer on the economic operation of the U.S.A. $1.00.

TEACHERS' GUIDE TO DEVELOPMENTAL ECONOMICS EDUCATION PROGRAM. PART ONE: ECONOMIC IDEAS AND CONCEPTS. 1964. 46 pp. Outlines the basic concepts and terms of economics. $.50.

Joint Council on Economic Education, 2 W. 46th St., New York, N. Y. 10036.

THE AMERICAN COMPETITIVE ENTERPRISE ECONOMY. A set of 17 pamphlets in the form of an Economics Primer for study groups. Conservative in approach. $6.00 per set, $.50 each.

Chamber of Commerce of the U. S., 1615 H St., N. W., Washington, D. C. 20006.

THE BIBLE SPEAKS ON ECONOMICS. A brief pamphlet containing basic biblical teachings on economics. Advocates no specific economic system. $.02.

> Christian Life Commission, 206 Baptist Bldg., Dallas, Tex. 75201.

*ECONOMIC LIFE PACKET. Selected materials on labor, management, consumers, and the use of American abundance. $3.00.

> Church of the Brethren, Elgin, Ill. 60120.

HANDBOOK OF BASIC ECONOMIC STATISTICS. A manual of basic economic data on industry, commerce, labor, and agriculture in the U.S.A.

> U. S. Govt. Statistics Bureau, Washington, D. C.

WHAT KIND OF ECONOMICS SHOULD CHRISTIANS SELL? A pamphlet by Howard E. Kershner advocating capitalism as the best economic system from a Christian point of view. Contains answers to critics of this position.

> Christian Freedom Foundation, 250 W. 57th St., New York, N. Y. 10019.

*THE WORLD OF ECONOMICS. Simple, yet adequate, discussion of economic theories. Excellent basic booklet. $.60.

> Public Affairs Pamphlets, 381 Park Ave. S., New York, N. Y. 10016

AUDIO VISUALS

CAPITALISM. 16 mm. B&W 10 min. $2.35 rental. Shows examples of some important aspects of the capitalistic system—private property, profit, competition, freedom of contract, and free enterprise. A high-school radio forum provides an opportunity to listen to a variety of conflicting opinions concerning the functioning and merits of capitalism.

> Visual Aids Service, Div. University Extension, University of Illinois, Champaign, Ill. 61822.

*CAPITALISM, SOCIALISM, AND COMMUNISM. 60 min tape. $5.00 purchase. These words have served political ends for so long that the theories on which the systems are based have been taken as descriptions of the facts. Michael Harrington attempts a redefinition of the terms and gives a historical account of the origin of some of the distortions.

> Center for the Study of Democratic Institutions, Box 4068, Santa Barbara, Cal. 93103.

CHART ON FLOW OF INCOME AND EXPENDITURES IN THE U. S. Free single copy. An excellent visual aid of the American economy.

> Twentieth Century Fund, 41 E. 70th St., New York, N. Y. 10021

DOLLARS, SENSE AND CHOICES. 35 mm. color filmstrip. 80 frames. 33-⅓ rpm record. $3.50 rental. $8.00 purchase. Developing values in spending as a responsible Christian family.
Cokesbury Bookstores.

ECONOMIC DISORDER. Tape of address by Foy Valentine. 1963. Free loan. Sets forth many economic abuses in America.
Campus Tape Service, Broadman Films Dept., Baptist S. S. Board, 127 Ninth Ave., N., Nashville, Tenn. 37203.

THE GRAPES OF WRATH. 16 mm. B&W 128 min. $32.50 rental for no admission charge. $45.00 with admission charge. John Steinbeck's major novel about migrant workers during the Depression. Shows disruption and suffering, economic injustice, and labor disputes in dramatic way.
Brandon Films, Inc., 200 W. 57th St., New York, N. Y. 10019.

HOUSE OF TOYS. B&W 30 min. $10.00 rental. $15.00 color. Reveals "secular materialism" and its effect on one's personal life. A girl's future mother-in-law shows her the emptiness of a life built around things.

THE RICH FOOL. 16 mm. B&W 28 min. $9.00 rental. $15.00 color. A dramatic story presents the effects of materialism on a man and his family. Inspirational and stimulating. Highly recommended.
Southern Baptist Film Centers.

100 SELECTED FILMS IN ECONOMIC EDUCATION. 1960. 34 pp. $.75. Each film entry provides a synopsis, questions raised by the film, suggested activities, and appropriate age level.

OUR GROWING AMERICA. Filmstrip. 152 frames. Script. 1963 ed. $8.00 purchase. Indicates the basic facts about the American economy. Helpful for general understanding.

THE UNITED STATES ECONOMY IN ACTION. Five 35 mm. filmstrips in color with accompanying booklets for study groups. Write for description and price.
Joint Council on Economic Education, 1212 Ave. of the Americas, New York, N. Y. 10036.

PURSUIT OF HAPPINESS, THE MATERIALISTIC WAY. 16 mm. 4 min. Color. Guide. $3.50 rental. A commentary on materialistic plenty vs. hunger and deprivation. Sounds and visuals compel the viewer to think about the "facts of life" of our consumer-oriented economic system which results in our preoccupation with things and the "easy life" and to compare this to the hard life of hunger and want in so many other part of the world.

> Office for Audio Visuals, United Church of Christ, 1720 Choutea Ave., St. Louis, Mo. 63103.

*TWO VIEWS ON SOCIALISM. 1½ reels. 16 min. B&W $3.90 rental. Color $5.65. The aims of socialism and charges by so cialists against capitalism are presented to stimulate discussion

> Audio Visual Center, Indiana University, Bloomington, Ind. 4740

The Federal Reserve Banks have a number of excellent free film on economics. Write the bank nearest you for available films.

OTHER HELPS

ECONOMIC ETHICS BIBLIOGRAPHY. Documents some cur rent literature in economics, philosophical ethics, and theologi cal ethics. Frequent annotation. Very helpful. Free.

> Economics Dept., Agricultural Experiment Station, South Dakot State University, Brookings, S. D. 57006.

INTERNATIONAL BIBLIOGRAPHY OF ECONOMICS. multi-volume bibliography.

> UNESCO Publications Center, 317 E. 34th St., New York, N. Y 10016.

LIST OF FREE MATERIALS AVAILABLE TO PROFESSORS Revised every other year. Materials, organizations, and addresse

> Educational Service Bureau, Dow Jones and Co., Inc., 200 Burne Rd., Chicopee, Mass. 01020.

A LITERATURE OF FREEDOM. 1966. Annotated bibliograph of books and papers which are highly critical of the tren toward state intervention in human affairs. Ultra-conservativ Free.

> Foundation for Economic Education, Inc., Irvington-on-Hudso N. Y. 10533.

SUGGESTIONS FOR A BASIC ECONOMICS LIBRARY. 196 64 pp. Annotated bibliography designed to guide the buildin of an economics library. Works of more than 240 authors liste $.75.

> Joint Council on Economic Education, 1212 Ave. of the America New York, N. Y. 10036.

EUTHANASIA

(See also Abortion, Capital Punishment, Pacifism)

BOOKS

AMERICAN FREEDOM AND CATHOLIC POWER. Paul Blanshard. Beacon. 2nd Rev. ed. 1958. $2.25 paper.

> A strong stand for euthanasia and an attack on the Catholic opposition to euthanasia.

CRISES IN MORALITY. C. W. Scudder, ed. Chapter 5. Broadman. 1964. $3.50.

> An excellent chapter on the pros and cons of euthanasia with an examination of the Christian's position in relation to the Bible.

JEWISH MEDICAL ETHICS. Immanuel Jakobovits. Chapter 11. Philosophical Library. 1959. OP

> From the point of view of a Jewish authority; a stand against the practice of euthanasia. Represents one Jewish viewpoint.

LAW AND MORALS. Norman St. John-Stevas. Hawthorn Books. 1964. $3.50.

> Discussion against euthanasia. Describes Catholic position and legal barriers to the practice.

MEDICAL ETHICS. Edwin Healy. Loyola University Press. 1956. $6.00.

> Builds a strong case against the practice and bases the stand on religious grounds.

MEDICAL ETHICS. Charles McFadden. F. A. Davis Co. 1961. 5th ed. $4.75.

> A stand against the practice of euthanasia carefully outlined and defended from a Catholic perspective.

MORALS AND MEDICINE. Joseph Fletcher. Beacon. 1960. $1.95 paper.

> A study of the problem from an ethical and medical point of view by an Episcopal professor of ethics. Favors practice under certain situations. One chapter on the subject. See also Moral Responsibility by Fletcher. Westminster, 1967. $1.95 paper.

THE RIGHT TO LIFE. Norman St. John-Stevas. Holt, Rinehart and Winston. 1964. $2.95.

> Discusses the value of life in western civilization and the diverse circumstances in which the right to life may be challenged.

THE SANCTITY OF LIFE AND THE CRIMINAL LAW. Glanville Williams. Alfred A. Knopf. 1957. $5.95.

> One chapter deals with the legal, theological, moral, biological aspects of euthanasia. Describes the movement to legalize voluntary euthanasia.

ORGANIZATIONS AND SOURCES

AMERICAN MEDICAL ASSOCIATION. Reprints and publications deal with euthanasia from time to time.
535 N. Dearborn St., Chicago, Ill. 60610.

EUTHANASIA SOCIETY OF AMERICA. Pamphlets, reprints, periodic paper *The Euthanasia Society Bulletin*. Favors euthanasia.
139 E. 57th St., New York, N. Y. 10022.

FAMILY LIFE BUREAU, U.S. CATHOLIC CONFERENCE. Pamphlets and reprints against euthanasia.
1312 Mass. Ave., N. W., Washington, D. C. 20005.

PERIODICALS AND JOURNALS

THE EUTHANASIA SOCIETY BULLETIN. Q $5.00. Articles, book reviews, and quotations favoring euthanasia.
Euthanasia Society of America, Inc., 139 E. 57th St., New York, N. Y. 10022.

MEDICAL TRIBUNE. 3 times a W $12.50. (Without charge to qualified recipients.) Articles and editorials on controversial questions in medicine.
120 E. 56th St., New York, N. Y. 10022.

See also medical journals.

PRINTED MATERIALS

THE PATIENT'S RIGHT TO DIE. Joseph Fletcher. Reprint from article in Harper's Magazine, October, 1960. $.05.

WHY LEGALIZE VOLUNTARY EUTHANASIA. Howard W. Haggard. A tract advocating new laws on euthanasia. $.10.
Euthanasia Society of America, 139 E. 57th St., New York, N. Y. 10022.

THE RIGHT TO LIFE. Opposition to euthanasia. $.10.
Family Life Bureau, U. S. Catholic Conference, 1312 Mass. Ave., N. W., Washington, D. C. 20005.

AUDIO VISUALS

None available.

EXTREMISM

(See also Citizenship, Communism, Race Relations)

BOOKS

THE BLACK MUSLIMS IN AMERICA. Eric C. Lincoln. Beacon. 1961. $4.95, $1.75 paper.

> One of the best books on the subject. Includes a foreword by Gordon Allport and a thorough bibliography.

BLACK NATIONALISM: A SEARCH FOR AN IDENTITY IN AMERICA. E. U. Essien-Udom. University of Chicago. 1962. $6.95.

> Describes the ideology of black nationalism, its organizations, leaders, programs, focusing on the Nation of Islam. It attempts to explain the meaning and significance of the movement for the participants and society as a whole.

BLUE BOOK OF THE JOHN BIRCH SOCIETY. $1.00 paper.

WHITE BOOK OF THE JOHN BIRCH SOCIETY. Robert Welch. 3 vols. 1960, 1961. $5.00 each.

> Primary source material on beliefs of the John Birch Society. Write to the John Birch Society (Belmont, Mass. 02178) for copies.

THE CHRISTIAN AND THE JOHN BIRCH SOCIETY. Lester DeKoster. Eerdman. 1965. $.75 paper.

> A comparison of the principles and practices advocated by the *Blue Book* of the John Birch Society and by the Bible.

*DANGER ON THE RIGHT. Arnold Forster and Benjamin Epstein. Random House. 1964. $4.95, $2.95 paper.

> On the attitudes, personnel, practices, and influence of the Radical Right and Extreme Conservatives. Discusses specific groups and organizations.

HOODED AMERICANISM: THE FIRST CENTURY OF THE KU KLUX KLAN: 1865 TO THE PRESENT. David Chalmers. Doubleday. 1965. $5.95.

> A historical study with much information to help understand current conditions. Basic for knowledge of the KKK.

THE RADICAL RIGHT. Daniel Bell, ed. Doubleday Anchor Book. 1964. $1.45.

> A lengthy book comprised of essays by social scientists on the development of the radical right in America. Historical and contemporary material.

REPORT ON THE JOHN BIRCH SOCIETY: 1966. Benjamin R. Epstein and Arnold Forster. Alfred A. Knopf, Inc. 1966. $3.95, $1.45 paper.

> Based on a comprehensive year-long study on the strengths, organization, and activity of the John Birch Society. Specific information. Extensive bibliography.

*THE STRANGE TACTICS OF EXTREMISM. Harry and Bonaro Overstreet. W. W. Norton & Co. 1964. $4.50.
> Discusses both right and left-wing extremism. Carefully done. Helpful suggestions on how to deal constructively with extremism.

ORGANIZATIONS AND SOURCES

Note: The label "extremist" is loosely used in America. What organizations should be identified as such and exactly what "extremist" means are questions for which answers are subjective and debatable. The following organizations are listed according to frequent descriptions in books and periodicals; not everyone will agree with the classifications. The reader should secure material from the organizations and decide for himself how they should be classified.

The following have been cited as examples of "right-wing extremism":

AMERICAN COUNCIL OF CHRISTIAN CHURCHES. An organization which is fundamentalist in religious outlook and ultra-conservative on economics and political issues. Vast material against National Council of Churches and Communism.
> 15 Park Row, New York, N. Y. 10038.

CHRISTIAN ANTI-COMMUNISM CRUSADE. Though limited largely to anti-Communist efforts apart from racial and economic concerns, the organization is still often listed among extremist groups.
> 124 E. 1st St., Long Beach, Cal. 90801.

CHRISTIAN CRUSADE. Wages far-flung campaign against Communism. Also deals with the U. N., politics, economics, and related topics.
> Box 977, Tulsa, Okla. 74101.

THE JOHN BIRCH SOCIETY. American Opinion Booklist, bulletin and two magazines, *American Opinion* and *The Review of the News.*
> Belmont, Mass. 02178.

The following have been cited as examples of "left-wing extremism":

COMMUNIST PARTY, U.S.A. Papers, pamphlets, and materials available.
> 23 W. 26th St., New York, N. Y. 10010.

See also the *Guide to Subversive Organizations and Publications* of the Committee on Un-American Activities, U.S. House of Representatives, for a list of Communist front groups. $.70.
> Supt. of Documents, U. S. Government Printing Office, Washington, D. C. 20402.

The following have been cited as examples of racist extremism (though they also deal with political and economic issues):

THE WORLD VISION OF NATIONAL SOCIALISTS. Selection of literature describing the organization and its activities is available for $1.00. Publishes *National Socialists World*, Q $10.00.
P. O. Box 5505, Arlington, Va. 22205.

CITIZENS' COUNCIL. Dedicated to principle of white supremacy. Papers and policy statements available.
314-325 Plaza Bldg., Jackson, Miss. 39201.

THE KU KLUX KLAN. White Supremacy group publishes material on the organization.
Box 107, Tucker, Ga. 30084.

MUHAMMAD'S MOSQUE OF ISLAM. Newspaper *Muhammad Speaks*, book *Message to the Blackman in America* $5.00, and radio program. States position of the Black Muslims.
5333-35 S. Greenwood Ave., Chicago, Ill. 60615.

STUDENT NONVIOLENT COORDINATING COMMITTEE (SNCC). Has become advocate of Black Power and radical means to overthrow discrimination.
360 Nelson St., S. W., Atlanta, Ga. 30313.

UNITED KLANS OF AMERICA, INC. A phase of the Ku Klux Klan.
Suite 401, Alston Bldg., Tuscaloosa, Ala. 35401.

The following organizations have information on extremism:

AMERICAN FEDERATION OF LABOR-CONGRESS OF INDUSTRIAL ORGANIZATIONS.
815—16th St., N. W., Washington, D. C. 20006.

AMERICAN JEWISH COMMITTEE.
165 E. 56th St., New York, N. Y. 10022.

ANTI-DEFAMATION LEAGUE OF B'NAI B'RITH.
315 Lexington Ave., New York, N. Y. 10016.

CENTER FOR THE STUDY OF DEMOCRATIC INSTITUTIONS. Works to combat all efforts to curtail freedom of speech and press in America. Scholarly, yet popular, pamphlets on extremism.
Box 4068, Santa Barbara, Cal. 93103.

COUNCIL FOR CHRISTIAN SOCIAL ACTION, UNITED CHURCH OF CHRIST.
289 Park Ave., S., New York, N. Y. 10010.

EXECUTIVE COUNCIL, EPISCOPAL CHURCH, DEPT. OF CHRISTIAN SOCIAL RELATIONS.
    815—2nd Ave., New York, N. Y. 10017.

GENERAL BOARD OF CHRISTIAN SOCIAL CONCERNS, THE METHODIST CHURCH.
    100 Maryland Ave., N. E., Washington, D. C. 20002.

INFORMATION SERVICE, NATIONAL COUNCIL OF CHURCHES.
    475 Riverside Dr., New York, N. Y. 10027.

INSTITUTE FOR AMERICAN DEMOCRACY. Special reports and source materials on the far left and the far right. *Homefront* is monthly publication.
    1330 Mass. Ave., N. W., Washington, D. C. 20005.

UNITED NATIONS ASSOCIATION OF THE U.S.A., INC.
    345 E. 46th St., New York, N. Y. 10017.

PERIODICALS AND JOURNALS

THE COUNCILOR. $2.00 for 24 issues. White supremist paper. Deals with race, politics, Communism, and religion.
    228 Oil and Gas Bldg., Shreveport, La. 71101.

NATIONAL CHRISTIAN NEWS. M $2.00. Anti-Jew-Communist newspaper.
    Box 10924, St. Petersburg, Florida 33733.

POLITICAL AFFAIRS. M $5.00, $4.00 students. Publication of far left viewpoint, theoretical magazine.
    799 Broadway, New York, N. Y. 10003.

THE REVIEW OF THE NEWS. W $10.00. Publication of the John Birch Society.
    395 Concord Ave., Belmont, Mass. 02178.

THE STORMTROOPER MAGAZINE. Q $1.00, $.25 per copy. Magazine on U.S. and international Nazism.
    Box 5505, Arlington, Va. 22205.

THE THUNDERBOLT. M White supremist anti-semetic publication.
    Box 783, Birmingham, Ala. 35201.

THE WORKER. SW $7.00, $4.00 students. Paper; editorial policy reflects the Communist viewpoint.
    Communist Party, U. S. A., 23 W. 26th St., New York, N. Y. 10010.

PRINTED MATERIALS

*COUNTERING EXTREMISM: RIGHTISTS, RACISTS, AND

SEPARATIONISTS ($.35) and WHAT IS EXTREMISM? 10 questions and answers. $.10. Material designed to help a community actively counter extremism. Extensive list of books and resources.

> The American Jewish Committee, Institute of Human Relations, 165 E. 56th St., New York, N. Y. 10022.

EXTREMISM. Lists materials on Communism, Nazism and the radical right. Free on request.

HOW TO LISTEN TO A JOHN BIRCH SOCIETY SPEAKER. Designed to help community leaders analyze the charges of John Birch spokesmen. $.35.

THE RADICAL RIGHT AND RELIGION. On the religiously-oriented radical right organizations. $.25.

REPORT ON THE KU KLUX KLAN. The history and current activities of the KKK. $.50.

> Anti-Defamation League, 315 Lexington Ave., New York, N. Y. 10016.

EXTREMISM-LEFT/RIGHT. Issue of *Social Progress* devoted to discussion of extremism. Bibliography. $.25.

> Board of Christian Education, United Presbyterian Church in the U. S. A., 1009 Sloan St., Crawfordsville, Ind. 47933.

*GUIDE TO SUBVERSIVE ORGANIZATIONS AND PUBLICATIONS. This list indicates which of the extremist groups are considered by Congress to be subversive. $.70.

> U. S. Government Printing Office, Washington, D. C. 20402.

INFORMATION SERVICE, Vol. XLIII, No. 16. Special issue on "The Radical Right." $.10 each, $4.50 for 50 copies.

> Office of Information, National Council of Churches, 475 Riverside Dr., New York, N. Y. 10027.

LABOR FIGHTS THE ENEMIES OF DEMOCRACY. Booklet describing why labor is opposed to extremism and what it is doing about the problem. $7.50 per 100.

> AFL-CIO, 815—16th St., N.W., Washington, D. C. 20006.

*LEFT-CENTER-RIGHT. An excellent chart comparing and contrasting the characteristics of radical left, radical right, and moderate middle organizations. $.05.

> All-American Conference, 1028 Conn. Ave., N. W., Washington, D. C. 20036.

AUDIO VISUALS

DANGER ON THE RIGHT. 16 mm. B&W 57 min. $7.00 rental. A documentary on various types of political extremism. It includes filming of an actual John Birch meeting as well as personal interviews with top leaders of the Birth Society.

> Office for Audio Visuals, United Church of Christ, 1720 Chouteau Ave., St. Louis, Mo. 63103.

DANGER ON THE RIGHT. Two 7½ IPS tapes. Free.

> Tape 1. Running time: 14:10. John Wingate moderates a discussion on the extreme Right Wing.
>
> Tape 2. Running time: 28:40. Dore Schary discusses the Radical Right with Benjamin Epstein, Arnold Forster and moderator David Susskind.

THE RADICAL RIGHT. 16 mm. B&W 30 min. $5.00 rental. A comprehensive treatment and analysis of the Right Wing extremist groups, ranging from the violently fanatic to their Extreme Conservative sympathizers.

*STAR-SPANGLED EXTREMISTS. 16 mm. B&W 30 min. $5.00 rental. A documentary which traces the historical development of the Radical Right from the time of the Know-Nothings of the 1850's to the John Birch Society of the 1960's. Illustrates the activities of extremist groups, analyzes their impact in American life, and demonstrates the similarities and differences between the radical right and the radical left.

> Anti-Defamation League of B'nai B'rith, 315 Lexington Ave., New York, N. Y. 10016.

*THE EXTREMISTS. Filmstrip. 25 min. $3.00 rental. Describes the wide range of extremist organizations that comprise the radical right-wing in the nation and their use of political action to achieve goals.

> AFL-CIO, Dept. of Education, 815—16th St., N. W., Washington, D.C. 20006.

*THE EXTREMISTS. 16 mm. B&W 28 min. $4.15 rental. Uses still photographs to review activities of right-wing extremist groups in the U.S. in recent years. Discusses examples of right-wing extremist groups by name, shows examples of their publications, and names their radio programs. Made in early 1960's, somewhat dated.

> Visual Aids Service, Div. University Extension, University of Illinois, Champaign, Ill. 61822.

THE KKK. 16 mm. B&W 28 min. Free. ABC-TV Scope documentary on the origins and operation of the Ku Klux Klan.

> Community Relations Service, Dept. of Justice, Washington, D. C. 20535.

OTHER HELPS

THE RADICAL RIGHT. From the Information Service of the

National Council of Churches. Book reviews and bibliography.
$.10.

475 Riverside Dr., New York, N. Y. 10027.

SELECTED BIBLIOGRAPHY ON EXTREMISM. Lists 17 books
and articles on various extremist groups in the U.S. $.05.

Service Dept. Methodist Church, 100 Maryland Ave., N. E., Washington, D. C. 20002.

FAMILY

(See also Abortion, Aging, Artificial Insemination, Juvenile Delinquency, Mental Health, Planned Parenthood, Sex, Unwed Parents)

BOOKS

THE AMERICAN FAMILY. Ruth S. Cavan. 3rd ed. Thomas Y.
Crowell. 1963. $6.50.

A sociological analysis of the contemporary family. This edition
is extensively revised to take into account recent research and
changes in social conditions.

A CHRISTIAN INTERPRETATION OF MARRIAGE. Henry A.
Bowman. Westminster. 1959. $2.50.

A brief and practical book on marriage from a Christian point of
view by an outstanding sociologist.

CHRISTIAN PARENTHOOD: A LIFETIME GUIDE. Helen
Hardwicke Sherrill. John Knox. 1964. $1.75.

The author follows parenthood through early years to old age. This
view of the life cycle is intended to help parents to be alert to the
emotional as well as the physical needs of their children. Furnishes
husbands and wives insights about handling their own personal
problems with maturity. For all parents.

THE ENCYCLOPEDIA OF CHILD CARE AND GUIDANCE.
Sidonie M. Gruenberg, ed. Doubleday. 1954. $8.50.

A new revised edition of a comprehensive reference book covering all phases of a child's growth—physical, psychological, and educational—from birth through adolescence.

FAMILIES IN THE CHURCH. Roy W. Fairchild and John Charles Wynn. Association. 1961. $5.75.

    Survey of church families plus data from other sources. A new look at today's family and guidelines for the church helping families.

FAMILY DEVELOPMENT. Evelyn Duvall. J. B. Lippincott. 1957 $8.75, text ed. $6.95.

    A study about the family from the family cycle point of view. Very helpful book from one of America's leading authorities of family life.

*THE FAMILY IN CHRISTIAN PERSPECTIVE. C. W. Scudder. Broadman. 1962. $3.50.

    A guide for marriage written from a theological viewpoint. Practical and helpful. Good bibliography for further study.

IF YOU MARRY OUTSIDE YOUR FAITH. James A. Pike. Harper and Brothers. Rev. ed. 1962. $3.50, $1.25 paper.

    A discussion from several points of view on the problems related to interfaith marriage. Helpful for those considering interfaith marriage and for those already involved.

INTERMARRIAGE—INTERFAITH, INTERRACIAL, INTER ETHNIC. Albert Gordon. Beacon. 1964. $2.95 paper.

    The most complete survey available of the attitudes, problems, and possibilities of intermarriage in the U. S. A. today.

*MARRIAGE FOR MODERNS. Henry A. Bowman. McGraw-Hill. 5th ed. 1965. $11.50, text ed. $8.50. Teacher's manual $1.50.

    One of the best books on problems of today's marriages. A total guide for preparation for and involvement in marriage. Useful as a text for courses in marriage preparation.

PASTORAL COUNSELING IN SOCIAL PROBLEMS. Wayne Oates. Westminster. 1966. $.75 paper.

    Helpful information on several subjects including sex and divorce. Valuable reference book.

PREMARITAL PASTORAL CARE AND COUNSELING. Wayne E. Oates. Broadman. 1958. $1.00.

    A leader in the field of family counseling sets forth ways to effectively guide couples into happy marriages.

SEX, MARRIAGE, AND SOCIETY IN THEOLOGICAL FOCUS. John C. Wynn, ed. Association. 1966. $4.95.

    Brings theological perspective to bear on current issues related to sex and family. Useful in balancing some of the more secular books on the subject. Highly recommended by authorities on the family field.

*SUCCESS IN MARRIAGE. David R. Mace. Abingdon. 1958. $2.95, $1.00 paper.

    A simple, readable book for those looking toward marriage, th average married couple, and the married couple in trouble. By one of the world's leading authorities on family life.

WHAT CHRISTIANITY SAYS ABOUT SEX, LOVE, AND MARRIAGE. Roland H. Bainton. Association. 1957. $.75 paper.
Helpful historical insights by a leading historian. Current debates are more clearly understood in the light of past teachings.

ORGANIZATIONS AND SOURCES

AMERICAN ASSOCIATION OF MARRIAGE COUNSELORS, INC. No material or publications available to general public except the annual *Directory of Members* to be used for referral purposes. $2.00.
27 Woodcliff Dr., Madison, N. J. 07940.

AMERICAN HOME ECONOMICS ASSOCIATION. Practical information for smoother-running families.
1600—20th St., N.W., Washington, D. C. 20009.

THE AMERICAN INSTITUTE OF FAMILY RELATIONS. Educational, counseling, and research organization publishes *Family Life*, publications list available.
5287 Sunset Blvd., Los Angeles, Cal. 90027.

*AMERICAN SOCIAL HEALTH ASSOCIATION.** Several pamphlets and material on children and family life available. List of film sources and bibliographies available.
1790 Broadway, New York, N. Y. 10019.

THE ASSOCIATION FOR FAMILY LIVING. Several pamphlets and reprints available. Membership $5.00 includes free subscription to publication *Your Family*. Pamphlets include "Bibliography and Film Guide," $.35.
32 W. Randolph St., Chicago, Ill. 60601.

BUREAU OF FAMILY SERVICES, WELFARE ADMINISTRATION. Public assistance to help needy people. Their material is available from:
Supt. of Documents, U. S. Government Printing Office, Washington, D. C. 20402.
U. S. Dept. of Health, Education, and Welfare, Washington, D. C. 20201.

CHILD STUDY ASSOCIATION OF AMERICA. Publications list available dealing with children and parent-child relations. Excellent source.
9 E. 89th St., New York, N. Y. 10028.

CHILDREN'S BUREAU, U. S. DEPT. OF HEALTH, EDUCA-

TION, AND WELFARE. Send for list of available materials related to child care and welfare.

Washington, D. C. 20201.

CHRISTIAN FAMILY MOVEMENT. Catholic apostolic movement for married couples. Tapes for sale or rent and monthly publication *Act*. Suggests ways families can minister to the needs of the world.

1655 Jackson Blvd., Chicago, Ill. 60612.

FAMILY LIFE BUREAU, U.S. CATHOLIC CONFERENCE. Reprints, pamphlets, and bimonthly bulletin *Catholic Family Leader*. Guidance for Catholic families; helpful insight for all into many aspects of family life.

1312 Mass. Ave., N. W., Washington, D. C. 20005.

FAMILY LIFE DEPARTMENT OF THE SOUTHERN BAPTIST CONVENTION. Publishes *Home Life* magazine. Pamphlets and tracts available.

127 Ninth Ave., N., Nashville, Tenn. 37203.

FAMILY LIFE PUBLICATIONS, INC. Counseling aids and newsletter which includes bibliography. Many helpful materials on family.

Box 6725, Durham, N. C. 27708.

FAMILY SERVICE ASSOCIATION OF AMERICA. Catalog of books and pamphlets for the social worker, psychiatrist, educator, student, community leader, clergy available. Publish quarterly magazine *Family Service Highlights*.

44 E. 23rd St., New York, N. Y. 10010.

LARGE FAMILIES OF AMERICA, INC. Educational organization devoted to the common interests of responsible parents and their children in large families. They re-distribute material published by others and publish monthly newsletter *LF. News* for members.

Box 885, Norwalk, Conn. 06852.

*MARRIAGE AND FAMILY LIFE, EDUCATIONAL DEVELOPMENT DEPT., NATIONAL COUNCIL OF CHURCHES. Lists of suggested materials, tracts, and pamphlets.

475 Riverside Dr., New York, N. Y. 10027.

NATIONAL ASSOCIATION FOR MENTAL HEALTH. Materials on family life, especially helpful for preventing mental illness and responding to the needs of the mentally ill within a family.

10 Columbus Circle, New York, N. Y. 10019.

NATIONAL CONGRESS OF PARENTS AND TEACHERS. Booklets and information on family life, especially as it relates to education.

700 N. Rush St., Chicago, Ill. 60611.

NATIONAL COUNCIL ON FAMILY RELATIONS. A fellowship of professional family life specialists, publish *Journal of Marriage and the Family* and a bibliography.

1219 University Ave. S. E., Minneapolis, Minn. 55414.

PARENTS WITHOUT PARTNERS, INC. An international, nonprofit, non-sectarian, educational organization devoted to the interests and welfare of single parents and their children. They publish *The Single Parent* magazine, chapter newsletters, manuals· and pamphlets of organization instructions. A number of regional chapters exist.

80 Fifth Ave., New York, N. Y. 10011.

*PUBLIC AFFAIRS PAMPHLETS.** A large number of excellent booklets on many phases of family life. $.25 each.

381 Park Ave., S., New York, N. Y. 10016.

In addition, most of the religiously-oriented organizations listed in the appendix have material on marriage and family life.

PERIODICALS AND JOURNALS

CATHOLIC FAMILY LEADER. BM $1.00. Service bulletin. Book recommendations, articles, notes on family life issues.

Family Life Bureau, U. S. Catholic Conference, 1312 Mass. Ave., N. W., Washington, D. C. 20005.

CHILD WELFARE. M (except Aug. & Sept.) $3.00, $.60 per copy. Methods, research, and education as they relate to child welfare services.

Child Welfare League of America, 44 E. 23rd St., New York, N. Y. 10010.

CHRISTIAN HOME. M $3.00. A magazine directed toward Christian families with practical information and inspiration.

TOGETHER. M $5.00. A Methodist family magazine, helpful for all Christian-oriented families.

201—8th Ave., S., Nashville, Tenn. 37203.

FAMILY LIFE. M $2.00. Service bulletin. Promotion material with some content on family problems and ministry.

American Institute of Family Relations, 5287 Sunset Blvd., Los Angeles, Cal. 90027.

*FAMILY SERVICE HIGHLIGHTS. M $1.50. Articles on family life, particularly on resolving problem situations.
> Family Service Association of America, 44 E. 23rd St., New York, N. Y. 10010.

HOME LIFE. M $3.00. A Southern Baptist family magazine with practical suggestions for all families especially those with a Christian perspective.

LIVING WITH CHILDREN. Q $1.25. Practical guides for activities with children; emphasis on religious education and character development.
> Sunday School Board, 127 Ninth Ave., N., Nashville, Tenn. 37203.

*JOURNAL OF MARRIAGE AND THE FAMILY. Q $12.00 membership includes subscription. (Students $5.00). $2.00 per copy. A medium for the presentation of original theory, research, interpretation, and critical discussion of materials that have to do with marriage and family.
> National Council of Family Relations, 1219 University Ave., S.E., Minneapolis, Minn. 55414.

PARENT'S MAGAZINE. M $4.00. For parents of children of all ages. Articles on parent-child relations, health, finances, and recreation. Lists books and pamphlets available.
> Parent's Magazine Subscription Office, Bergenfield, N. J. 07621.

THE SINGLE PARENT. M $5.00. Journal devoted to welfare and interests of single parents and their children.
> Parents Without Partners, Inc., 80 Fifth Ave., New York, N. Y. 10011.

PRINTED MATERIALS

THE AMERICAN FAMILY IN A CHANGING WORLD. A very good series on family life. Alerts families to changes and pressures from their culture.
> American Association of University Women, 2401 Virginia Ave., N. W., Washington, D. C. 20037.

THE BIBLE SPEAKS ON FAMILY and CHRISTIAN PRINCIPLES APPLIED TO FAMILY. Two brief pamphlets outlining and applying biblical teachings. $.02 each.

CHRISTIAN COUNSELING SERIES. Three pamphlets on adoption, unwed mothers, and mental illness to help families in crisis. $.02 each.

CHRISTIAN FAMILY LIFE EDUCATION CONFERENCE. A booklet of suggestions, sources, and bibliography on structuring family life ministry in the church. $1.00.
> Christian Life Commission, 206 Baptist Bldg., Dallas, Tex. 75201.

*CHILD GUIDANCE, FAMILY WELL-BEING, and MARRIAGE AND SPECIAL FAMILY CONCERNS. 3 packets of 18 pamphlets each. Very readable and helpful. $3.50 for one packet; $6.00 for two; $8.50 for three.

*WHAT MAKES A MARRIAGE HAPPY. David Mace. A superb booklet on married life as a whole. $.25.

> Public Affairs Pamphlets, 381 Park Ave., S., New York, N. Y. 10016.

*CHRISTIAN ANSWERS TO FAMILY PROBLEMS. A series of 15 pamphlets on family life dealing with divorce, planned parenthood, maturity for marriage, working wives, relation to relatives, conflict in marriage, parent-teenager relations, teenage marriage, discipline, finances, marital adjustment, religion, recreation, the aged, and interfaith marriage. Concise, colorful, helpful. $.02 each.

> Christian Life Commission, Southern Baptist Convention, 460 James Robertson Parkway, Nashville, Tenn. 37219.

DIRECTORY OF MEMBERS, AMERICAN ASSOCIATION OF MARRIAGE COUNSELORS, INC. A list, by states and alphabetically, of marriage counselors who are members of the American Association of Marriage Counselors, Inc. Helpful in locating competent persons for help with family counseling. $2.00.

> 27 Woodcliff Dr., Madison, N. J. 07940.

THE FAMILY TODAY. A well-written analysis of family life under present strains and how it can be improved. $.30.

> Executive Council, Episcopal Church, 815 2nd Ave., New York, N. Y. 10017.

THE MOTHER WHO WORKS OUTSIDE THE HOME. Violet Weingarten. A 25-page booklet exploring the problems of the working mother. $.50.

> Child Study Association of America, 9 E. 89th St., New York, N. Y. 10028.

THE NEW SHAPE OF THE AMERICAN FAMILY. Helpful overview of changes in and pressures on the American family. $.07.

> Commission on Research and Social Action, American Lutheran Church, 422 S. 5th St., Minneapolis, Minn. 55415.

*SERIES ON FAMILY PROBLEMS: A HANDBOOK FOR HUSBANDS AND WIVES, HOW TO KEEP ROMANCE IN YOUR MARRIAGE, HUSBANDS AND PREGNANCY, HOW TO RETIRE AND LIKE IT. Readable, up-to-date and inexpensive material. $.75 each.

> Family Life Library, Association Press, 291 Broadway, New York, N. Y. 10007.

WHAT MAKES FOR STRONG FAMILY LIFE. A brief survey of what makes for the type of family which can successfully survive stress. From a secular point of view. $.20.
>   Family Association of America, 44 E. 23rd St., New York, N. Y. 10010.

AUDIO VISUALS

Numerous films are available on family life. Films should be selected to suit the purpose, age group, and perspective of those involved in the showing. Collect film catalogues and then make selections as needed. Catalogues can be obtained from the following. Ask for lists of films on the family.

ASSOCIATION FILMS, INC.
>   35 W. 45th St., New York, N. Y. 10019.

CENTER FOR MASS COMMUNICATION.
>   Columbia University, 1125 Amsterdam Ave., New York, N. Y. 10025.

CHURCHILL FILMS.
>   662 N. Robertson Blvd., Los Angeles, Cal. 90069.

CORONET FILMS.
>   65 E. South Water St., Chicago, Ill. 60601.

FAMILY FILMS.
>   5823 Santa Monica Blvd., Hollywood, Cal. 90038.

McGRAW-HILL BOOK COMPANY.
>   Text-Film Division, 30 W. 42nd St., New York, N. Y. 10036.

MEDICAL ARTS PRODUCTIONS.
>   Box 4042, Stockton, Calif. 95204.

MENTAL HEALTH FILM BOARD.
>   164 E. 38th St., New York, N. Y. 10016.

MENTAL HEALTH MATERIALS CENTER.
>   104 E. 25th St., New York, N. Y. 10010.

NATIONAL FILM BOARD OF CANADA.
>   Room 819, 680 Fifth Ave., New York, N. Y. 10019.

In addition, the following lists of audio visuals are available:

AUDIO-VISUAL MATERIALS FOR FAMILY LIFE PROGRAMS.
>   Dept. of Christian Family, Board of Education, The Methodist Church, Box 871, Nashville, Tenn. 37202.

BIBLIOGRAPHY AND FILM GUIDE.
>   The Association for Family Living, 32 W. Randolph St., Chicago, Ill. 60601.

FAMILY LIFE: LITERATURE AND FILMS.

Minnesota Council on Family Life, 1219 University Ave., S. E., Minneapolis, Minn. 55414.

LIST OF FILMS ON FAMILY RELATIONS AND CHILD DEVELOPMENT.

American Home Economics Association, 1600—20th St., N. W., Washington, D. C. 20009.

PUBLICATIONS.

Family Service Association of America, 44 E. 23rd St., New York, N. Y. 10010.

The following are samples of the many materials available:

A CHANGING VIEW OF THE CHANGE OF LIFE. Color 28 min. Free. Many vital questions concerning menopause are answered in this candid and informative film for women of all ages and their families.

Association Films, Inc.

A FAMILY AFFAIR. 16 mm. B&W 30 min. $7.50 rental. Helps family members see how they make each other unhappy and how they can learn to create a more harmonious family.

International Film Bureau, 332 S. Michigan Ave., Chicago, Ill. 60604.

*THE FAMILY NEXT DOOR. 16 mm. B&W 30 min. $8.00 rental. Helps parents understand what makes a Christian home by observing events in the life of one family.

GETTING ALONG WITH YOUR PARENTS. 35 mm. filmstrip. 38 frames. $3.00 purchase. For youth and adults. Practical suggestions on better parent-youth relations.

ONE LOVE—CONFLICTING FAITHS. 16 mm. B&W 30 min. $6.00 rental. Color $9.00. Presentation of problem of interfaith marriage and possible responses.

PREPARATION FOR MARRIAGE SERIES. Five 35 mm. filmstrips. 33-⅓ rpm recording. B&W $8.50 each purchase. $35.00 for set. Script written by Evelyn Millis Duvall. Concerning dating, engagement, and general marriage preparation.

SHOULD I MARRY OUTSIDE MY FAITH? 16 mm. B&W 30 min. $10.00 rental. A study of the religious problems faced by a boy and girl who are in love but of different faiths, and what they learn from friends of a mixed marriage.

WORSHIP, A FAMILY'S HERITAGE. 16 mm. B&W 30 min. $7.00 rental. Color $11.00. Help and incentive for family worship.

Cokesbury.

*The following six films, produced for the Department of National Health and and Welfare, present a study of child behavior at various age levels, and stage-to-stage guidance about what children need from parents:

HE ACTS HIS AGE. 16 mm. 14 min. 15 sec. 1949. B&W $6.00 rental. Color $8.50.

THE TERRIBLE TWOS AND THE TRUSTING THREES. 16 mm. 21 min. 22 sec. 1950. B&W $6.00 rental. Color $8.50.

THE FRUSTRATING FOURS AND FASCINATING FIVES. 16 mm. 21 min. 30 sec. 1952. B&W $6.00 rental. Color $8.50.

FROM SOCIABLE SIX TO NOISY NINE. 16 mm. 21 min. 3 sec. 1953. B&W $6.00 rental. Color $8.50.

FROM TEN TO TWELVE. 16 mm. 25 min. 18 sec. 1956. B&W $8.00 rental. Color $11.00.

THE TEENS. 16 mm. 25 min. 23 sec. 1957. B&W $8.00 rental. Color $11.00.

Contemporary Films Inc., 267 W. 25th St., New York, N. Y. 10001.

OTHER HELPS

BIBLIOGRAPHY AND FILM GUIDE. Suggestions for family life resources. $.35.

The Association for Family Living, 32 W. Randolph St., Chicago, Ill. 60601.

BOOKS FOR THE MARRIAGE AND FAMILY COUNSELOR, INFORMATION ABOUT COUNSELING AND TEACHING AIDS. Description of materials available. Free on request.

Family Life Publications, Box 6725, Durham, N. C. 27708.

THE CHILDREN'S BOOKSHELF: A GUIDE TO BOOKS FOR AND ABOUT CHILDREN. Parents' guide to good books for boys and girls, including special section of more than 300 books for parents about family life. $.95.

A PARENT'S BOOKSHELF. Annotated, classified list of 50 books and pamphlets selected from among the most helpful published in the field of child development and family life in recent years. $.10.

Child Study Association of America, 9 E. 89th St., New York, N. Y. 10028.

FAMILY LIFE AND FAMILY LIFE EDUCATION. A list of selected and annotated readings prepared to answer the question, "What are a few good basic books about family life and family life education?"

American Social Health Association, 1790 Broadway, New York, N. Y. 10019.

FAMILY LIFE REFERENCES. Annotated listings of family life sources. $1.00.

RECENT PUBLICATIONS IN HUMAN DEVELOPMENT AND FAMILY RELATIONS. Selected important recent publications listed. $1.00.
> Dept. of Human Development and Family Relationships, Brigham Young University, Provo, Utah 45180.

PUBLICATIONS. List of books, pamphlets, films, plays and magazines of most phases of family life.
> Family Service Association of America, 44 E. 23rd St., New York, N. Y. 10010.

RECOMMENDED PUBLICATIONS ON MARRIAGE AND THE FAMILY. Classified and annotated. A bibliography for Christian formation in the family. $.95. Books, Inc. 1963. $.75.
> Family Life Bureau, U. S. Catholic Conference, 1312 Mass. Ave., N. W., Washington, D. C. 20005.

RESOURCES FOR CHRISTIAN FAMILY LIFE EDUCATION. A pamphlet listing books, pamphlets, motion pictures, filmstrips, recordings and tracts on family. Single copy free.
> Family Life Dept., Education Div., Baptist Sunday School Board, 127 Ninth Ave., N., Nashville, Tenn. 37203.

GAMBLING

(See also Crime, Decision Making, Juvenile Delinquency)

BOOKS

COMPLETE GUIDE TO GAMBLING. John Scarne. Simon & Schuster. 1961. $10.00.
> Basic information on all phases of gambling. An encyclopedia-type book.

GAMBLERS' MONEY. Wallace Turner. The Riverside Press, Houghton Mifflin Co. 1965. $5.95.

     A comprehensive investigation by a prize-winning reporter of the influence of gambling in the U. S. Links gambling and big-time crime.

*THE GAMBLING MENACE. Ross Coggins, ed. Broadman. 1966. $2.95.

     The best volume available on all phases of gambling. Biblical, sociological, and psychological studies. A leading economist shows the relation of gambling to taxation and other economic issues. Contains a comprehensive plan of action.

GAMBLING, SHOULD IT BE LEGALIZED? Virgil Peterson. Charles Thomas Publishers. 1951. OP

     An expert in law enforcement discusses why he opposes the legalization of gambling.

GREEN FELT JUNGLE. Ed Reid and Ovid Demaris. Pocket Books, Inc. 1963. $.75.

     A vivid account of gambling in the U.S. today. Behind the respectable front is a vicious operation.

*MONEY, MANIA, AND MORALS: THE CHURCH AND GAMBLING. Lycurgus M. Starkey, Jr. Abingdon. 1964. $1.50 paper.

     An excellent volume on the extent and effect of gambling with a careful ethical evaluation. Unique in its discussion of the theological implications in gambling.

THE NATURE OF GAMBLING. David D. Allen. Coward McCann, Inc. 1952. OP

     A secular study of the subject with an approach to control of gambling.

PLAY THE DEVIL. Henry Chafetz. Clarkson N. Potter, Inc. 1960. $1.98.

     A rather comprehensive history of gambling in the U.S. from 1492 until 1955.

THE PSYCHOLOGY OF GAMBLING. Edmund Bergler. Hill and Wang. 1957. OP

     A physician takes a look at the psychological reasons behind gambling. Devoted largely to the study of the compulsive gambler and the possibility of his cure.

A TWO DOLLAR BET MEANS MURDER. Fred Cook. Dial. 1961. OP.

     Relates gambling and crime. Shows how innocent small betting contributes to large scale crime in the U. S.

YOU CAN'T WIN. Ernest E. Blanche. Public Affairs Press. 1949. OP

     A discussion of the foolishness of gambling and the improbability of the gambler beating the professional.

ORGANIZATIONS AND SOURCES

BACK TO GOD TRACT COMMITTEE.
2850 Kalamazoo Ave., S. E., Grand Rapids, Michigan 49508.

BOARD OF CHRISTIAN EDUCATION, PRESBYTERIAN CHURCH U. S.
Box 1176, Richmond, Va. 23209.

BOARD OF SOCIAL MINISTRY, LUTHERAN CHURCH IN AMERICA.
231 Madison Ave., New York, N. Y. 10016.

CHRISTIAN LIFE COMMISSION OF THE BAPTIST GENERAL CONVENTION OF TEXAS.
206 Baptist Bldg., Dallas, Tex. 75201.

CHRISTIAN LIFE COMMISSION OF THE SOUTHERN BAPTIST CONVENTION.
460 James Robertson Parkway, Nashville, Tenn. 37219.

CONCORDIA TRACT MISSION.
Box 201, St. Louis, Mo. 63166.

EPISCOPAL CHURCH CENTER.
815—2nd Ave., New York, N. Y. 10017.

GAMBLERS ANONYMOUS, NATIONAL SERVICE OFFICE.
Materials on gambling and information on local chapters of G. A.
Box 17173, Los Angeles, Cal. 90017.

METHODIST CHURCH, GENERAL BOARD OF CHRISTIAN SOCIAL CONCERNS.
100 Maryland Ave., N. E., Washington, D. C. 20002.

NATIONAL COUNCIL OF CHURCHES OF CHRIST.
475 Riverside Dr., New York, N. Y. 10027.

UNITED STATES DEPT. OF JUSTICE.
Washington, D. C. 20535.

PRINTED MATERIALS

THE ANNALS OF THE AMERICAN ACADEMY OF POLITICAL AND SOCIAL SCIENCE. The May, 1950, issue is devoted to a study of gambling. $2.00.
3937 Chestnut St., Philadelphia, Pa. 19104.

COMPULSIVE GAMBLING. A tract produced and distributed by the Gamblers Anonymous National Service Office. $.05.
Box 17173, Los Angeles, Cal. 90017.

THE FAMILY AND GAMBLING, WHAT'S SO BAD ABOUT GAMBLING and PARIMUTUEL GAMBLING. Tracts helpful in deciding what to do about and how to deal with the issue of gambling. $.02 each.

      Christian Life Commission, 206 Baptist Bldg., Dallas, Tex. 75201.

GAMBLING AND ORGANIZED CRIME. A report on the close connection of organized crime and gambling. Excellent source material.

      U. S. Government Printing Office but out of print. Consult library for a copy.

GAMBLING IS FOR SUCKERS. Cartoon illustrated booklet on the harm involved in gambling. $.75

      Texas Alcohol Narcotics Education, Inc., 2814 Oak Lawn Ave., Dallas, Tex. 75219.

GAMBLING: ISSUES AND ANSWERS SERIES. A brief up-to-date analysis of the problem with suggested courses of action. $.05 each.

      Christian Life Commission, Southern Baptist Convention, 460 James Robertson Parkway, Nashville, Tenn. 37219.

REPORT ON LEGALIZED GAMBLING. Facts and insight into the issue of whether or not to legalize gambling. 1963. $1.25.

      Baltimore Criminal Justice Commission, 22 Light St., Baltimore, Maryland 21202.

REPORT ON ORGANIZED GAMBLING. A comprehensive report issued in 1967. $.30.

*MATERIALS FROM THE 1964 NATIONAL CONFERENCE ON GAMBLING. Much useful information on gambling from competent spokesmen dealing with all phases of the gambling problem. $.30.

      National Council of Churches, 475 Riverside Dr., New York, N. Y. 10027.

SHOULD WE LEGALIZE GAMBLING? A helpful report on the dangers of legalized gambling. 1962. $.10.

      New England Citizens Crime Commission, 3 Joy St., Boston, Mass. 02108.

*WHEN YOU GAMBLE—YOU RISK MORE THAN YOUR MONEY. Excellent pamphlet on the harm caused by gambling to the individual and to society. $.25.

      Public Affairs Pamphlets, 381 Park Ave., S., New York, N. Y. 1001

AUDIO VISUALS

BIG STEVE. 16 mm. B&W 27 min. 1964. $9.00 rental. Color $13.50. "Big Steve" Johnson is a moderately successful business man who becomes a compulsive gambler. The film traces his degeneration as the habit engulfs him, swallowing his home and job and threatening his life by suicide. The steadfast love and encouragement of his wife influence him to recognize the problem and join the organization Gamblers Anonymous.

The Hour of St. Francis, 1224 S. Los Angeles St., Los Angeles, Cal. 90015.

GAMBLING AND THE CHURCH. 3-part filmstrip. 126 frames. 17 min. Color. Script. Guide. Record. $14.75 purchase. 1964. Produced by General Board of Christian Social Concerns, The Methodist Church. Part 1 discusses what gambling is, describing chance as the determining factor in gambling. Part 2 discusses why the church is concerned, showing some of the economic, social, personal and spiritual effects of gambling. Part 3 asks what can Christians do, placing responsibility on Christians to be alert and informed and to take action.

HOW FREE ARE YOU? 35 mm. filmstrip. 75 frames. 33-1/3 rpm record. $7.50 purchase. Shows how gambling enslaves men's wills. Good discussion starter.

Service Dept., Methodist Church, 100 Maryland Ave., N.E., Washington, D. C. 20002.

GAMBLING IS FOR SUCKERS. Color filmstrip and recording. Complete with script. $6.95 purchase with set of two filmstrips, the other being on alcohol. Discusses harm of gambling.

TANE Press, 2814 Oak Lawn Dr., Dallas, Tex. 75219.

ON THE RIGHT SIDE. 16 mm. B&W 20 min. $6.00 rental. A young man addicted to gambling nearly breaks up his home when he fails to heed his wife's pleas to give it up. Through the help of a judge the family is reunited, and their home is strengthened by the efforts of their pastor and congregation.

WHERE FORTUNE SMILES. 16 mm. B&W Sound. 30 min. $9.00 rental. Color $13.00. Shows what can happen to a person when the "something for nothing" philosophy gains control of his life.

Cokesbury.

HOMOSEXUALITY

(See also Family, Mental Health, Sex)

BOOKS

CHRIST AND THE HOMOSEXUAL. Robert W. Wood. Vantage. 1960. OP.

> An appeal by a churchman for compassion and ministry in respect to the homosexual. Some defense offered for homosexuality.

*CRISES IN MORALITY. C. W. Scudder, ed. Chapter 3. Broadman. 1964. $3.50.

> An excellent brief chapter on a Christian appraisal of homosexuality. Sets forth several aspects of the problem and suggests a response for Christians.

THE HOMOSEXUAL OUTLOOK. Donald W. Cory. Peter Nevill. 1953. OP.

> Written by a homosexual, the book gives an inside view of homosexual life in America. Albert Ellis says, ". . . the best non-fictional picture of the American homosexual and his problems."

HOMOSEXUALITY AND THE WESTERN CHRISTIAN TRADITION. Derrick S. Bailey. Longmans, Green, & Co. 1955. OP.

> A very helpful historical study of homosexuality from Bible times to the present. The theological and moral aspects of homosexuality are not discussed.

HOMOSEXUALITY—DISEASE OR WAY OF LIFE? E. Bergler. Collier. 1962. $.95 paper.

> A psychological approach. Offers hope for cure if the individual really wants help. Popular rather than technical.

HOMOSEXUALITY: ITS CAUSES AND CURE. Albert Ellis. Lyle Stuart. 1965. $7.95.

> A rational psychotherapy approach to the cure. Tape-recorded interviews helpful to understanding the homosexual and Ellis' approach.

LAW AND MORALS. Norman St. John-Stevas. Hawthorn. 1964. $3.50.

> A brief chapter on the legal and Catholic moral position on homosexuality.

MORALITY AND THE HOMOSEXUALS. Michael J. Buckley. Newman. 1959. OP.

> A Catholic approach to the problem of homosexuality. Covers the subject from a moral as well as psychological perspective.

STRANGERS IN OUR MIDST. Alfred A. Gross. Public Affairs Press. 1961. $4.50.

> A discussion of the homosexual in American society. Chapters on the law and the church in relation to the homosexual.

*TOWARD A CHRISTIAN UNDERSTANDING OF THE HOMOSEXUAL. H. Kimball Jones. Association. 1966. $4.95.
> Examines the nature of the problem using the most recent psychological and sociological studies. Good bibliography. Contains names and addresses of some homosexual organizations.

*TOWARD AN UNDERSTANDING OF HOMOSEXUALITY. Daniel Cappon. Prentice-Hall, Inc. 1965. $6.95.
> Competent but easily read, this book explores every facet of the homosexual problem and offers hope for a changed way of life to the homosexual.

THE WOLFENDEN REPORT. Lancer Books. 1964.
> An English study of homosexuality and the law.

ORGANIZATIONS AND SOURCES

AMERICAN PSYCHOLOGICAL ASSOCIATION. Mainly an organization for professionals in the field of psychology.
> 1200—17th St., N. W., Washington, D. C. 20036.

GLIDE URBAN CENTER and COUNCIL ON RELIGION AND THE HOMOSEXUAL. A religious organization which specializes in ministry to the out groups of society, such as homosexuals. Pamphlets and other materials.
> 330 Ellis St., Room 100, San Francisco, Cal. 94102.

GROUP FOR THE ADVANCEMENT OF PSYCHIATRY, INC. Reports and study papers available.
> 104 E. 25th St., New York, N. Y. 10010.

THE MATTACHINE SOCIETY OF WASHINGTON. Specialized concern about homosexuality.
> P. O. Box 1032, Washington, D. C. 20013.

PUBLIC HEALTH SERVICE. References and materials available.
> U. S. Dept. of Health, Education, and Welfare, Washington, D. C. 20201.

SEX INFORMATION AND EDUCATION COUNCIL OF THE U. S. Newsletters and discussion guides with homosexuality as one topic of consideration.
> 1885 Broadway, New York, N. Y. 10023.

PERIODICALS AND JOURNALS

None specifically devoted to the subject. See journals in medicine, psychology, sociology, and law for occasional articles.

PRINTED MATERIALS

THE CHURCH AND THE HOMOSEXUAL. Suggested approaches. $1.00.

HOMOSEXUALITY: A CONTEMPORARY VIEW OF THE BIBLICAL PERSPECTIVE. An example of radical new approaches. $.50.
>   Glide Urban Center, 330 Ellis St., Room 100, San Francisco, Cal. 94102.

HOMOSEXUALITY and ANOMALY. Rev. Kenneth B. Murphy. Two brief but helpful pamphlets. Single copies free.
>   Rescue, Inc., 115 Southampton St., Boston, Mass. 02118.

REPORT OF THE COMMITTEE ON HOMOSEXUAL OFFENSES AND PROSTITUTION. A report of a study done in England, 1957. Also known as Wolfenden Report.
>   Sales Section, British Information Services, 845 Third Ave., New York, N. Y. 10022.

REPORT ON HOMOSEXUALITY WITH PARTICULAR EMPHASIS ON THIS PROBLEM IN GOVERNMENTAL AGENCIES. Jan. 1955. $.25.
>   Group for the Advancement of Psychiatry, Inc., 104 E. 25th St., New York, N. Y. 10010.

SIECUS DISCUSSION GUIDE: HOMOSEXUALITY. A guide for discussion leaders and for individuals interested in intensive self-motivated study. $.50.
>   SIECUS, 1855 Broadway, New York, N. Y. 10023.

TOWARDS A QUAKER VIEW OF SEX. A liberal treatment of the problem. Indicates an approach toward acceptance of the homosexual as he is. $.50.
>   Friends Home Service Committee, Friends House, Euston Rd., London, N. W. I.

UNDERSTANDING HOMOSEXUALITY. A pamphlet by Catholics on causes, cure, and morality of homosexuality. $.15.
>   Claretian Publications, 221 W. Madison St., Chicago, Ill. 60606.

AUDIO VISUALS

None available for general public.

INTERNATIONAL RELATIONS

(See also Citizenship, Communism, Extremism, Pacifism,
United Nations, War-Peace)

BOOKS

CHRISTIAN ETHICS AND THE DILEMMA OF FOREIGN POLICY. Kenneth W. Thompson. Duke University Press. 1959. $3.50.

> A Christian realist examines the difficulty and possibility of relating Christian ethical insights to foreign policy issues.

*CHRISTIANITY AND WORLD ISSUES. T. B. Maston. Macmillan. 1957. $5.95.

> A heavily documented volume dealing with a number of issues relating to international affairs, such as race, war and peace, and the world crisis.

CONTEMPORARY THEORY IN INTERNATIONAL RELATIONS. Stanley Hoffmann, ed. Prentice-Hall. 1960. $7.50.

> A collection of writings giving different concepts of the nature of international relations. Technical, but helpful as introduction to various points of view.

ETHICAL RESOURCES FOR INTERNATIONAL RELATIONS. Harvey Seifert. Westminster. 1964. $1.25.

> An approach to Christian action for influencing foreign policy. Written to help the layman think theologically about difficult problems. Special emphasis on relation of U. S. A. and U. S. S. R.

ETHICS AND UNITED STATES FOREIGN POLICY. Ernest Lefever. Meridian. 1958. $1.45 paper.

> A study of the ethics of world diplomacy and law. First Section relates international ethics to theology. Discusses cold war diplomacy, U. S. security aims, and lobbying techniques.

*FOREIGN POLICY IN CHRISTIAN PERSPECTIVE. John C. Bennett. Scribner. 1966. $3.50, $1.25 paper.

> By one of America's foremost thinkers in the area of ethics and politics, this book discusses foreign policy from a Christian point of view. Emphasized are the cold war, the ethics of atomic weapons, international goals, and the role of the church.

HUMAN RIGHTS AND THE INTERNATIONAL COMMUNITY. Egon Schwelb. Quadrangle Books. 1967. $1.45 paper.

> A probing of the roots of the Universal Declaration of Human Rights and developments connected with its adoption from 1948 to the present.

INTERNATIONAL CONFLICT IN THE TWENTIETH CENTURY: A CHRISTIAN VIEW. Herbert Butterfield. Harper. 1960. OP.

Views the problems of war and revolution from a Christian perspective, with realistic assessment of methods and politics used in war.

*MAN AMID CHANGE IN WORLD AFFAIRS. Leonard J. Kramer, ed. Friendship. 1964. $1.95.

Speaks to laymen and clergy about the chief disturbing issues in international affairs and their relation to Christian faith and practice.

STATESMAN'S YEARBOOK. Macmillan. Annual.

Manual on the governments of the world, including a variety of statistical and other information.

THE STRUCTURES OF NATIONS AND EMPIRES. Reinhold Neibuhr. Chas. Scribner. 1959. $5.95.

Neibuhr gives a critical analysis of the two great world powers (U.S.A. and U.S.S.R.) with reference to their political structure. A good book for insights into political theory and power structures.

WHOSE WORLD? John S. Wood. Friendship. 1960. $1.00 paper.

A handbook for youth on international relations. Included are questions for discussion and program plans.

ORGANIZATIONS AND SOURCES

BROOKINGS INSTITUTION. A non-partisan organization devoted to research, education, and publication in foreign policy studies.

1775 Mass. Ave., N. W., Washington, D. C. 20036

*CENTER FOR STUDY OF DEMOCRATIC INSTITUTIONS. An academic center to gather specialists for discussions on current important issues. Supported by the Fund for the Republic. Numerous publications and tapes on foreign policy. Write for publications list.

Box 4068, Santa Barbara, Cal. 93103.

COMMISSION OF THE CHURCHES ON INTERNATIONAL AFFAIRS, WORLD COUNCIL OF CHURCHES. To serve churches in their approach to international problems by suggesting means of action, by relating the problems of Christian issues, by the study of problems and approaching materials focusing on the issues, by assigning persons, committees and organizing conferences to approach problems under consideration, and by serving as a contact between the churches and international bodies.

297 Park Ave., S., New York, N. Y. 10010.

*COUNCIL ON RELIGION AND INTERNATIONAL AFFAIRS. To further the supposition that insights of religion are basic to any sound attempt to cope with the complexities of international

problems and that moral imperatives must be related to the realities of power. Series on ethics and foreign policy, $.50 each.
170 E. 64th St., New York, N. Y. 10021.

DEPARTMENT OF STATE, U.S.A. Vast amount of material on international affairs. Constantly updated.
Washington, D. C. 20520.

DIVISION OF CHRISTIAN CITIZENSHIP. EXECUTIVE COUNCIL. EPISCOPAL CHURCH. Pamphlets and papers on Christian responsibility in citizenship affairs.
815 2nd Ave., New York, N. Y. 10017.

*DIVISION OF PEACE AND WORLD ORDER OF THE GENERAL BOARD OF CHRISTIAN SOCIAL CONCERNS OF THE METHODIST CHURCH. Audio visuals, articles, and pamphlets. Order list available.
100 Maryland Ave., N. E., Washington, D. C. 20002.

FOREIGN POLICY ASSOCIATION, INC. Serves as a non-profit, non-partisan, non-governmental education agency dealing in citizenship education in world affairs. Publications and seminars.
345 E. 46th St., New York, N. Y. 10017.

INTERNATIONAL AFFAIRS DEPT., THE NATIONAL COUNCIL OF CHURCHES. Materials available on international affairs from a church-related perspective.
475 Riverside Dr., New York, N. Y. 10027.

WORLD LAW FUND. Tapes, reprints, study materials, catalogue available. The World Law Fund is a special project of the Institute for International Order. The Fund aids and encourages educational institutions and organizations throughout the world to offer programs of study relating to the basic requirements of an adequate war-prevention system.
11 W. 42nd St., New York, N. Y. 10036.

WORLD PEACE FOUNDATION. Strives to make the facts of international relations available in clear and undistorted form.
40 Mt. Vernon St., Boston, Mass. 02108.

PERIODICALS AND JOURNALS

THE ANNALS OF THE AMERICAN ACADEMY OF POLITICAL AND SOCIAL SCIENCE. BM $8.00. A Journal of factual information and expert interpretation of national and international affairs.
3937 Chestnut St., Philadelphia, Pa. 19104.

BETWEEN THE LINES. BM $2.50. A newsletter with an interpretation of current events, generally from a strong anti-war stance.

    BTL Circulation Dept., Newtown, Pa. 18940.

CURRENT HISTORY. M $7.50. Scholarly but readable articles on international affairs, book reviews, and statistics.

    1822 Ludlow St., Philadelphia, Pa. 19103.

DEPARTMENT OF STATE BULLETIN. W $8.50, $.25 per copy. Provides information on the development of foreign relations, operations of the State Dept., statements of the President and Secretary of State, and special articles on international affairs.

    Supt. of Documents, Washington, D. C. 20402.

*FOREIGN AFFAIRS. Q $6.00, $1.50 per copy. A non-parisan review of current ideas and policies affecting U.S. relations in all parts of the world, including international political, commercial and cultural relations. Majority of contributors are from academic, government, and business communities.

    Council on Foreign Relations, Inc., 58 E. 68th St., New York, N. Y. 10021.

*INTERCOM. 7 times a year. $5.00, $.75 per copy. New books, pamphlets, documents, audio-visual aids, conferences and special events, governmental and voluntary agencies concerned with foreign policy and international affairs.

    Foreign Policy Association, 345 E. 46th St., New York, N. Y. 10017.

*JOURNAL OF INTERNATIONAL AFFAIRS. SA $2.50, $1.25 per copy. Analysis of international affairs. Aids in the further understanding of international problems.

    Columbia University School of International Affairs, 409 W. 117th St., New York, N. Y. 10027.

THE PROGRESSIVE. M $5.00, $.50 per copy. Reports and interprets national and world affairs—political, economical, social, etc. from a liberal viewpoint.

    408 W. Gorham, Madison, Wis. 53703.

WORLD POLITICS. Q $6.00, $2.00 per copy. Problems of international relations of a general and theoretical nature, emphasizing social change and employing multidisciplinary methods and concepts; review articles on major books in politics and economics.

    Princeton University Press, Woodrow Hall, Princeton, N. J. 08540.

WORLDVIEW: A JOURNAL OF RELIGION AND INTERNATIONAL AFFAIRS. M $4.00. $.40 per copy. Book reviews, articles, and notes regarding materials on international relations. 170 E. 64th St., New York, N. Y. 10021.

PRINTED MATERIALS

CAREERS IN WORLD AFFAIRS. Discusses career opportunities, governmental and non-governmental, in international relations. $.75.

*DECISION MAKING IN WORLD AFFAIRS. A 48-page booklet about the role of Christians in international relations. $.50. Matching leaflet, $4.00 per 100.

PEOPLE AND NATIONS. Booklet illustrating statistics of 128 nations including population, literacy, language, religion, etc. $.75.

*RELIGION AND WORLD AFFAIRS. Discusses the relevance and resources of religious groups in international affairs. $1.00.

THE UNITED STATES AND THE NEW NATIONS. Helps to understanding the social, political, cultural, and economic forces shaping the new nations of the world. $1.00. Study guide, $.50.
   Service Dept., 100 Maryland Ave., N. E., Washington, D. C. 20002.

DISARMAMENT KIT, $2.50. PEACE THROUGH LAW RESOURCE GUIDE KIT, $2.00. These two compilations of material are designed for use with high school students.

INTRODUCTORY PEACE THROUGH LAW KIT. A collection of study materials for adults. $.75.
   World Law Fund, 11 W. 42nd St., New York, N. Y. 10036

*ETHICS AND NATIONAL PURPOSE. Kenneth W. Thompson. Explores the tensions which exist between ethic and foreign policy today. $.50.

FOREIGN AID: MORAL AND POLITICAL ASPECTS. Victor Ferkiss. A 48-page booklet outlining reasons and purposes for foreign aid. $.50.

*MORAL TENSIONS IN INTERNATIONAL AFFAIRS. John C. Bennett. Sets forth difficulties and guidelines for relating moral principles to political decisions. $.50.

THE MORALITY AND POLITICS OF INTERVENTION. Manfred Halpern. Evaluation of American intervention in the lives of other nations. $.50.

THE RECOVERY OF ETHICS. Paul H. Nitze. An analysis of decision-making at top government levels. $.50.

*RELIGION AND INTERNATIONAL RESPONSIBILITY. Robert Gordis. An argument that the religious and ethical heritage of the Judio-Christian tradition is relevant to international relations today. $.50.

Council on Religion and International Affairs, 170 E. 64th St., New York, N. Y. 10021.

*INTERNATIONAL RELATIONS PACKET. Materials on American foreign policy, the U. N., disarmament, economic aid, and related subjects. $3.00.

Church of the Brethren, Elgin, Ill. 60120.

SOCIAL ACTION. Issues related to peace and international relations, Sept. 1966, Feb. 1967, April 1967. $.35 each.

289 Park Ave. S., New York, N. Y. 10010.

*UNDERSTANDING FOREIGN POLICY. A non-partisan approach designed to help the citizen understand how foreign policy is developed. $.25.

Public Affairs Pamphlets, 381 Park Ave., S., New York, N. Y. 10016.

AUDIO VISUALS

*FILMS ON WORLD AFFAIRS. A directory of more than 150 films on world affairs screened and evaluated by the INTERCOM staff, what they are about, where to get them, what audiences they best serve. $1.00.

INTERCOM Foreign Policy Associations, Inc., 345 E. 46th St., New York, N. Y. 10017.

FOR THE HEALING OF THE NATIONS. Filmstrip with record. $5.00 purchase. Describes the history and purposes of the Church Center for the United Nations.

Service Dept. Methodist Church, 100 Maryland Ave., N. E., Washington, D. C. 20002.

*THE HAT. 16 mm. Sound. Color. 18 min. $15.00 rental. Explores the complicated questions related to the organization of a peaceful world. With study guide. Produced for World Law Fund, a special project of the Institute for International Order.

Sterling Educational Films, Inc., 241 E. 34th St., New York, N. Y. 10016.

THE ONLY WAR WE SEEK. 16 mm. B&W Sound 28 min. $5.00 rental. Produced by Agency for International Development. Shows how new nations are being given assistance by the U. S. government.

Cokesbury.

OUR SHRINKING WORLD. 16 mm. B&W Sound 11 min. $2.15 rental. Treats the development of transportation, the development of communications, and the resultant bringing together of the world. Closes with a plea for international understanding and cooperation which has been made necessary by the nearness of the nations of the world.

Audio Visual Center, Indiana University, Bloomington, Ind. 47405.

*THE TOYMAKER. 16 mm. Color 12 min. $5.50 rental. ($3.50 to UCC) Two puppets first play together until they discover differences in their appearance. They build up a wall between them, then find out how to get around the wall to fight. Finally they discover they are created by the same person and are really part of each other. They no longer need to be afraid or to fight.

Office for Audio Visuals, United Church of Christ, 1720 Chouteau Ave., St. Louis, Mo. 63103.

*WORLD AFFAIRS ARE YOUR AFFAIRS. 16 mm. B&W 25 min. $5.65 rental. Points out that decisions made by one group of people will influence other groups. As a result, it is essential for everyone to understand the issues involved in a decision and to have a voice in the making of the decision. Stresses the importance of being informed and taking part in current affairs.

Visual Aids Service, Division University Extension, University of Illinois, Champaign, Ill. 61822.

OTHER HELPS

ECONOMIC, POLITICAL, AND SOCIAL FACTORS IN INTERNATIONAL AFFAIRS. Annotated listing of materials and sources. $3.00.

National Conference on Social Welfare, 22 W. Gay St., Columbus, Ohio 43215.

ETHICAL STUDIES: ECONOMIC ETHICS BIBLIOGRAPHY. Annotated bibliography in economics and ethics. Related to international affairs in regard to economic factors in foreign policy. Free.

Economics Dept., South Dakota State University, Brookings, S. D. 57006.

JUVENILE DELINQUENCY

(See also Alcohol, Crime, Family, Mental Health, Narcotics,
Sex, Unwed Parents, Venereal Disease)

BOOKS

ACTION PROGRAMS FOR DELINQUENCY PREVENTION.
William E. Amos and others. Charles C. Thomas. 1965. $6.75.

> Positive suggestions for preventing delinquency. Valuable from individual, community, and church point of view.

DELINQUENCY, THE JUVENILE OFFENDER IN AMERICA
TODAY. Herbert A. Bloch and Frank T. Flynn. Random
House. 1956. $6.00.

> Deals with the meaning, scope, pressures, prevention and treatment agencies of delinquency.

DELINQUENTS IN THE MAKING. Sheldon and Eleanor Glueck.
Harper. 1952. $3.95.

> Over ten years old but still helpful in understanding the factors which make for delinquency. By two of the leading experts in the field.

*FAMILY ENVIRONMENT AND DELINQUENCY. Sheldon and
Eleanor Glueck. Houghton Mifflin. 1962. $6.95.

> An attempt to predict delinquency on the basis of family life. Furnishes guidelines for building healthy homes to develop stable personalities.

*HOW THE CHURCH CAN HELP WHERE DELINQUENCY
BEGINS. Guy L. Roberts. John Knox. 1958. $1.50.

> Practical suggestions to churches on a role in preventing juvenile delinquency. Of particular use to urban churches.

*JUVENILE DELINQUENCY: ITS NATURE AND CONTROL.
Sophia Robison. Holt, Rinehart and Winston. 1960. $10.75,
text ed. $7.95.

> Excellent book. Many case studies. Positive suggestions for control. Highly recommended by authorities in the field.

READINGS IN JUVENILE DELINQUENCY. Ruth S. Cavan.
Lippincott. 1964. $3.50 paper.

> Information from many different perspectives on the problem of delinquency. Provides broad background and insight from scholarly perspective.

THE SHOOK-UP GENERATION. Harrison E. Salisbury. Harper
and Brothers. 1958. $4.50, $.50 paper (Fawcett).

> A Pulitzer Prize winning newspaperman analyzes the factors that cause delinquency and suggests approaches and programs as solutions.

STATISTICS ON DELINQUENTS AND DELINQUENCY.
Walter A. Lunden. Charles C. Thomas. 1964. $11.50.
> Valuable statistical information necessary for an adequate study
> of the problem.

*UNDERSTANDING AND PREVENTING JUVENILE DELIN-
QUENCY. Haskell M. Miller. Abingdon. 1958. $2.75, $1.25
paper.
> This book contains practical resources for the individual, family,
> and the church in dealing with juvenile delinquency and problems.

ORGANIZATIONS AND SOURCES

*CHILD STUDY ASSOCIATION OF AMERICA. An extensive
list of pamphlets available.
> 9 E. 89th St., New York, N. Y. 10028.

*CHILDIEN'S BUREAU, U. S. DEPT. OF HEALTH, EDUCA-
TION AND WELFARE. Much material on delinquency.
Write for list and prices.
> Washington, D. C. 20201.

FAMILY LIFE BUREAU, U. S. CATHOLIC CONFERENCE.
Write for list of available information. Informative and motiva-
tional materials.
> 1312 Mass. Ave., N. W., Washington, D. C. 20005.

HOME MISSION BOARD OF THE SOUTHERN BAPTIST
CONVENTION. A special program of work with delinquents.
Pamphlets and study guide available.
> 161 Spring St., N. W., Atlanta, Ga. 30303.

MOBILIZATION FOR YOUTH, INC. Reprints. A non-profit corporation for planning, study, and research.
> 214 E. 2nd St., New York, N. Y. 10009.

NATIONAL ASSOCIATION OF TRAINING SCHOOLS AND
JUVENILE AGENCIES. Publish the proceedings of their annual meetings. $2.00 each. Primarily for professional workers
in prevention and correction of delinquency.
> Glen Mills, Pa. 19342.

NATIONAL COMMITTEE FOR CHILDREN AND YOUTH.
Maintain resource library. Materials from White House Conference for Children and Youth, 1960.
> 1145—19th St., N. W., Washington, D. C. 20036.

NATIONAL CONGRESS OF PARENTS AND TEACHERS. Conferences and materials on delinquency problems.
> 700 N. Rush St., Chicago, Ill. 60611.

NATIONAL COUNCIL OF JUVENILE COURT JUDGES. Several booklets and curriculum units available in single copies free.

> American Bar Center, 1155 E. 60th St., Chicago, Ill. 60637.

*NATIONAL COUNCIL ON CRIME AND DELINQUENCY. Pamphlets and reprints, excellent bibliography. It is the only nationwide voluntary organization of citizens and officials organized to prevent and control crime and delinquency. Membership minimum $5.00, includes quarterly magazine *Crime and Delinquency* and bi-monthly *NCCD News*.

> 44 E. 23rd St., New York, N. Y. 10010.

U. S. FEDERAL BUREAU OF INVESTIGATION. Papers and reprints on delinquency, mainly from viewpoint of law enforcement.

> 9th St. and Penn. Ave., N. W., Washington, D. C. 20535.

In addition most of the Religiously-Oriented Organizations listed in the Appendix have information.

PERIODICALS AND JOURNALS

*CRIME AND DELINQUENCY. Q $4.50. Excellent competent information in general on delinquency.

JOURNAL OF RESEARCH IN CRIME AND DELINQUENCY. SA $4.50, $2.50 per copy. Description and reports from significant research on delinquency.

NCCD NEWS. 5 issues per year. $1.50, $.35 per copy. News related in main to the organization.

> National Council on Crime and Delinquency, 44 E. 23rd St., New York, N. Y. 10010.

*FEDERAL PROBATION. Q Free to persons actively engaged in correctional work or allied fields and to graduate students majoring in these fields. The journal covers all phases of preventive and correctional activities in delinquency and crime.

> Federal Prison Industries, Inc., Supreme Court Bldg., Washington, D. C. 20543.

FROM THE STATE CAPITALS—JUVENILE DELINQUENCY & FAMILY RELATIONS. 14 or more issues per year. $21.00. Covers state and local action throughout the nation dealing with juvenile delinquency, marriage and divorce, adoptions and other family relations matters.

> Bethune Jones, 321 Sunset Ave., Asbury Park, N. J. 07712.

PRINTED MATERIALS

ANNALS OF THE AMERICAN ACADEMY OF POLITICAL AND SOCIAL SCIENCE, March, 1959. Entire issue devoted to nature, cause, and prevention of juvenile delinquency. $2.00.

American Academy of Political and Social Science, 3937 Chestnut St., Philadelphia, Pa. 19104.

BACK TO WHAT WOODSHED? Analyzes approaches to dealing with problem youth. $.25.

THE DELINQUENT AND THE LAW. Discussion of role of courts and police and plea for wider community action. $.25.

Public Affairs Pamphlets, 381 Park Ave., S., New York, N. Y. 10016.

*CHILDREN OF THE MIST. A program kit on juvenile delinquency. Free.

National Association of Manufacturers, 277 Park Ave., New York, N. Y. 10017.

*DELINQUENCY: EVERYBODY'S PROBLEM — A BRIEF GUIDE TO A COMMUNITY STUDY. A 46-page introduction to the delinquency problem and suggestions for community response. $.50.

TRENDS IN JUVENILE DELINQUENCY. A 56-page booklet by the World Health Organization. $.60.

*YOU AND THE LAW. Very helpful booklet. Tells how the law affects youth, why they get into trouble, and what the penalties are. Lists films and other references. $.25.

YOUR COMMUNITY SHOULD COUNT . . . TO 10. A 31-page booklet outlining ten basic steps a community should take to prevent and control delinquency. $.25, first copy free.

National Council on Crime and Delinquency, 44 E. 23rd St., New York, N. Y. 10010.

FACTS ABOUT JUVENILE DELINQUENCY. Excellent study discussion resource. $.75.

Science Research Associates, 259 E. Erie St., Chicago, Ill. 60611.

JUVENILE DELINQUENCY: A PLAN OF ATTACK. A general outline of suggested action. Especially for church-related groups. $.02.

*JUVENILE DELINQUENCY: ISSUES AND ANSWERS SERIES. Facts about delinquency and a specific set of suggestions as to what to do about it. $.05.

Christian Life Commission, Southern Baptist Convention, 460 James Robertson Parkway, Nashville, Tenn. 37219.

JUVENILE DELINQUENCY SERVICES. Pamphlet outlining services available to help with delinquency.

Children's Bureau, U. S. Dept. of Health, Education, and Welfare, Washington, D. C. 20201.

*STUDIES IN DELINQUENCY. A 1967. Series of pamphlets by the Dept. of Health, Education, and Welfare. Write for complete list. $.20 each.

Dept. of Public Documents, U. S. Govt. Printing Office, Washington, D. C. 20402.

UNIFORM CRIME REPORT. Annual publication giving statistical information on crime in the U. S. Free.

F. B. I., Dept. of Justice, Washington, D. C. 20535.

AUDIO VISUALS

ASK ME, DON'T TELL ME. B&W 22 min. 1961. $5.00 rental Restless and unemployed teenagers in San Francisco are helped to help themselves. Insight into causes, attempts to explain a human condition, and an approach to redeem it.

THE QUIET ONE. B&W 70 min. $25.00 rental. The classic documentary about a delinquent boy (a child of a disrupted home in New York's Harlem), offering insight into methods and approaches for understanding and rehabilitation. Somewhat dated in clothing, style and surroundings (1948), but still very good insight into the problem.

Contemporary Films Inc., 267 W. 25th St., New York, N. Y. 10001.

*BUCK AND I. 16 mm. B&W 16 min. $10.00 rental. Reenactment of a true story about the efforts of a Christian layman to help a boy in trouble.

Home Mission Board, Southern Baptist Convention, 161 Spring St., N. W., Atlanta, Ga. 30303.

*BOY WITH A KNIFE. 16 mm. B&W 19 min. 1956. $4.15 rental. Using a youth service agency case history, this film delves into the family life of a delinquent adolescent to find the source of his maladjustment. Technically well done, it should be of interest to all who would be concerned with adolescents even though some may disagree with the realism of the treatment.

SEARCHLIGHTS ON DELINQUENCY. Series of 7 films. B&W 29 min. each. $4.90 rental each. Discusses many aspects of delinquency. Analytical rather than corrective. Secular. The following titles are included:

SEARCHLIGHTS ON DELINQUENCY: ADDICTION AMONG TEENAGERS.

SEARCHLIGHTS ON DELINQUENCY: DELINQUENCY AREAS

SEARCHLIGHTS ON DELINQUENCY: EDUCATION FOR CRIME

SEARCHLIGHTS ON DELINQUENCY: NARCOTICS TRAFFIC

SEARCHLIGHTS ON DELINQUENCY: THE CULTURE OF DELINQUENCY

SEARCHLIGHTS ON DELINQUENCY: THE DELINQUENT SELF

SEARCHLIGHTS ON DELINQUENCY: THE GANG

Audio-Visual Center, Indiana University, Bloomington, Ind. 47405.

*CALL FOR THE QUESTION. Filmstrip. $7.50 purchase. $10.00 with record narration. Reveals shocking facts of delinquency, particularly as related to housing and equal rights.

Union of American Hebrew Congregations, 838 Fifth Ave., New York, N. Y. 10021.

THE DOUBLE GUILT. 16 mm. B&W 30 min. $9.00 rental. Implies that juvenile delinquency is not always a sign of something wrong with the child, but may indicate a problem with the parent.

Southern Baptist Film Centers.

JUVENILE DELINQUENCY (THE SEARCH). 16 mm. B&W 27 min. $5.55 rental. Tells of the joint attack made on juvenile delinquency by Wayne University and the Detroit Police Dept. Shows four basic types of delinquents, and discusses factors contributing to their behavior. Presents interrogations, interviews, and some of the conclusions reached. Not available for use in Michigan, Ohio, or Ontario.

Visual Aids Service, Division University Extension, University of Illinois, Champaign, Ill. 61822.

PROTEST. 16 mm. B&W 25 min. $3.25 rental. Produced by the University of Southern California (Dept. of Cinema) 1958. The treatment given juvenile delinquents both from the standpoint of law and parental authority is presented here. It answers no questions but seeks to portray the juvenile problem as seen by those working with offenders.

University of Southern California, Film Distribution Div., University Park, Los Angeles, Cal. 90007.

WHO'S DELINQUENT? 16 mm. B&W Sound. 16 min. $3.75 rental. Features a newspaper investigating the causes of juvenile delinquency in the community and finding many inadequacies. Ends with the people of the town meeting in an effort to solve the delinquency problem.

The University of Texas, Visual Instruction Bureau, Austin, Tex. 78712.

OTHER HELPS

BIBLIOGRAPHY ON JUVENILE DELINQUENCY. Up-to-date bibliography on delinquency and research in delinquency.

Children's Bureau, U. S. Dept. of Health, Education, and Welfare, Washington, D. C. 20201.

COMMUNITY ORGANIZATION OF JUVENILE DELINQUENCY. Annotations on 24 documents. $2.00.

DELINQUENT ADOLESCENTS AND YOUNG ADULTS. Annotations on 33 documents. $2.50.

JUVENILE DELINQUENCY, GENERAL. Annotation of 26 key documents. $2.00.

National Conference on Social Welfare, 22 W. Gay St., Columbus, Ohio 43215.

MASTER ANNOTATED BIBLIOGRAPHY OF THE PAPERS OF MOBILIZATION FOR YOUTH. Description of many books and materials related to youth. $1.50.

Mobilization for Youth, Inc., 214 E. 2nd St., New York, N. Y. 10009.

INTERNATIONAL BIBLIOGRAPHY ON CRIME AND DELINQUENCY AND CURRENT PROJECTS IN THE PREVENTION, CONTROL, AND TREATMENT OF CRIME AND DELINQUENCY. Compiled by the Information Center on Crime and Delinquency and published six times yearly, available free to workers in the field.

National Clearing House for Mental Health Information, National Institute of Mental Health, Bethesda, Maryland 20014.

SELECTED READING LIST IN DELINQUENCY AND CRIME. 38 pages of excellent bibliography. Single copy free.

National Council on Crime and Delinquency, 44 E. 23rd St., New York, N. Y. 10010.

LABOR

(See also Daily Work, Economics, Leisure)

BOOKS

THE CHRISTIAN WITNESS IN AN INDUSTRIAL SOCIETY.
Horst Symanowski. Westminster. 1964. $3.75.

>A book that challenges the industrial world and the church to new
forms of organization and new patterns of responsibility which will
protect a man's humanity against dehumanizing processes. A strong
plea is made for the church as a catalyst to penetrate this industrial
world.

THE CHURCH AND THE WORKINGMAN. John F. Cronin
and Harry W. Flannery. Hawthorn. 1965. $3.50.

>Presents the social teaching of the Catholic Church in the area of
labor. Discusses such areas of concern as rights of man, a living
wage, church and unions, the right to strike, labor and management,
poverty and unemployment, and social legislation. Concludes with
a brief history of labor.

*A HISTORY OF AMERICAN LABOR. Joseph G. Rayback. Mac-
millan. 1959. $6.95, $3.50 paper.

>An excellent study of labor by historic periods from Colonial days
to the merger of AFL-CIO. Contains a good bibliography for each
period of study.

LABOR AND THE PUBLIC INTEREST. W. Willard Wirtz.
Harper. 1964. $3.95.

>Delves into the problems that labor must cope with—new federalism,
education and training of youth, more versatile labor force, job
creation vs. unemployment, new labor-management relationships,
international trade negotiations, and automation.

LABOR IN A CHANGING AMERICA. William Haber, ed. Basic
Books. 1966. $5.95.

>Twenty-four essays that seek to clarify the problems which face
labor and the American community, i.e. work and leisure, minority
groups, social security, class consciousness, etc.

*LABOR, INDUSTRY, AND THE CHURCH. J. Daniel. Con-
cordia. 1957. $3.00.

>A comprehensive discussion of industrial and labor problems with
Christian application.

LABOR TODAY, THE TRIUMPHS AND FAILURES OF
UNIONISM IN THE U. S. B. J. Widick. Houghton Mifflin.
1964. $4.50.

>Critically diagnoses the ills which beset the unions and probes
into the current situation for a cure to the trend of the movement's
hardening into a bureaucratic structure. Concludes with an analysis
of labor's leadership—James Hoffa, John L. Lewis, Walter Reuther,
and George Meany.

LABOR U. S. A. TODAY. Lester Velie. Harper Bros. 1964. $4.95.

> A series of studies of leading men in the development of labor
> unions in the U. S.—George Meany, Jim Hoffa, Walter Reuther,
> Sam Gompers, and John L. Lewis. Examines what unions do in
> negotiations as well as explores their extracurricular activities. Also
> includes a section on laws that regulate unions and union leaders
> and the future of the union in an automated age.

*THE PRACTICE OF UNIONISM. Jack Barbash. Harper. 1956.
$6.00.

> Intensive look at the way union people themselves look at what
> they are doing and why. The major sectors of union functioning—
> organizing, internal administration, collective bargaining, strikes,
> politics, use of technicians, and the impact of leadership—provide
> the scope of this work. Uses authentic illustrative material from
> union sources.

ORGANIZATIONS AND SOURCES

*AMERICAN FEDERATION OF LABOR AND CONGRESS OF
INDUSTRIAL ORGANIZATIONS (AFL-CIO). Numerous
pamphlets and films (listed in "Films for Labor") and several
periodicals.

> 815—16th St., N. W., Washington, D. C. 20006.

THE BUREAU OF NATIONAL AFFAIRS, INC. Maintains Labor Relations Information Services with numerous publications
on labor and labor unions.

> 1231—24th St., N.W., Washington, D. C. 20037.

CENTER FOR THE STUDY OF DEMOCRATIC INSTITU-
TIONS. Labor is one area of study. Booklets, tapes, and papers
available. Write for publications list.

> Box 4068, Santa Barbara, Cal. 93103.

*CHAMBER OF COMMERCE OF THE UNITED STATES. See
"Publications Directory" for a number of pamphlets related to
labor unions mainly from the perspective of management.

> 1615 H St., N. W., Washington, D. C. 20006.

CHURCH AND ECONOMIC LIFE, SOCIAL JUSTICE DEPT.,
THE NATIONAL COUNCIL OF CHURCHES. Continuing
study of labor with resultant publications.

> 475 Riverside Dr., New York, N. Y. 10027.

DIVISION OF HUMAN RELATIONS AND ECONOMIC AF-
FAIRS OF THE GENERAL BOARD OF CHRISTIAN SO-
CIAL CONCERNS OF THE METHODIST CHURCH.
Literature available for church study.

> 100 Maryland Ave., N. E., Washington, D. C. 20002.

INDUSTRIAL RELATIONS DIVISION, NATIONAL ASSO-

CIATION OF MANUFACTURERS. Pamphlets and boo' le s on labor-management relations from perspective of management.

277 Park Ave., New York, N. Y. 10017.

*U. S. DEPARTMENT OF LABOR. Papers and materials on labor history and problems.

Washington, D. C. 20210.

PERIODICALS AND JOURNALS

THE AFL-CIO NEWS. W $2.00. Official newspaper with broad national and international labor news and many special features.

AFL-CIO, 815—16th St., N. W., Washington, D. C. 20006.

INDUSTRIAL AND LABOR RELATIONS REVIEW. Q $6.00, $1.75 per copy. An academic look at labor relations.

New York State School of Industrial and Labor Relations, Cornell University, Ithaca, N. Y. 14850.

LABOR HISTORY. 3 times a year. $4.00, $1.50 per copy. Scholarly magazine dealing with phases of the American labor movement, and with topics and developments germane to it: politics, the law, ideology, labor leaders and historical events. Book reviews, and appraisals of libraries specializing in labor history.

Tamiment Institute, 7 E. 15th St., New York, N. Y. 10003.

*MONTHLY LABOR REVIEW. M $7.50, $.75 per copy. Report on trends of employment and payrolls, hourly and weekly earnings, weekly working hours, collective agreements, industrial accidents, disputes, etc. Subscribers receive an annual statistic supplement.

Supt. of Documents, Washington, D. C. 20402.

PRINTED MATERIALS

CYBERNATION: THE SILENT CONQUEST. Donald Michael. A study of the effects of cybernation on labor and employment. $.60.

Study of Democratic Institutions, Box 4068, Santa Barbara, Cal. 93103.

*LABOR AND THE PUBLIC. A frank appraisal of the role of labor unions in the economic life of the nation. $.25.

*THE LABOR MOVEMENT IN THE U. S. A. A discussion of the structures and development of the trade union movement in the U.S. $.25.

Public Affairs Pamphlets, 381 Park Ave., S., New York, N. Y. 10016.

THIS IS THE AFL-CIO. Booklet outlining the purpose and organization of the AFL-CIO. $4.00 per 100.

*WHY STRIKES: FACTS VS FICTION. Labor's argument why strikes are necessary and helpful to the economy. $10.00 per 100.

*WHY UNIONS? Booklet justifying unions and showing their place in the American economy. $7.50 per 100.

> AFL-CIO, 815—16th St., N. W., Washington, D. C. 20006.

AUDIO VISUALS

CHALLENGE OF CHANGE. 16 mm. 20 min. 1963. $3.00 rental. Traces the history of the Labor Department and indicates its areas of responsibility. Produced by the U.S. Dept. of Labor.

*STRIKE IN TOWN. 16 mm. 38 min. 1955. $3.00 rental. A dramatic though realistic portrayal of the effects of a strike on management, labor, families, and community. Produced by the National Film Board of Canada.

> AFL-CIO Film Div., 815—16th St., N. W., Washington, D. C. 20006. (Order catalog for complete listing, $.25.)

LABOR LOOKS AT LABOR. Tape. $5.00 purchase. Some officials of the United Auto Workers in a rare and revealing self-examination of the American labor movement. (Printed version, $.20)

> Center for the Study of Democratic Institutions, Box 4068, Santa Barbara, Cal. 93103.

THE LABOR MOVEMENT: BEGINNINGS AND GROWTH IN AMERICA. B&W Sound. 13 min. $2.90 rental. Color $4.15. Highlights the significant developments in labor's organization in the U.S. from 1873 through the merger of the AFL and CIO. Indicates some of the high points in the development of union strength. Excellent for historical perspective.

> Audio Visual Center, Indiana University, Bloomington, Ind. 47405.

*RISE OF ORGANIZED LABOR. B&W Sound. 18 min. $4.40 rental. Traces the development of organized labor, describing the early factory system, the conditions which produced the need for unions, and the significance of historical events during the rise of labor unions. Uses photographs and drawings of the period to indicate working conditions of men, women, and children during the early development of factories. Describes the events which inhibited and encouraged the development of union organization. Shows the wide range of means used by labor to achieve its end from violence and strikes to peaceful negotiations.

> The University of Texas, Visual Instruction Bureau, Austin, Tex. 78712.

*THE STRUCTURE OF UNIONS. B&W 10 min. 50 sec. 1954. $5.00 rental. Color $6.00. A cartoon film which examines the organization of labor unions today. Examples are given to illustrate the functioning of a union at its various levels, from union local to national body to labor congress.

> Contemporary Films, Inc., 267 W. 25th St., New York, N. Y. 10001.

LEISURE

(See also Daily Work, Economics, Labor, Poverty)

BOOKS

ARE WE READY FOR LEISURE? William P. H. Stevens, Jr. Friendship. 1966. $.65.

> Explores the way in which the capacity to transform simple free time into genuine leisure and authentic service is related to the individual's faith.

*THE CHALLENGE OF LEISURE. Charles Kestner Brightbill. Prentice Hall. 1963. $1.75 paper.

> In a non-technical way the author explores the challenge of leisure, its costs, and its relation to the varieties of human activity: recreation, religion, science, art, personal development, health, and education. Advocates leisure time as an opportunity for enriching our lives and developing our personalities in this day of tense living.

THE CHRISTIAN ENCOUNTERS THE NEW LEISURE. R. Norden. Concordia. 1965. $1.00 paper.

> Brings Christian insight to bear on leisure. Discusses the question, "How can Christians bring a new fullness to leisure-time living?"

LEISURE IN AMERICA: BLESSING OR CURSE? James Clyde Charlesworth, ed. American Academy of Political and Social Science. 1964. OP.

> Discusses the philosophy of leisure and its wise implementation in society. Deals with the question of how much leisure now and in the future.

OF TIME, WORK, AND LEISURE. Sebastian de Grazia. Doubleday-Anchor. 1964. $1.95 paper.
>A classic in the field of leisure. Solid statistical information. Informal
>in presentation.

*RELIGION AND LEISURE IN AMERICA. Robert Lee. Abing-
don. 1964. $4.50, $1.75 paper.
>A thorough discussion of leisure in America. Theological insight.
>A basic resource.

WHEN LEISURE IS THE LORD'S. Thomas L. Jones. John
Knox. 1964. $.75 paper.
>A devotional challenge to use new-found leisure in a creative way
>for God.

WORK AND LEISURE. Nels Anderson. The Free Press of Glencoe, Inc. 1961. $5.50.
>Discusses the relationship of work and leisure. He concludes that
>a key to coping with leisure is strong family life.

ORGANIZATIONS AND SOURCES

*AFL-CIO RESEARCH DEPT. Many pamphlets and booklets re-
lated to work, leisure, and automation.
>815—16th St., N. W., Washington, D. C. 20006.

BOARD OF CHRISTIAN EDUCATION, PRESBYTERIAN
CHURCH, U.S.
>Box 1176, Richmond, Va. 23209.

CHRISTIAN LIFE COMMISSION, BAPTIST GENERAL CON-
VENTION OF TEXAS.
>206 Baptist Bldg., Dallas, Tex. 75201.

CHRISTIAN LIFE COMMISSION, SOUTHERN BAPTIST
CONVENTION.
>460 James Robertson Parkway, Nashville, Tenn. 37219.

*CHURCH AND CULTURE DEPT. and THE DEPT. OF
CHURCH AND ECONOMIC LIFE, NATIONAL COUN-
CIL OF CHURCHES. Pamphlets, booklets, audio visuals.
>475 Riverside Dr., New York, N. Y. 10027.

CHURCH RECREATION DEPT. OF THE SUNDAY SCHOOL
BOARD OF THE SOUTHERN BAPTIST CONVENTION.
Pamphlets and publications primarily related to church and
church-related recreation activity.
>127 Ninth Ave., N., Nashville, Tenn. 37203.

DEPT. OF CHRISTIAN ACTION IN COMMUNITY SERVICE
OF THE UNITED CHRISTIAN MISSIONARY SOCIETY.
>Missions Bldg., Indianapolis, Ind. 46207.

DIVISION OF CHRISTIAN EDUCATION: LEISURE TASK FORCE. United Church of Christ.
  1505 Race St., Philadelphia, Pa. 19102.

DIVISION OF CHRISTIAN SOCIAL CONCERN OF AMERICAN BAPTIST CONVENTION.
  Valley Forge, Pa. 19481.

DIVISION OF HUMAN RELATIONS AND ECONOMIC AFFAIRS, GENERAL BOARD OF CHRISTIAN SOCIAL CONCERN OF THE METHODIST CHURCH. Pamphlets and resource materials.
  100 Maryland Ave., N. E., Washington, D. C. 20002.

ECONOMICS-ETHICAL STUDIES. Publish *Management Ethics Guide,* 1.50 and the following free materials: *Economic Ethics Bibliography, Rationale for Management Ethics Guide, Ethical Perspectives in Marketing Decisions.*
  South Dakota State University, Brookings, South Dakota 57006.

*LEISURE RESEARCH, INSTITUTE OF ETHICS AND SOCIETY. A study of leisure in America. Emphasis on research, reports, and bibliography.
  San Francisco Theological Seminary, San Anselmo, Cal. 94960.

NATIONAL RECREATION AND PARK ASSOCIATION. Citizen's organization concerned with all aspects of free time and its use. Publishes *Parks and Recreation* magazine monthly and various special publications.
  1700 Penn. Ave., N. W., Washington, D. C. 20006.

PUBLIC AFFAIRS PAMPHLETS. Write for a current list of practical, brief pamphlets, most for only $.25.
  381 Park Ave., S., New York, N. Y. 10016.

PERIODICALS AND JOURNALS

CHURCH RECREATION. Q $2.00. Magazine related to church programs for recreation for all ages. Useful material for a limited area of the leisure question.
  Church Recreation Dept., Baptist Sunday School Board, 127 Ninth Ave. N., Nashville, Tenn. 37203.

PARKS AND RECREATION. M. $5.00, $.60 per copy. On the use of leisure time for recreation.
  National Recreation and Parks Association, Oglebay Park, Wheeling, W. Va. 26003.

PRINTED MATERIALS

*THE CHALLENGE OF LEISURE. A report and discussion guide. 1962. 18 pages. $.15.
> National Social Welfare Assembly, Inc., 345 E. 46th St., New York, N. Y. 10017.

CHRISTIANITY AND THE WORKADAY WORLD. A series of speeches on daily work and leisure by leading authorities. Much helpful material. $1.00.
> Christian Life Commission, 206 Baptist Bldg., Dallas, Tex. 75201.

HELPING YOUTH WITH LEISURE TIME CHOICE. A brief pamphlet to help youth plan for constructive leisure activity. $.30 per doz.
> Gen. Board of Education, The Methodist Church, Box 871, Nashville, Tenn. 37202.

*LEISURE IN AMERICA: BLESSING OR CURSE? April, 1964, *The Annals*. Excellent material from the American Academy of Political and Social Science. $2.00.
> 3937 Chestnut St., Philadelphia, Pa. 19104.

LEISURE, THE BASIS OF CULTURE. Josef Pieper. Classic Catholic interpretation of leisure. $.60.
> Pantheon Books, Inc., 22 E. 51st St., New York, N. Y. 10022.

AUDIO VISUALS

AUTOMATION. B&W Sound. 27 min. $5.50 rental. For sr. hi.-adult. Under the guidance of Automatic Control research engineers, takes viewers on a cross-country tour of laboratories which are pioneering in the development of new robot machines designed to take over some of the duties once performed only by the human nervous system.
> The University of Texas, Visual Instruction Bureau, Austin, Tex. 78712.

*EDEN, U.S.A. 16 mm. Color 25 min. $12.00 rental. Provides impetus for discussion of the "new" leisure, man's relation to the machine and what the church will do when much traditional work is no longer necessary. Opens issues, does not provide answers.
> Audio-Visual Dept., United Church of Christ, 1501 Race St., Philadelphia, Pa. 19102.

*OF TIME, WORK AND LEISURE. B&W 30 min. motion picture. $5.45 rental. Produced by National Educational Television, 1965. Through dramatization, film clips, narration and exposition, this film examines modern ideas about time, work and leisure. It presents the problem of the enslavement of people in a society dominated by machines and clocks. The film asks such questions as "What is leisure?" and "What is man's real purpose in life?"

Audio Visual Center, Indiana University, Bloomington, Ind. 47405.

WHAT IS AUTOMATION? Color and B&W 14 min. $7.50 rental. This film shows an automated factory where automation is in action. A few skilled workers supervise the machines and check the quality of the product. Demonstrates the factors making for increased leisure in America.

Film Associates, 11559 Santa Monica Blvd., Los Angeles, Cal. 90025.

OTHER HELPS

"A COMPREHENSIVE BIBLIOGRAPHY ON LEISURE, 1900-1958," MASS LEISURE. Eric Larrabee and Rolf Meyersohn, ed. The Free Press. 1958 (pp. 389-419). $6.95.

ECONOMIC ETHICS BIBLIOGRAPHY. An annotated bibliography of recent and classic publications. Very useful. Free.

Ethical Studies, South Dakota State University, Brookings, South Dakota 57006.

MEANINGFUL LEISURE. An interpretive bibliographic essay by William G. Doty, Institute of Ethics and Society, San Francisco Theological Seminary, San Anselmo, Cal., for Dept. of Evangelism, National Council of Churches.

AN OVERVIEW OF LITERATURE ON LEISURE. A bibliographic essay by Marjorie L. Casebier. Available only by making copies of the original. $12.00 approximate cost.

Institute of Ethics and Society, San Francisco Theological Seminary, San Anselmo, Cal. 94960.

LITERACY
(See also Population Explosion, Poverty, United Nations)

BOOKS

BIG CITY DROP OUTS AND ILLITERACY. Robert A. Dentler. Center for Urban Education. 1965. $3.00.
> A study of the relation between literacy and economic security.

DRIVE AGAINST ILLITERACY. Irwin Isenberg. Wilson. 1964. $3.00.
> Description of extent and effects of illiteracy and what can be and is being done about the problem.

HOW TO TEACH ONE AND WIN ONE FOR CHRIST. Frank Laubach. Zondervan. 1964. $1.95.
> A brief book with simple directions for conducting literacy classes. Practical suggestions.

LITERACY: THE ESSENTIAL SKILL. Samuel Habib and others. World Literacy. 1965. $2.00 paper.
> Presentation of the case that literacy is the basic skill necessary for improving the people's living standards in underdeveloped areas.

THIRTY YEARS WITH THE SILENT BILLION. Frank Laubach. Revell. 1960. $3.95.
> The story of Frank Laubach's literacy campaigns throughout the world over a thirty-year period. Provides insight into the staggering amount of illiteracy in the world and the obstacles to an effective campaign to overcome it.

TOWARD WORLD LITERACY. Frank Laubach. Syracuse University Press. 1960. $4.95.
> An illustrated "How To" book with suggestions and concrete directions on teaching the illiterate to read and establishing literacy programs.

WAY OF THE WORD. K. D. Bengt. World Literacy. 1965. $2.00 paper.
> Informative, inspirational, up-to-date reading on the world's problem of illiteracy.

ORGANIZATIONS AND SOURCES

COMMITTEE ON WORLD LITERACY AND CHRISTIAN LITERATURE. Coordinating body for 40 mission boards and church agencies. Works in 54 countries to provide literacy programs.
> 475 Riverside Dr., New York, N. Y. 10027.

LAUBACH LITERACY FUND. Active in literacy programs in the U. S. and abroad. Prepares materials and trains teachers.
> Box 131, University Station, Syracuse, N. Y. 13210.

UNITED NATIONS EDUCATIONAL, SCIENTIFIC, AND CULTURAL ORGANIZATION (UNESCO). Programs for literacy. Informational material available describing the work and setting forth the extent of world literacy.

317 E. 34th St., New York, N. Y. 10016.

U. S. DEPT. OF HEALTH, EDUCATION, AND WELFARE. Information of literacy in the U. S. and programs to improve it.

Washington, D. C. 20201.

U. S. OFFICE OF ECONOMIC OPPORTUNITY. Parts of its programs directed toward eliminating illiteracy. Write for information.

Washington, D. C. 20506.

PERIODICALS AND JOURNALS

LIT-LIT NEWSLETTER. Q $1.00. Interprets the literacy work of the agency and stimulates literacy programs.

LIT-LIT REPORTING. Q $1.00 airmail; surface mail free. Presents new developments in literacy programs for persons responsible for such programs and affords an opportunity for such workers to share experiences.

Committee on World Literacy and Christian Literature, 475 Riverside Dr., New York, N. Y. 10027.

UNESCO COURIER. M $5.00. Illustrated magazine. World literacy is one of concerns.

UNESCO INTERNATIONAL JOURNAL OF ADULT AND YOUTH EDUCATION. Q $1.75. Information on education programs around the world.

317 E. 34th St., New York, N. Y. 10016.

PRINTED MATERIALS

ABC OF LITERACY. A 64-page, illustrated booklet on world illiteracy and efforts to deal with it. $.30.

UNESCO Publication Center, 317 E. 34th St., New York, N. Y. 10016.

UNESCO STATISTICAL YEARBOOK. Statistics for more than 200 nations and territories with some material related to education and literacy. $5.00.

317 E. 34th St., New York, N. Y. 10016.

WORLD LITERACY MANUAL. A resource and guide for literacy workers.

Lit-Lit, Box 180, New York, N. Y. 10010.

For materials to use in literacy programs write:
    New Readers Press, Box 131, Syracuse, N. Y. 13210.
    Lit-Lit, Box 180, New York, N. Y. 10010.

AUDIO VISUALS

CHAINS. The story of two young men from Mexico who leave the barren soil of the farms to seek a better home in the city—how literacy helps them help themselves. A professionally written and acted film.

IT TAKES ONLY TWO. The story of a community "Each One Teach One" literacy program in Syracuse, N. Y. Shows how the church women of Syracuse organized and are presently carrying out the program. Of inspirational and informational value especially for those in other communities interested in promoting volunteer literacy teaching on the local level.

PLIGHT OF THE DESPERATE BILLION. A stirring talk-on-film by Frank C. Laubach; as he looks the audience in the eye and tells of the plight of the illiterates—the "desperate billion"— the camera takes the audience to lands on every continent to show their plight, and how literacy may help them.

    Each of these 16 mm sound films is approximately 30 min. in length, sent without charge, asking only that a free-will offering be taken, using contribution envelopes supplied.

    Laubach Literacy Fund, Box 131, University Station, Syracuse, N. Y. 13210.

EACH ONE TEACH ONE. 16 mm. Color 20 min. $3.65 rental. Explains Frank Laubach's "each one teach one" program of combating illiteracy in the world. Then shows how he teaches reading to a beggar in India.

    Audio-Visual Service, University of Illinois, Champaign, Ill. 61822.

LIT-LIT COLOR FILMSTRIPS. Reading script with each. $2.50 rental, $5.00 purchase.

    LITERACY FRONTIERS IN BOLIVIA. For adults, 75 frames. The picture story of three Alfalit ventures into newly colonized areas, army camps and city slums. 1966.

    NOW I CAN READ. For adults, 75 frames. A thrilling story from Tanzania, told by Marian Halvorson. She is Lit-Lit's coordinator for literacy work in Africa. Watch an African woman emerge from the cocoon of illiteracy and try her literary wings.

    TI-TI IN HONG KONG. For children, 60 frames. Lit-Lit's best story for boys and girls. Feel how a boy's need to learn motivates his family, even amid refugee conditions.

VILLAGE REBORN. For adults, 67 frames. A pictorial record
from the Nile Valley, showing how literacy work and community development overcome the blight of poverty.
Lit-Lit, Box 180, New York, N. Y. 10010.

MASS COMMUNICATION AND MORALITY

(See also Pornography)

BOOKS

CATHOLIC VIEWPOINT ON CENSORSHIP. Harold Charles
Gardiner. Doubleday. 1958. $.75 paper.
A substantial and authoritative view by a Roman Catholic. Discusses
thoroughly the pro and anti-censorship views.

THE CHRISTIANS AND THE MOVIES. Stephen W. Paine.
Eerdmans. 1957. $1.00.
A thorough condemnation of movies. Sets forth reasons from a
conservative perspective why Christians should not attend and
answers arguments in favor of attending.

*CRISES IN MORALITY. C. W. Scudder, ed. Broadman. 1964.
$3.50.
A chapter on censorship and mass communication sets forth the
key issues involved.

THE FACE ON THE CUTTING ROOM FLOOR. Murray
Schumach. Morrow. 1964. $6.95.
The history of movie and Hollywood censorship. A call for self-
classification of films by Hollywood producers.

THE IMAGE INDUSTRIES. William Lynch. Sheed & Ward. 1959.
$3.50.
A Catholic priest considers the theological implications of the impact
made by motion pictures and television.

JUSTICE AND THE PRESS. John Lofton. Beacon. 1966. $5.95.

>A lengthy (462 pages) study of the press in American life with special emphasis on its impact on and responsibility to the public, particularly in regard to justice.

*MOVIES, CENSORSHIP, AND THE LAW. Ira H. Carmen. University of Michigan Press. 1966. $7.95.

>Both a current and historical study of censorship laws in the U.S.A. as applied to movies. Examines current censorship practices on a state and local basis.

MOVIES, MORALS, AND ART. Frank Getlein and Harold C. Gardiner. Sheed and Ward. 1961. $3.50.

>A discussion by a movie reviewer and a priest on movies from the perspective of art and morality. Provocative discussion with guidelines for positive response to and by the movie industry.

*RESPONSIBILITY IN MASS COMMUNICATION. Wilber Schramm. Harper. 1957. $5.50.

>An examination of how the freedom of the individual and the vitality of the culture can be maintained at a time of bigness in communication.

THE RESPONSIBILITY OF THE PRESS. Gerald Gross, ed. Fleet Publishing Co. 1966. $8.50.

>An appeal for more responsibility in every area of mass communication by 31 contributors well aware of the need to which they speak.

TELEVISION AND SOCIETY: AN INQUEST AND AGENDA FOR IMPROVEMENT. Harry J. Skornia. McGraw-Hill. 1965. $7.50, $2.45 paper.

>A study of television as it affects life and culture. Discusses the economics, public relations, political, and language problems associated with television.

TELEVISION IN THE LIVES OF OUR CHILDREN. Wilbur Schramm and others. Stanford. 1961. $2.95 paper.

>A lengthy technical study of television as it relates to children—how much they watch, what they watch, what effect it has on them. Also an evaluation of television programs in general.

*VERSIONS OF CENSORSHIP. John McCormick and M. MacInnes, eds. Doubleday. 1962. $1.45 paper.

>Text of materials in various periods of history which have been criticized by religious, political, and literary censorship. A plea for a critical examination of censorship with the ideal being self censorship.

ORGANIZATIONS AND SOURCES

AMERICAN CIVIL LIBERTIES UNION. Pamphlets and statements on censorship. Generally opposed to all censorship.
156 Fifth Ave., New York, N. Y. 10010.

CENTER FOR THE STUDY OF DEMOCRATIC INSTITU-
TIONS. Study center for study of many areas, including com-
munications, of American life. Scholarly, non-partisan stance.
Write for list of materials.
Box 4068, Santa Barbara, Cal. 93103.

CITIZENS FOR DECENT LITERATURE, INC. Publish a National Decency Report on the problem of obscenity and pornography.
3309 Carew Tower, Cincinnati, Ohio 45202.

FEDERAL COMMUNICATIONS COMMISSION. Office of Reports and Information. (FCC). Information on government
regulations on broadcasting.
Washington, D. C. 20554.

FILM ESTIMATE BOARD OF NATIONAL ORGANIZA-
TIONS. Distributes evaluations of movies.
522 Fifth Ave., New York, N. Y. 10036.

GENERAL BOARD OF CHRISTIAN SOCIAL CONCERNS OF
THE METHODIST CHURCH. Source lists and pamphlets
available in quantity.
100 Maryland Ave., N. E., Washington, D. C. 20002.

INFORMATION SERVICE, NATIONAL COUNCIL OF
CHURCHES. Material on censorship and obscenity.
475 Riverside Dr., New York, N. Y. 10027.

NATIONAL ASSOCIATION FOR BETTER BROADCASTING.
Quarterly publication *Better Radio and Television*. Limited
materials on family and mass communications.
373 North Western Ave., Los Angeles, Cal. 90004.

NATIONAL ASSOCIATION OF BROADCASTERS. Code
adopted for broadcasters available.
1771 N St., N.W., Washington, D. C. 20036.

NATIONAL CATHOLIC OFFICE FOR MOTION PICTURES.
Prepares and distributes description and classification of home
and foreign films.
453 Madison Ave., New York, N. Y. 10022.

NATIONAL COUNCIL OF THE ARTS. Information on art, but
some information on relation of arts to mass media. Write also
for information on the AMERICAN FILM INSTITUTE.
Suite 1149, 1800 G St., N.W., Washington, D. C. 20506.

NATIONAL OFFICE FOR DECENT LITERATURE. Established by the Roman Catholic bishops of the U.S. to review

and evaluate comic books, magazines, and pocket size books.
Evaluations available. $.75 a year.

    33 E. Congress Parkway, Chicago, Ill. 60605.

OFFICE OF THE CLERK, SUPREME COURT OF THE UNITED STATES. Contact for copies of court decisions relating to censorship and obscenity.

    Washington, D. C. 20543.

PROTESTANT MOTION PICTURE COUNCIL. Distributes reviews and ratings of current films.

    405 W. 23rd St., New York, N. Y. 10011.

U.S. CATHOLIC CONFERENCE. Many materials on censorship, obscenity, and mass communication.

    1312 Mass. Ave., N.W., Washington, D. C. 20005.

UNITED STATES POST OFFICE DEPT. Information on postal laws and regulations related to obscenity and censorship.

    Washington, D. C. 20260.

Movie studios and addresses:

ALLIED ARTISTS.

    4376 Sunset Blvd., Hollowood, Cal. 90028; 165 W. 46th St., New York, N. Y. 10036.

COLUMBIA PICTURES.

    1711 Fifth Ave., New York, N. Y. 10022.

METRO-GOLDWYN-MAYER.

    1350 Broadway, New York, N. Y. 10019.

PARAMOUNT.

    1501 Broadway, New York, N. Y. 10036.

TWENTIETH CENTURY FOX.

    444 W. 56th St., New York, N. Y. 10019.

UNITED ARTISTS CORPORATION.

    729—7th Ave., New York, N. Y. 10019.

UNIVERSAL-INTERNATIONAL PICTURES CORP.

    445 Park Ave., New York, N. Y. 10022.

WALT DISNEY.

    500 S. Buena Vista, Burbank, Cal. 91505.

WARNER BROTHERS.

    666 Fifth Ave., New York, N. Y. 10019.

National Radio-Television networks:

ABC-TV (American Broadcasting Company).

    7 W. 66th St., New York, N. Y. 10023.

CBS (Columbia Broadcasting System).

    51 W. 52nd St., New York, N. Y. 10019.

NBC-TV (National Broadcasting Company).

    30 Rockefeller Plaza, New York, N. Y. 10020.

PERIODICALS AND JOURNALS

BETTER RADIO AND TELEVISION. Q $2.50. Helpful analysis of television programs, particularly in reference to effect on children and discussions of rights and responsibilities related to commercial broadcasting.

> National Association for Better Radio and Television, 373 Northwestern Ave., Los Angeles, Cal. 90004.

CONSUMER BULLETIN. M $5.00. Contains ratings of current motion pictures.

> Consumer's Research Inc., Washington, N. J. 07882.

THE GREEN SHEET. Film evaluations. Clergy mainly. Free on request.

> Film Estimate Board of National Organizations, 522 Fifth Ave., New York, N. Y. 10036.

NCOMP OFFICIAL BI-WEEKLY CLASSIFICATION ON FILMS. BW. $5.00. Contains concise description, evaluation, and classification of current films. Positive approach to encourage better films.

> National Catholic Office for Motion Pictures, 453 Madison Ave., New York, N. Y. 10022.

PARENTS' MAGAZINE. M $4.00, $.50 per copy. Contains ratings of current films.

> 52 Vanderbilt Ave., New York, N. Y. 10017.

*REVIEWS AND RATINGS OF CURRENT FILMS. Free on request.

> Protestant Motion Picture Council, 405 W. 23rd St., New York, N. Y. 10011.

PRINTED MATERIALS

CHILDREN AND TV. Josette Frank. Evaluations and positive suggestions. $.25.

*MOVIES AND CENSORSHIP. Bosley Crowther. Discussion of pros and cons of movie censorship. $.25.

> Public Affairs Pamphlets, 381 Park Ave., S., New York, N. Y. 10016.

THE CHURCH, ENTERTAINMENT MEDIA, AND MORAL VALUES. Report of a seminar in which leaders from the field of entertainment met with churchmen to discuss factors affecting moral values, mass media controls, etc. $.50.

SEX IN FILMS AND LITERATURE. Attractive, well-written pamphlet. $.20.

A SICKNESS IN SOCIETY. A booklet by Ralph Cannon setting

forth the nature of obscenity in American publications, mainly magazines. $.25.

> Methodist General Board of Christian Social Concerns, 100 Maryland Ave., N. E., Washington, D. C. 20002.

*THE CHURCH LOOKS AT IMMORALITY IN PRINT AND ON SCREEN. A 14-page booklet outlining problems, setting forth positive suggestions, and providing discussion guides. Free.

> Commission on Research and Social Action, American Lutheran Church, 422 S. 5th St., Minneapolis, Minn. 55415.

*MASS MEDIA: ISSUES AND ANSWERS SERIES. Sets forth problems related to mass media and what responses ought to be made. $.05.

> Christian Life Commission, Southern Baptist Convention, 460 James Robertson Parkway, Nashville, Tenn. 37219.

THE NEW MASS MEDIA: CHALLENGE TO A FREE SO-CIETY. Gilbert Seldes. Investigation of the social significance of the mass media. $1.50.

> American Association of University Women, 2401 Virginia Ave., N. W., Washington, D. C. 20037.

THE PRESS. A 49-page discussion by leading figures in the world of journalism on the place of the press in American life. $.20.

STAGE AND SCREEN. By a drama critic and a film producer and director, a 56-page analysis of these two aspects of communication-entertainment. $.25.

TELEVISION. Jack Gould, TV critic, *The New York Times*. A 36-page evaluation of TV in America. $.15.

> Center for the Study of Democratic Institutions, Santa Barbara, Cal. 93103.

TELEVISION: HOW TO USE IT WISELY WITH CHILDREN. A 28-page pamphlet dealing with practical questions. $.25.

> Child Study Association of America, 9 E. 89th St., New York, N. Y. 10028.

AUDIO VISUALS

*THE CONSTITUTION AND CENSORSHIP. 16 mm. B&W 28 min. 1958. $5.65 rental. Produced by Columbia University. Presents the question of the right of a state to censor motion pictures on the grounds of religion. Develops the various arguments pro and con, tracing the legal actions taken through the courts. Although the Supreme Court made a final decision, lower courts had taken the opposite stance for reasons which are brought out in the narration.

> Visual Aids Service, University of Illinois, 704 S. 6th St., Champaign, Ill. 61820.

LEARNING ABOUT LOVE. Color filmstrips. 40-44 frames each. $3.00 purchase for each filmstrip with teacher's guide. $10.80 for set of four filmstrips with teacher's guides. Interesting and unusual filmstrips contrast ideas about love from four different sources. The Bible, the comics, the newspapers, and the movies. Help to counteract false impressions created by fictional stories in mass communication media.

LEARNING ABOUT LOVE—FROM THE BIBLE PN 784-4

LEARNING ABOUT LOVE—FROM THE COMICS PN 784-1

LEARNING ABOUT LOVE—FROM THE MOVIES PN 784-2

LEARNING ABOUT LOVE—FROM THE NEWSTANDS PN 784-3

> Luthern Church Supply Stores, 2900 Queen Lane, Philadelphia, Pa. 19129.

*TIME FOR TELEVISION. 16 mm. 17 min. $4.00 rental. A boy's life is monopolized by television, shutting out family, teacher, schoolmates, friends. He finally realizes how much he has been losing and works out his own way of letting TV take its place as a natural and interesting part of his daily existence.

> Association Films Inc.

MENTAL HEALTH

(See also Aging, Alcoholism, Family)

BOOKS

BASIC HANDBOOK ON MENTAL ILLNESS. Harry Milt. Scientific Aids Publications. 1965. $1.50.

> A 91-page book setting forth main types and characteristics of mental illness.

*CHRISTIAN ENCOUNTERS MENTAL ILLNESS. Harold I. Haas. Concordia. 1966. $1.00 paper.

> A readable, positive approach to help Christians who must deal with mental illness in their own lives or in the lives of others.

THE CHURCH AND MENTAL HEALTH. Paul B. Maves. Scribners. 1953. OP.

> A compilation attempt to help ministers carry on a more adequate ministry which will foster mental health and help the mentally ill. It is an aid to help physicians and welfare workers understand and use the resources of the church. It attempts to foster closer cooperation between the professions concerned with mental health. It contains a good strategy for the churches in relating to illness and health and an extensive bibliography.

EMOTIONAL ILLNESS: HOW FAMILIES CAN HELP. Earl R. Beutner and Nathan G. Hale. Putnam. 1957. OP

> This will be of particular help in allaying the relatives' anxiety and guilt about illness and in contributing to the family's own self-understanding.

THE FAMILY AND MENTAL ILLNESS. Samuel Southard. Westminster. 1957. OP.

> The author gives helpful suggestions from a keen understanding of the mentally ill and their families. The Christian dimension adds uniqueness to this volume.

MENTAL HEALTH THROUGH CHRISTIAN COMMUNITY. Howard J. Clinebell. Abingdon. 1965. $4.75.

> A challenging and effective guide for making the church's ministry more effective in the mental health field.

*MENTAL ILLNESS. A GUIDE FOR THE FAMILY. Edith M. Stern. Harper. 4th ed. 1962. $3.00.

> This has been the classic manual for the families of the mentally ill. Practical answers to the "What do we do now?" questions are set forth beginning at the first sign of illness and continuing throughout hospitalization and discharge.

THE MENTALLY RETARDED IN SOCIETY. Stanley P. Davies and K. G. Ecob. Columbia. 1958. $6.00.

> Comprehensive treatment of the problem with suggested approaches for helping the retarded.

MINISTERING TO DEEPLY TROUBLED PEOPLE. Ernest E. Bruder. Prentice-Hall. 1963. $2.95.

> A book on mental disturbance with a strong emphasis on the helping role of the church.

THE MINISTRY AND MENTAL HEALTH. Hans Hofmann, ed. Association. 1960. OP.

> The result of a National Institute of Mental Health grant. It copes with the problem which arises from the juxtaposition of religion and mental health. Suggests enhancing a personality growth of ministers at the seminary education level. It offers to the minister

the assurance that in his struggle to be relevant to the mental health of his parishioners he is in the good company of many who will help him.

RELIGIOUS FACTORS IN MENTAL ILLNESS. Wayne Oates. Association. 1955. $4.00.

> Presents the religion of the mentaly ill person from his point of view and interprets his religious experiences as it goes on within him. From both theological and psychiatrical points of view. Helpful to the minister who seeks to understand the mentally ill's world of religion and their particular outlooks.

ORGANIZATIONS AND SOURCES

THE AMERICAN ASSOCIATION ON MENTAL DEFICIENCY. Membership available to professionals and others with interest in this field. Dues from $8.00 to $25.00. They publish *American Journal of Mental Deficiency, Mental Retardation* and the *Directory of the AAMD.*

> Box 96, Willimantic, Conn. 06226.

AMERICAN ASSOCIATION OF PASTORAL COUNSELORS.

> Garrett Biblical Seminary, Evanston, Ill. 60201.

AMERICAN PSYCHIATRIC ASSOCIATION. List of publications available from Publications Services Division. Mainly professional materials.

> 1700—18th St., N. W., Washington, D. C. 20009.

CHILD STUDY ASSOCIATION OF AMERICA, INC. Materials related to mental health, illness, and emotional crises of youth. Write for list of materials.

> 9 E. 89th St.., New York, N. Y. 10028.

COMMISSION ON MENTAL RETARDATION, THE LUTHERAN CHURCH-MISSOURI SYNOD. Superb materials, special emphasis on children.

> 210 N. Broadway, St. Louis, Mo. 63102.

THE HOGG FOUNDATION FOR MENTAL HYGIENE. Some booklets available, mainly related to Texas, but helpful for all.

> The University of Texas, Austin, Tex. 78712.

HUMAN BETTERMENT LEAGUE OF NORTH CAROLINA, INC. Materials on mental illness, largely advocating moral reasons for sterilization of the mentally ill.

> Box 3036, Winston-Salem, N. C. 27102.

METHODIST GENERAL BOARD OF CHRISTIAN SOCIAL CONCERN. Materials and source lists. Particularly helpful in regard to the role of the church in ministering to the mentally ill.

> 100 Maryland Ave., N.E., Washington, D. C. 20002.

*THE NATIONAL ASSOCIATION FOR MENTAL HEALTH, INC. Several excellent pamphlets available. Most states and many cities have associations for mental health. Write for list of publications.

> 10 Columbus Circle, New York, N. Y. 10019.

*U. S. DEPT. OF HEALTH, EDUCATION, AND WELFARE, PUBLIC HEALTH SERIVCE, NATIONAL INSTITUTE OF MENTAL HEALTH, Bethesda, Maryland. 20014.

> Reprints and other materials available for sale by: Supt. of Documents, U. S. Government Printing Office, Washington, D. C. 20402.

THE WORLD FEDERATION FOR MENTAL HEALTH: UNITED STATES COMMITTEE, INC. Associated with many mental health agencies. Material and information from a world-wide perspective.

> Publication Office, 104 E. 25th St., New York, N. Y. 10010.

PERIODICALS AND JOURNALS

AMERICAN JOURNAL ON MENTAL DEFICIENCY. BM Sent to members of the Association. Annual dues $12.00.

> American Association on Mental Deficiency, Box 96, Willimantic, Conn. 06226.

AMERICAN JOURNAL OF PSYCHIATRY. M $12.00. Official journal of American Psychiatric Association.

> Publications Service Div., American Psychiatric Assn., 1700—18th St., N. W., Washington, D. C. 20009.

INSIGHT. Q $5.00. Review of religion and mental health.

> 1831 College Ave., Quincy, Ill. 62301.

*JOURNAL OF PASTORAL CARE. Q $5.00. Articles written by clergymen and psychiatrists to help the pastor in counseling. Many articles related to mental health and illness.

> The Council for Clinical Training, Inc., 1312 I St., N. W., Washington, D. C. 20005.

MENTAL HYGIENE. Q $8.00. Journal of the National Association for Mental Health, Inc. Contains original papers by writers of authority plus book reviews, surveys, and new methods of prevention and treatment.

> The National Association for Mental Health, Inc., 10 Columbus Circle, New York, N. Y. 10019.

PASTORAL PSYCHOLOGY. M (except July, Aug.) $5.00, $.50 per copy. Reading references in the field of pastoral psychology. Pastoral Psychology Press, Great Neck, New York 11020.

PRINTED MATERIALS

CHRISTIAN FAITH AND EMOTIONAL HEALTH. A sound but non-technical description of the meaning of emotional health in the Christian sense. $.45. Leader's Guide. $.25.

THE METHODIST CHURCH AND MENTAL HEALTH. A report of discussions and suggestions for positive steps. Excellent list of sources. $.50.

Service Dept., 100 Maryland Ave., N. E., Washington, D. C. 20002.

*THE CLERGY AND MENTAL HEALTH. $.10.

*CLERGYMAN'S GUIDE TO RECOGNIZING MENTAL ILL-NESS. $.10.

DIRECTORY OF OUTPATIENT PSYCHIATRIC CLINICS AND OTHER MENTAL HEALTH RESOURCES IN THE UNITED STATES AND TERRITORIES. $1.50.

MENTAL AND EMOTIONAL ILLNESS. Free.

*MENTAL ILLNESS: A GUIDE FOR THE FAMILY. $.50.

MINISTERING TO FAMILIES OF THE MENTALLY ILL. $.10.

PASTORAL HELP IN SERIOUS MENTAL ILLNESS. $.10.

A PSYCHIATRIC GLOSSARY. $1.00.

12 FACTS ABOUT MENTAL ILLNESS. $.03.

*WHEN MENTAL ILLNESS STRIKES YOUR FAMILY. $.25.
All excellent materials on mental illness.

National Association for Mental Health, Inc., 10 Columbus Circle, New York, N. Y. 10019.

*HELP FOR THE FAMILY OF THE MENTALLY ILL. A pamphlet designed to help in counseling. $.02.

Christian Life Commission, 206 Baptist Bldg., Dallas, Tex. 75201.

MENTAL HEALTH IS A FAMILY AFFAIR. Tells the causes for many personality problems in families and offers some ideas for helping prevent these problems. $.25.

SERIOUS MENTAL ILLNESS IN CHILDREN. A discussion to alert parents and others to signs of mental illness in children and what to do about it. $.25.

*TOWARD MENTAL HEALTH. Suggestions for achieving and maintaining good mental health. $.25.

Public Affairs Pamphlets, 381 Park Ave., S., New York, N. Y. 10016.

PROVIDING A PROGRAM OF CHRISTIAN EDUCATION FOR THE MENTALLY RETARDED. Guide for church program with suggested resources. Single copy free.

Board of Parish Education, The Lutheran Church—Missouri Synod. 3558 S. Jefferson Ave., St. Louis, Mo. 63118.

SERVING THE MENTALLY RETARDED IN CHURCH AND COMMUNITY. Pamphlet with practical suggestions.

Dept. of Social Welfare of the Lutheran Church of the Missouri Synod, 210 N. Broadway, St. Louis, Mo. 63102.

WHEN A PARENT IS MENTALLY ILL. A most helpful booklet for the parent who must tell a child that his father or mother is mentally ill. $.50.

WHEN CHILDREN NEED SPECIAL HELP WITH EMOTIONAL PROBLEMS. How to recognize abnormal behavior in children and where to go for help. $.50.

Child Study Association of America, 9 E. 89th St., New York, N. Y. 10028.

AUDIO VISUALS

For extensive listing of audio visuals see *Catalog: Mental Health,* Film Board Films, 332 S. Michigan Ave., Chicago, Ill. 60604.

ABOUT PEOPLE: EMOTIONAL ILLNESS. Sound B&W 30 min. $5.40 rental. Shows a young husband whose wife has suddenly had a nervous breakdown and must be hospitalized. Discusses his reactions of fear and guilt, and also explodes some of the destructive myths about mental disturbance and psychiatry. Gives answers to such questions as: Can a psychiatrist change your personality? Is sex the main concern of psychiatry? Is insanity hereditary? Defines neurotic, psychotic, and psychosomatic disorders.

ESCAPE FROM THE CAGE SERIES. 11 films. B&W 29 min. each. $5.40 rental each. Presents basic information on the subject of mental health and illness. Discusses the history of the treatment of the mentally ill from earliest times to the present, techniques currently in use, and theories which guide research in the field. Defines psycho-surgery, drug therapy, the open hospital, child psychology and psycho-therapy and organic and psychodynamic research. Uses film clips to show hospitals, patients, therapeutic measures, and research centers. Features doctors and psychiatrists currently working in different areas of the field.

EARLY TREATMENT OF THE MENTALLY ILL

THE MENTALLY ILL: 16th TO 20th CENTURIES

THE MENTALLY ILL: PRESENT DAY PROBLEMS

THE MENTALLY ILL: HOSPITAL ADMINISTRATION

THE MENTALLY ILL: THE PSYCHODYNAMIC AP-
PROACH
THE MENTALLY ILL: PSYCHOSURGERY AND SHOCK
TREATMENT
THE MENTALLY ILL: DRUG THERAPY
THE OPEN HOSPITAL
THE MENTALLY ILL: ORGANIC RESEARCH
THE MENTALLY ILL: TREATMENT OF CHILDREN
MISCONCEPTIONS ABOUT MENTAL ILLNESS
Audio Visual Center, Indiana University, Bloomington, Ind. 47405.

BITTER WELCOME. B&W 36 min. Guide. 1958. $8.50 rental. A
newly-discharged mental patient fights to regain his place in
society against the prejudices and fears of his co-workers and
neighbors. With the help of his wife and doctor, he gains self-
confidence and is gradually accepted as a normal person again.
Unfortunately, there is no mention of religion as a factor in rehabilitation.
Contemporary Films, 267 W. 25th St., New York, N. Y. 10001.

A CHANGING VIEW OF THE CHANGE OF LIFE. 16 mm.
Color. 28 min. Free. Many vital questions concerning menopause are answered in this candid and informative film for
women of all ages and their families.

*THE 91st DAY. 16 mm. B&W 58 min. Free. User pays postage
only. This film was produced to stimulate interest in improving
the care and treatment of the mentally ill. It is the dramatic
story of a man's mental breakdown, his admission to a mental
hospital and his wife's determined struggle to get him the treatment he needs for a successful return to society.

*TUESDAY'S CHILD. Color 14 min. $3.50 rental. This film is ex-
ceptionally valuable as an introduction to the subject of mental
retardation among children.
Association Films, Inc.

*MOMENT TO ACT. 16 mm. B&W Sound. 29 min. $8.00 rental.
Story of a young woman who returns to her home after an
extended stay in a mental institution and of the misunderstand-
ing she encounters at home and church. Produced by National
Council of Churches.
Cokesbury.

OTHER HELPS

DIRECTORY OF FACILITIES FOR THE MENTALLY ILL

AND THE MENTALLY RETARDED IN THE U.S. Prepared
by APA Mental Hospital Service. 40 pp. $1.00.

> Publications Services Div., American Psychiatric Assoc., 1700—18th
> St., N. W., Washington, D. C. 20009.

DIRECTORY OF PSYCHIATRIC CLINICS IN THE UNITED
STATES. Lists by state: community psychiatric clinics; state
institutions for the mentally ill, mentally deficient, and epi-
leptics; psychiatric hospitals and facilities operated by the Vet-
erans Administration and other federal agencies. Also lists state
mental health associations and state governmental departments.
144 pp. 1.25.

> The National Assoc. for Mental Health, Inc., 1790 Broadway, New
> York, N. Y. 10019.

NARCOTICS

(See also Alcoholism, Decision Making, Mental Illness, Tobacco)

BOOKS

THE ADDICT AND THE LAW. Alfred R. Lindesmith. Indiana
University Press. 1965. $7.50.

> Author contends drug addiction should be treated as disease, not
> crime. Condemns prohibition as contributing to the problem.

THE BEYOND WITHIN: THE LSD STORY. Sidney Cohen.
Atheneum. 1965. $5.00.

> Description of the nature and effect of LSD from first-hand reports
> under carefully described conditions of observation.

*DRUG ADDICTION: CRIME OR DISEASE. Joint Committee
of the American Bar Association and the American Medical
Association on Narcotic Drugs. Indiana University Press. 1961.
$5.00, $2.50 paper.

> Report of joint committee of the American Bar Association and

the American Medical Association. Argues for treatment of addiction as a disease, not a crime.

*DRUG ADDICTION IN YOUTH. Ernest Harms, ed. Pergamon Press. 1965. $9.50.

Recommended by American Social Health Association and The National Council on Crime and Delinquency. Sets forth extent, cause, and suggestions for dealing with the problem.

DRUG ADDICTION: PHYSIOLOGICAL, PSYCHOLOGICAL, AND SOCIOLOGICAL ASPECTS. David P. Ausubel. Random House. 1958. $.95 paper.

A rather technical study, but helpful in understanding the complex problem of addiction.

DRUGS AND THE MIND. Robert S. DeRopp. Grove. 1960. $.95 paper.

A thought-provoking book on modern drugs and their good and harmful effects. Utilizes a number of good case studies and has an excellent bibliography.

THE ENIGMA OF DRUG ADDICTION. Thorwald T. Brown. C. C. Thomas. 1961. $11.50.

A good overall study. Includes description of drugs, law enforcement, effects of narcotics, procedures for cure.

MAINLINE TO NOWHERE. Yves J. Kron and Edward M. Brown. Pantheon Books. 1965. $4.95. Meridian $1.95 paper.

Story of how addiction develops. Throws problem in a personal light.

PROBLEMS IN ADDICTION: ALCOHOLISM AND NARCOTICS. William C. Bier. Fordham University Press. 1962. $5.00.

Delineation of problems caused by narcotic and alcoholic addiction, with suggestions for treatment and cure from the viewpoints of law, medicine, and clergy.

*UNDERSTANDING AND HELPING THE NARCOTIC ADDICT. Tommie Duncan. Prentice-Hall. 1965. $2.95.

A practical approach with a special emphasis on the church working and helping addicts.

ORGANIZATIONS AND SOURCES

ADDICTS ANONYMOUS ASSOCIATION. Similar in pattern, though smaller, to Alcoholics Anonymous.

Box 2000, Lexington, Kentucky 40501.

*AMERICAN MEDICAL ASSOCIATION, MENTAL HEALTH AND DRUGS COMMITTEE. Research and publications on the medical aspects of narcotic addiction.

535 N. Dearborn St., Chicago, Ill. 60610.

*AMERICAN SOCIAL HEALTH ASSOCIATION. Reprints and pamphlets, mostly $.10-$.20 each. Performs studies and pilot projects. Designated by National Institute of Mental Health, an arm of the Dept. of Health, Education, and Welfare, to be officially responsible for serving as its information center on narcotics.

    1790 Broadway, New York, N. Y. 10019.

CHRISTIAN ANTI-NARCOTIC ASSOCIATION. Distributes narcotics literature from a Christian perspective.

    Box 946, Hesperia, Cal. 92345.

CHRISTIAN LIFE COMMISSION OF THE SOUTHERN BAPTIST CONVENTION. Pamphlets and periodic publications on the cause and cure of narcotic addition.

    460 James Robertson Parkway, Nashville, Tenn. 37219.

DEPT. OF SOCIAL AFFAIRS, UNITED NATIONS. Bulletins on narcotics from an international perspective.

    United Nations Bldg., New York, N. Y. 10017.

GENERAL BOARD OF CHRISTIAN SOCIAL CONCERNS, METHODIST CHURCH. Pamphlets and source lists. Particularly helpful to churches.

    The Methodist Bldg., 100 Maryland Ave., N. E., Washington, D. C. 20002.

NARCOTICS EDUCATION, INC. Catalog of material available. Books, films, pamphlets.

    6840 Eastern Ave., N. W., Takoma Park, Washington, D. C. 20012.

NATIONAL ASSOCIATION FOR THE PREVENTION OF ADDICTION TO NARCOTICS. Advocates treatment of addiction as medical problem. Several action projects. Information available.

    250 W. 57th St., New York, N. Y. 10019.

NATIONAL COUNCIL OF CHURCHES, DEPT. OF SOCIAL WELFARE. Materials and source lists available on narcotics. Write for list of publications.

    475 Riverside Dr., New York, N. Y. 10027.

PUBLIC HEALTH SERVICE, U.S. DEPT. OF HEALTH, EDUCATION, AND WELFARE. A number of booklets and pamphlets available.

    Washington, D. C. 20201.

U. S. TREASURY DEPARTMENT, BUREAU OF NARCOTICS. Many booklets and reprints.

    Washington, D. C. 20226.

PERIODICALS AND JOURNALS

FEDERAL PROBATION. Q Free to persons actively engaged in correctional work or to students majoring in the study of crime and penology. Covers all phases of preventive and correctional activities in crime.

U. S. Dept. of Justice, Washington, D. C. 20535.

THE INTERNATIONAL JOURNAL OF THE ADDICTIONS. SA $6.00.Scientific information on drug, alcohol, tobacco, and food misuse from international sources.

Institute for the Study of Drug Addiction, 680 W. 3rd Ave., New York, N. Y. 10025.

*LISTEN. BM $2.50, $.45 per copy. Problems of drug addiction and alcoholism for popularized reading and study purposes. Very attractive, well-done publication.

Pacific Press Publishing Assoc., 6840 Western Ave., N. W., Washington, D. C. 20015.

NAPAN NEWSLETTER. $10.00. Information on treatment of narcotic addiction as medical problem.

Hotel Astor, New York, N. Y. 10036.

*SOCIAL HEALTH NEWS. M (except July, Aug.) $5.00. Free to persons with interest and activity in various fields of ASHA's program. Highlights ASHA program activities in fields of venereal disease, prostitution, narcotic addiction and family life education. Includes reviews of important literature in these fields and surveys other activities of importance.

American Social Health Association, 1790 Broadway, New York, N. Y. 10019.

UN BULLETIN ON NARCOTICS. Periodic publication. Information mainly from an international perspective. $.50 a copy. $2.00 for annual subscription.

United Nations Bldg., New York, N. Y. 10017.

See also leading medical journals and social issues publications.

PRINTED MATERIALS

THE CONTROL OF NARCOTICS. Background readings, bibliography, discussion questions, action suggestions. $.50.

Distribution Center, Unitarian Universalist Assoc., 25 Beacon St., Boston, Mass. 02108.

FACTS ABOUT NARCOTIC DRUG ADDICTION. Facts about use, extent, and laws. $.10.

*PROCEEDINGS OF THE WHITE HOUSE CONFERENCE ON NARCOTICS AND DRUG ABUSE, 1962. $1.00.

NARCOTICS AND DRUG ABUSE. Task force report by the President's Committee on Law Enforcement and Administration of Justice, 1967.

> Supt. of Documents, U. S. Government Printing Office, Washington, D. C. 20402.

*FIRST FACTS ABOUT DRUGS. Pamphlet giving essential information on narcotics. $.15 from Supt. of Documents, U. S. Govt. Printing Office, Washington, D. C. 20402.

> Food and Drug Administration, U. S. Dept. of Health, Education, and Welfare, Washington, D. C. 20204.

THE GLUE SNIFFING PROBLEM $.20.
THE LIFE CYCLE OF THE NARCOTICS ADDICT AND OF ADDICTION. $.10.
*THE NARCOTIC ADDICTION PROBLEM. $.15.

> Excellent brief pamphlets. Bibliographical information. Other materials available.
>
> American Social Health Association Publications, 1790 Broadway, New York, N. Y. 10019.

*HOOKED. A full color, 32-page comic book style story of an addict tracing the development of his problem. Produced for the National Institute of Mental Health. $.15.

> Information Materials Press, 25 W. 45th St., New York, N. Y. 10036.

INTERNATIONAL CONTROL OF NARCOTIC DRUGS. A U.N. publication of 44 pages describing international efforts to control narcotics. $.25.
THE UNITED NATIONS AND NARCOTIC DRUGS. A 31-page history of the struggle against narcotics. $.15.

> Sales Section, United Nations, New York, N. Y. 10017.

LIVING DEATH. A brief but shocking pamphlet. Helpful to distribute among young people. Free in small numbers.
*PREVENTION AND CONTROL OF NARCOTIC ADDICTION. A superb 32-page booklet presenting facts and a government program for control. $.15.
TRAFFIC IN OPIUM AND OTHER DANGEROUS DRUGS. Annual report. No charge in small amounts.

> United States Treasury Dept., Bureau of Narcotics, Washington, D. C. 20226.

THE METHODIST CHURCH AND THE NARCOTICS PROBLEM. A report of discussions concerning narcotics, the area of involvement, and the plans and attitude of the church in meeting this problem. Excellent bibliography. $.50.

NARCOTICS AND OTHER ADDICTING DRUGS. A BACK-
GROUND PAPER. E. Clinton Gardner. A 1962 paper still
helpful in background and suggestions for practical action. $.05.

> Service Dept., Methodist Church, 100 Maryland Ave., N. E., Wash-
> ington, D. C. 20002.

NARCOTIC DRUG ADDICTION. Suggestions for dealing with
addiction. $.35.

REHABILITATION IN DRUG ADDICTION. A brief explanation
of the cause and effect of addiction. Single copies free.

> U. S. Dept. of Health, Education, and Welfare, Public Health
> Service, Washington, D. C. 20201.

REPORT ON NARCOTIC ADDICTION. The narcotic problem
presented from a medical viewpoint. Single copy free.

> Council on Mental Health, American Medical Assoc., 535 N. Dear-
> born St., Chicago, Ill. 60610.

*SPECIAL ISSUE ON NARCOTICS AND ADDICTION: LIGHT.
An excellent piece directed in the main to churches. Section
devoted to positive, helpful response of churches to the problem.
Free.

> Christian Life Commission Southern Baptist Convention, 460 James
> Robertson Parkway, Nashville, Tenn. 37219.

*WHAT WE CAN DO ABOUT THE DRUG MENACE. Albert
Deutsch. A pamphlet setting forth a positive note and call to
action. $.25.

> Public Affairs Pamphlets, 381 Park Ave., S., New York, N. Y. 10016.

AUDIO VISUALS

THE HOOK. 64 frame filmstrip. B&W $6.00 purchase. Narcotic
addiction in young people and the church's responsibility.

> National Council of Churches, 475 Riverside Dr., New York, N. Y.
> 10027.

*HOOKED? IT COULD NEVER HAPPEN TO ME. 2 full-color
filmstrips. 2 12″ lp records. $29.95 total purchase. Cuts through
to the heart of the teenage drug "experiment." Material defines
the most common drug families—including LSD and other
hallucinatory drugs—and explores the causes that underlie the
teenager's search for "kicks." *Hooked* will dramatize the real
horror and helplessness of the addict.

> Guidance Associates, Pleasantville, N. Y. 10570.

HOW FREE ARE YOU? 75 frame color filmstrip with 33-⅓ rpm
record. $7.50 purchase. Shows how one loses freedom of choice
as he is dominated by narcotics.

Service Dept. Methodist Church, 100 Maryland Ave., N. E., Washington, D. C. 20002.

MONKEY ON THE BACK. B&W 29 min. 27 sec. 1955. $8.00 rental. This documentary drama, based on the real-life experiences of a drug addict, not only portrays the terrible consequences of the misuse of narcotics but presents the general problem of addiction and particularly, of the addict as an individual.

Contemporary Films Inc., 267 W. 25th St., New York, N. Y. 10001.

*NARCOTICS AND YOU. Two color filmstrips, 39 and 46 frames, with captions. $6.75 purchase each. Part I covers growth, cultivation, and medicinal use of narcotics. Part II treats illegal trade and habitual use.

McGraw-Hill Text Film Dept., 330 W. 42nd St., New York, N. Y. 10036.

NARCOTICS: THE DECISION. 30 min. Color. Guide. $15.00 rental. Produced by United Research and Training, Inc., 1960. A teenage girl is trapped into drug addiction. She proceeds from mild barbituates through marijuana to heroin. This film shows methods of drug traffic, law enforcement efforts, and effects of withdrawal process. Animated sequences show the effect of various narcotics on the nerve center. Further, the film points up emotional disturbances of users.

Film Distributors International, 2223 S. Olive St., Los Angeles, Cal. 90007.

*SEARCHLIGHTS ON DELINQUENCY. Two films. Sound. B&W 29 min. each. $4.90 rental each.

ADDICTION AMONG TEENAGERS. Discusses the conditions and effects of drug addiction among young people. Explains how an individual may be enticed to use narcotics. Outlines some of the causes of addiction and considers the possibilities of treatment and cure.

NARCOTICS TRAFFIC. Outlines some of the factors contributing to the narcotics traffic. Suggests possible ways to prevent drug addiction and to treat addicts. Shows how drugs are distributed and used. Includes an interview with an addict.

Audio Visual Center, Indiana University, Bloomington, Ind. 47405.

SEDUCTION OF THE INNOCENT. B&W 10 min. $4.00 rental. Color $8.00. Produced by Sid Davis Productions, 1961. Accepting a dare, a high school girl smokes some marijuana. This leads to heroin, and she eventually becomes a drug addict. The girl, from a respectable middle-class home, is forced into prostitution to pay for her expensive habit. Her life becomes hopeless.

Independent Film Distributors of America, 30 E. 40th St., New York, N. Y. 10016.

OTHER HELPS

THE METHODIST CHURCH AND THE NARCOTIC PROBLEM. Contains excellent bibliography and resource suggestions. $.50.

Service Dept. Methodist Church, 100 Maryland Ave., N. E., Washington, D. C. 20002.

PACIFISM—CONSCIENTIOUS OBJECTORS

(These materials present the pacifist position. See also War-Peace, International Affairs for material counter to pacifist position.)

BOOKS

BIBLICAL REALISM CONFRONTS THE NATION. Paul Peachey, ed. Herald. 1963. $4.00.

A collection of essays by Christians, most of whom are biblical scholars. Largely related to nuclear war, the material sets forth strong pacifist arguments.

*CHRISTIAN ATTITUDES TOWARD WAR AND PEACE. Roland H. Bainton. Fellowship Publications. 1960. $2.50 paper.

A study of pacifism, the just war and the crusade, encompassing the entire Christian era up to and including the nuclear age. An authoritative book in its field, written vividly with no sacrifice of sound scholarship.

CHRISTIANS IN THE ARENA. Allan A. Hunter. Fellowship Publications. $1.50 paper.

The true stories of eight contemporary men and women who have pitted nonviolence and faith in the gospel of love against war and totalitarianism.

*THE DAGGER AND THE CROSS. Culbert G. Rutenber. Fellowship Publications. 3rd ed. $1.50 paper.

> A careful survey of the biblical foundations of pacifism, written in the context of contemporary Christian thought.

*THE NEW TESTAMENT BASIS OF PACIFISM AND THE RELEVANCE OF AN IMPOSSIBLE IDEAL. G. H. C. Macgregor. Fellowship Publications. 1950. $1.25 paper.

> Two books in one volume, respectively setting forth scriptural evidence for this faith and replying to the critique of pacifism presented by Reinhold Niebuhr.

NON-VIOLENCE AND THE CHRISTIAN CONSCIENCE. P. Regamey. Herder and Herder. 1966. $5.95.

> Highly recommended by Catholic scholars on Christianity and violence.

PACIFISM: AN HISTORICAL AND SOCIOLOGICAL STUDY. David A. Martin. Schochen Books. 1966. $6.95.

> Sets forth the different types of pacifists, discusses their arguments and presents an historical background. British point of view.

*THE PACIFIST CONSCIENCE. Peter Mayer, ed. Holt, Rinehart and Winston, Inc. 1966. $7.95.

> A collection of peace statements by leading thinkers from Buddha to the present. Presents views of the absolutist, internationalist and nuclear pacifists.

REINHOLD NIEBUHR AND CHRISTIAN PACIFISM. John H. Yoder. Herald. 1955. $.35 paper.

> A former pacifist, Niebuhr makes a distinction between pacifism as a political policy for states and pacifism as an ethical principle for Christians. Yoder, a pacifist, refutes this distinction.

WAR AND THE GOSPEL. Jean Lasserre. Herald. 1962. $3.75.

> A forthright statement on pacifism from a Christian point of view by a traveling secretary for the Fellowship of Reconciliation. Strong appeal to the individual Christian to avoid serving in the military.

ORGANIZATIONS AND SOURCES

*AMERICAN FRIENDS SERVICE COMMITTEE. Distributes large quantities of peace material. Write for list of resources.

> 160 N. 15th St., Philadelphia, Pa. 19102.

AMERICAN PEACE SOCIETY. One of the oldest peace organizations, founded in 1828. Publishes *World Affairs*.

> 1307 New Hampshire Ave., N. W., Washington, D. C. 20036.

CATHOLIC PEACE FELLOWSHIP. Much material from the Catholic slant.

> 5 Beekman St., New York, N. Y. 10038.

CATHOLIC WORKER. Outspoken against war. Urges non-participation. No official connection with the Catholic Church.
>175 Chrystie St., New York, N. Y. 10002.

CENTRAL COMMITTEE FOR CONSCIENTIOUS OBJECTORS. List of counseling materials and other publications available. They publish bi-monthly *News Notes*.
>2016 Walnut St., Philadelphia, Pa. 19103.

CHURCH OF THE BRETHREN SERVICE COMMISSION. Pamphlets and study materials from a generally pacifist position.
>1451 Dundee Ave., Elgin, Ill. 60120.

COMMITTEE FOR NONVIOLENT ACTION. List of literature and materials available. Urges open opposition to war. Sympathetic, related organizations at same address: Student Peace Union and War Resisters League.
>5 Beekman St., Room 1033, New York, N. Y. 10038.

THE COMMITTEE ON CONSCIENTIOUS OBJECTORS, NATIONAL COUNCIL OF CHURCHES. No official pacifist position taken, but distributes information related to the Christian conscience and war.
>475 Riverside Dr., New York, N. Y. 10027.

DIVISION OF PEACE AND WORLD ORDER, GENERAL BOARD OF CHRISTIAN SOCIAL CONCERNS OF THE METHODIST CHURCH. No official pacifist position taken, but material available on pacifism and the conscientious objector.
>100 Maryland Ave., N. E., Washington, D. C. 20002.

*THE FELLOWSHIP OF RECONCILIATION. Literature catalog available. Reprints, leaflets, etc. Some of the best material available on pacifism and the conscientious objector.
>Box 271, Nyack, N. Y. 10970.

*NATIONAL SERVICE BOARD FOR RELIGIOUS OBJECTORS. Literature order blank available. They have leaflets, booklets, government releases, a film, case helps, and other information helpful to religious objectors. They publish a newsletter *The Reporter*.
>550 Washington Bldg., 15th and New York Ave., N. W., Washington, D. C. 20005.

NOTE: Most major religious denominations have some members which have organized peace fellowships. The names and addresses of these fellowships can be secured from the religiously-oriented agencies listed in the appendix.

PERIODICALS AND JOURNALS

CNVA BULLETIN. No definite publication time. $2.00. Urges opposition to war.

> Committee for Nonviolent Action, 5 Beekman St., Room 1033, New York, N. Y. 10038.

NEWS NOTES OF THE CENTRAL COMMITTEE FOR CONSCIENTIOUS OBJECTORS. BM Free on request. News related to war and conscientious objectors.

> 2006 Walnut St., Room 300, Philadelphia, Pa. 19103.

*THE REPORTER. M $1.00. Brief paper counseling pacifism and conscientious objection. Includes book reviews.

> National Service Board for Religious Objectors, Washington Bldg., 15th and New York Ave., N. W., Washington, D. C. 20005.

WORLD AFFAIRS. Q $3.00. Journal of opinion, quotations, book reviews.

> American Peace Society, 1307 New Hampshire Ave., N. W., Washington, D. C. 20036.

PRINTED MATERIALS

ALTERNATIVES TO MILITARY SERVICE. Attractive, positive pamphlet on ways men can serve other than in military service. Single copy free.

> American Friends Service Committee, 1600 N. 15th St., Philadelphia, Pa. 19102.

THE CHRISTIAN CONSCIENCE AND WAR. An evaluation by leading theologians of the positions Christians take on war. Generally sympathetic with the pacifist position. $.25.

CONSCIENTIOUS OBJECTOR'S PACKET. A selection of materials providing information and guidance on draft procedure. $.50.

*HANDBOOK FOR CONSCIENTIOUS OBJECTORS. A detailed statement on facts and procedure about conscientious objection. 110 pp. $.50.

THE PACIFISM OF KARL BARTH. A booklet setting forth the position of one of the best-known contemporary theologians. Important because it sets forth the theological undergirding for his stand on war and peace. $.25.

> Service Dept. Methodist Church, 100 Maryland Ave., N. E., Washington, D. C. 20002.

THE DRAFT LAW AND YOUR CHOICES. Clear statements on the draft law. $3.00 per 100.

THE USE OF FORCE IN INTERNATIONAL AFFAIRS. A

study of the different kinds of force and an evaluation from the Friends' position. $.10.

> Friends Peace Committee, 1520 Race St., Philadelphia, Pa. 19102.

*PEACE PACKET. An assorted packet of up-to-date materials on the pacifist position. Excellent single source. $3.00.

> Brethren Service Commission, 1451 Dundee Ave., Elgin, Ill. 60120.

QUESTIONS AND ANSWERS ON THE CLASSIFICATION AND ASSIGNMENT OF CONSCIENTIOUS OBJECTORS. Booklet on steps a conscientious objector follows within the law. 38 pp. $.25.

STATEMENTS OF RELIGIOUS BODIES ON THE CON-SCIENTIOUS OBJECTOR. A compilation of statements by the religious bodies of the U. S. on the conscientious objector. 62 pp. $.50.

> National Service Board for Religious Objectors, 550 Washington Bldg., 15th and New York Ave., N. W., Washington, D. C. 20005.

*THINK ON THESE THINGS. A positive presentation of the case for conscientious objection.

> Mennonite Central Committee, Akron, Pa. 17501.

AUDIO VISUALS

*ALTERNATIVES. 16 mm. Sound. 24 min. $7.50 rental. It includes both art and live action sequences showing conscientious objectors at work in various kinds of alternative service.

> National Service Board, 604 Washington Bldg., 15th and New York Ave., N. W., Washington, D. C. 20005.

HENRY HITT CRANE SPEAKS. B&W 30 min. Free loan. 1959. Henry Hitt Crane presents the pacifist point of view in this filmed sermon, which pleads for peace.

> American Friends Service Committee, 160 N. 15th St., Philadelphia, Pa. 19102.

MY PACIFISM. 14 min. 7½ ips tape recording. $1.50 rental. $3.50 purchase. This document excerpts key segments from a debate between the Rev. Henry Hitt Crane, minister-emeritus of De-troit's Central Methodist Church, and Methodist Bishop G. Bromley Oxnam. Crane takes the more pacifistic position of the two.

NOT BY MIGHT. B&W 15 min. $5.00 rental. The various argu-ments for passive resistance to evil and for national disarmament are presented with portrait of Gandhi, pictured as a prime example of true pacifism's practical manifestation and success.

> Fellowship of Reconciliation, Box 271, Nyack, N. Y. 10970.

*WHICH WAY TO PEACE? B&W 30 mn. $7.50 rental. Produced
by the Methodist Church, 1955. Methodist Bishop Gerald Kennedy moderates a discussion between Dr. Henry Hitt Crane and
Bishop G. Bromley Oxnam. Crane defines and defends his
position as a pacifist Christian; Oxnam does the same for his
non-pacifist views. They clearly state that both positions are
well-founded in Christian tradition.

> University of Southern California, Film Distribution Div., Uni-
> versity Park, Los Angeles, Cal. 90007.

OTHER HELPS

CLASSIFIED CATALOG OF LATE LITERATURE ON PEACE,
NONVIOLENCE AND RECONCILIATION. Annotated
bibliography of materials available.

> Fellowship Publications, Box 271, Nyack, N. Y. 10970.

PEACE LITERATURE. A listing of materials which set forth the
pacifist position.

> American Friends Service Committee, 160 N. 15th St., Phila-
> delphia, Pa. 19102.

PLANNED PARENTHOOD

*(See also Abortion, Artificial Insemination, Family, Population
Explosion, Sex)*

BOOKS

AND THE POOR GET CHILDREN. Lee Rainwater assisted by
Karol Weinstein. Quadrangle Books, 1960. $4.75.

> A study of sex, contraception and family planning among the
> working class. This was sponsored by the Planned Parenthood
> Federation of America.

*CATHOLICS AND BIRTH CONTROL. Dorothy Bromley. The Devin-Adair Co. 1965. $4.95.

> An excellent summary of all the current Catholic discussions on the doctrine of birth control. It was written for the purpose of achieving a mutual understanding on the subject in the Church.

CONTRACEPTION: A HISTORY OF ITS TREATMENT BY THE CATHOLIC THEOLOGIANS AND CANONISTS. John T. Noonan, Jr. Harvard University Press. 1965. $7.95.

> First book to document thesis that Church teaching on contraception could be changed radically yet remain within the tradition and laws of Church. Historically significant book.

CONTRACEPTION AND CATHOLICS: A NEW APPRAISAL. Louis Dupre. Helicon. 1964. $1.95.

> Catholic historical analysis of the Church's position against artificial birth control.

MEDICAL HISTORY OF CONTRACEPTION. Norman E. Himes. Gamut Press. 1963. $7.50.

> Helpful background information for current issues on birth control.

THE PILL AND BIRTH REGULATION. Leo Pyle. ed. Helicon. 1964. $1.65 paper.

> Current Catholic debate over use of birth control pill. Clearly reveals pro and con arguments.

*PLANNED PARENTHOOD. Alfred M. Rehwinkel. Concordia. 1959. $1.50 paper.

> A discussion of planned parenthood and birth control in the light of Christian ethics. Historical materials and pro and con discussion for different methods included.

*PLANNING YOUR FAMILY: THE COMPLETE GUIDE TO CONTRACEPTION AND FERTILITY. Alan F. Guttmacher, M. D. with Winfield Best and Frederick S. Jaffe. Macmillan. 1964. $5.95.

> Covers all aspects of family planning and methods of contraception in readable and concise language.

*RELIGION AND BIRTH CONTROL. John Clover Monsma, ed. Doubleday. 1963. OP

> Symposium of Protestant, Jewish and Catholic physicians discuss ethics of contraception, abortion, artificial insemination and related subjects.

ORGANIZATIONS AND SOURCES

The following organizations either deal extensively with planned parenthood or have a great deal of helpful material:

HUMAN BETTERMENT LEAGUE OF NORTH CAROLINA, INC. Pamphlets and information, particularly on sterilization.
Box 3036, Winston-Salem, N. C. 27102.

INTERNATIONAL PLANNED PARENTHOOD FEDERATION. News of planned parenthood efforts around the world. Newsletter available.
51 E. 42nd St., New York, N. Y. 10017.

PLANNED PARENTHOOD—WORLD POPULATION. Catalogs available "Publications about Planned Parenthood" and "List of PP-WP Publications for Professionals." Also "Guide to Films" and bibliographies.
515 Madison Ave., New York, N. Y. 10022.

The following organizations can supply material or suggest sources on planned parenthood:

THE CHRISTIAN LIFE COMMISSION OF THE BAPTIST GENERAL CONVENTION OF TEXAS.
206 Baptist Bldg., Dallas, Tex. 75201.

DIVISION OF ALCOHOL PROBLEMS AND GENERAL WELFARE, GENERAL BOARD OF CHRISTIAN SOCIAL CONCERNS OF THE METHODIST CHURCH.
100 Maryland Ave., N. E., Washington, D. C. 20002.

DIVISION OF PASTORAL SERVICES, EXECUTIVE COUNCIL, EPISCOPAL CHURCH.
815—2nd Ave., New York, N. Y. 10017.

FAMILY LIFE BUREAU, U. S. CATHOLIC CONFERENCE.
1312 Mass. Ave., N. W., Washington, D. C. 20005.

NATIONAL CONFERENCE OF CHRISTIANS AND JEWS.
43 W. 57th St., New York, N. Y. 10019.

PUBLIC AFFAIRS PAMPHLETS.
381 Park Ave., S., New York, N. Y. 10016.

PERIODICALS AND JOURNALS

INTERNATIONAL PLANNED PARENTHOOD NEWS. 10 times a year. $2.00.
International Planned Parenthood Federation, 18/20 Lower Regent St., London, S. W. 1, England.

PLANNED PARENTHOOD NEWS. 9 issues $1.50. Information on birth control, new developments, legal issues, and activity of Planned Parenthood-World Population.
515 Madison Ave., New York, N. Y. 10022.

POPULATION BULLETIN. 8 times a year. $3.00. Statistics and information. Some material related to birth control.
Population Reference Bureau Inc., 1507 M St., N. W., Washington, D. C. 20005.

PRINTED MATERIALS

*BIRTH CONTROL AND PUBLIC POLICY. Norman St. John-Stevas. A thorough study of the issues in the birth control controversy with a superb bibliography. $.50.
> Center for the Study of Democratic Institutions, Box 4068, Santa Barbara, Cal. 93103.

THE CHURCHES SPEAK UP ON BIRTH CONTROL. Statements by major religious groups and leaders. $.10.

*THE COMPLETE BOOK OF BIRTH CONTROL. Comprehensive, clearly-written, paperback manual on all aspects and methods of contraception. $.50.

THE CONTROL OF FERTILITY. Report on evaluation of all methods of birth control. Presented by Committee on Human Reproduction of the American Medical Association. $.15.

MODERN METHODS OF BIRTH CONTROL. A discussion of birth control techniques in booklet form. $.10.

*THE MORALITY OF BIRTH CONTROL. Short statements on the attitude toward birth control by Protestant, Roman Catholic, and Jewish faith. $.10.

TO THOSE DENIED A CHILD. Information on treatment of infertility and centers giving such treatment. $.10.
> Planned Parenthood-World Population, 515 Madison Ave., New York, N. Y. 10022.

THE METHODIST CHURCH AND PLANNED PARENTHOOD. A report of discussions on the major problems and issues in planned parenthood, goals for immediate action, and a theological approach to planned parenthood. Contains excellent source list. $.50.

RESPONSIBLE PARENTHOOD FROM A CHRISTIAN PERSPECTIVE. A brief pamphlet which sets forth persuasive arguments from a biblical perspective for planned parenthood. $.04.
> Service Dept. Methodist Church, 100 Maryland Ave., N. E., Washington, D. C. 20002.

NEW FACTS ABOUT BIRTH CONTROL. An easily understood booklet by Allan Guttmacher and Joan Gould setting forth new developments in birth control—attitudes and techniques. $.25.

*WHY CAN'T YOU HAVE A BABY? Planned parenthood also involves overcoming obstacles to pregnancy as this booklet by Guttmacher and Gould indicates. $.25.
> Public Affairs Pamphlets, 381 Park Ave., S., New York, N. Y. 10016.

*ORAL CONTRACEPTIVES and MORALITY AND THE PILL. Two pamphlets presenting reasons for Catholic opposition to the birth control pill. $.05 each.

STERILIZATION AND PUBLIC POLICY. Norman St. John-
Stevas. A balanced treatment of the subject as it relates to
traditional moral teaching, civil law and public policy. $.50.
   Family Life Bureau, U. S. Catholic Conference, 1312 Mass. Ave.,
   N. W., Washington, D. C. 20005.

*PLANNED PARENTHOOD. A brief pamphlet setting forth dif-
ferent viewpoints on birth control and evaluating them. $.02.
   Christian Life Commission, 206 Baptist Bldg., Dallas, Tex. 75201.

AUDIO VISUALS

For an extensive listing, order *Guide to Films* from Planned Parenthood-World Population, 515 Madison Ave., New York, N. Y.
10022.

*BEFORE THEY SAY "I DO." 16 mm. Color. Sound. 28 min. $6.00
rental. As a young couple walks down the aisle to be married,
a series of flashbacks traces the role of the clergyman and the
physician in pre-marital counseling. The minister deals skillfully
and sympathetically with the physical aspects of marriage and
its relation to the spiritual. The physician explains methods of
birth control. The young couple emerge with a new understanding of themselves and each other.
   Cokesbury.

*BIRTH CONTROL AND THE LAW. B&W 52 min. 1962. $9.40
rental. From the CBS Reports series, this film analyzes the problem of whether a tax-supported institution such as a hospital
should give out information on birth control. It examines legal,
moral, medical and social implications of birth control and
presents views of clergymen, doctors, social workers and patients.
   Audio Visual Center, Div. of University Extension, Indiana University, Bloomington, Ind. 47405.

FAIR CHANCE. 16 mm. Color. 14½ min. $3.55 rental. In a hos-
pital maternity ward, a new father explains how planned parenthood made it possible for him and his wife to have children
when they were ready and on their schedule. As he recounts
his experience to a troubled stranger, awaiting news of the birth
of his fourth unwanted baby, the camera shows every phase of
a typical Planned Parenthood visit.
   Visual Aids Service, University of Illinois, Div. of University Extension, Champaign, Ill. 61820.

*INTRODUCTION TO BIRTH CONTROL. Filmstrip and record.
Color. 15 min. $4.00 purchase. A straightforward presentation
of the accepted methods of contraception—rhythm, withdrawal,

diaphragm, condom, jellies, creams and foams, pills and intra-uterine devices—preceded by basic facts about reproduction. Presented by use of colorful and clear diagrams and accompanied by a good, brief explanation on a synchronized record. Recommended for patient groups, professional training sessions, colleges and universities, marriage counseling courses.

OPEN END—BIRTH CONTROL. 16 mm. B&W Sound. 40 mn. $7.00 rental. Reveals strikingly the changing climate in the Catholic Church on birth control.

> Planned Parenthood-World Population, 515 Madison Ave., New York, N. Y. 10022.

OTHER HELPS

BOOKS ABOUT POPULATION AND FAMILY PLANNING AND RELATED SUBJECTS. Handy reference for the busy worker; information offered is authentic yet understandable to the lay reader. Small pamphlet.

LIST OF PP-WP PUBLICATIONS FOR PROFESSIONALS. A list of material for doctors, ministers, social workers, counselors, and educators on planned parenthood. Very helpful.

A SELECTED BIBLIOGRAPHY—FAMILY PLANNING, POPULATION, RELATED SUBJECTS. More extensive listing. Single copy free.

> Planned Parenthood-World Population, 515 Madison Ave., New York, N. Y. 10022.

POPULATION EXPLOSION

(See also International Relations, Planned Parenthood)

BOOKS

FERTILITY AND SURVIVAL: POPULATION PROBLEMS FROM MALTHUS TO MAO TSE-TUNG. Alfred Sauvy.

Criterion Books. 1961. $7.50. Collier, $.95 paper.

> Historical study of population problems and the way people have dealt with the problems. Recommended by Population Reference Bureau, Inc.

*OVERPOPULATION: A CATHOLIC VIEW. George A. Kelly. National Catholic Welfare Conference. 1960. $.75.

> A recognition of population problems in some areas, but a refusal to recognize artificial birth control as necessary to meet the problem.

THE POPULATION CRISIS, IMPLICATIONS AND PLANS FOR ACTION. Larry K. Y. Ng and Stuart Mudd, eds. Indiana University Press. 1965. $2.95.

> Discusses world population growth in relationship to world resources. Valuable appendix of voluntary organizations and research programs.

*THE POPULATION DILEMMA. Philip Hauser, ed. Prentice-Hall. 1963. $1.95.

> The nature of the population problem, ways to deal with the problem, and difficulties in solving the problem are all ably set forth. Highly recommended by authorities.

POPULATION, EVOLUTION AND BIRTH CONTROL. Garrett Hardin, ed. Freeman. 1964. $2.00 paper.

> Collection of the most effective published statements in support of and in opposition to the questions at issue, arranged to reveal the historical development of major ideas.

*THE POPULATION EXPLOSION AND CHRISTIAN RESPONSIBILITY. Richard M. Fagley. Oxford University Press. 1960. $4.25.

> Discussion of the church's growing awareness of the population problem, governmental neglect, religious obstacles and the need for a clear stand. Highly recommended by experts in the field.

POPULATION: THE VITAL REVOLUTION. Ronald Freedman, ed. Doubleday-Anchor. 1964. $1.25.

> Nineteen experts analyze important world population trends in non-technical language.

THE SILENT EXPLOSION. Philip Appleman. Beacon. 1965. $4.95, $1.95 paper.

> Outlines in a dramatic way the problem of a population out of control in growth. Catholic, Communist, liberal responses set forth. Excuses for not taking the problem seriously are answered.

SRO, OVERPOPULATION AND YOU. M. L. Bracher. Fortress. 1966. $3.50.

> A presentation of the problems created by overpopulation, its effect on the individual, and what the individual's responsibility is.

TO HUNGER NO MORE. I. W. Moomaw. Friendship. 1963. $1.95.

> Outlines what the problems are in attempting to feed the hungry. Also spells out in detail the work of the churches in coming to grips with those problems. Examples are drawn from all over the world. Suggests that the only kind of efforts that will succeed are those which "help people help themselves."

ORGANIZATIONS AND SOURCES

ASSOCIATION FOR VOLUNTARY STERILIZATION. Research, education, and service in regard to sterilization as means of population control.

> 14 W. 40th St., New York, N. Y. 10018.

*FAMILY LIFE BUREAU, U. S. CATHOLIC CONFERENCE. Materials available on the Catholic position in regard to birth control as a way of meeting population problems.

> 1312 Mass. Ave., N. W., Washington, D. C. 20005.

*PLANNED PARENTHOOD-WORLD POPULATION. To make available to all peoples of the world the most effective and scientific means of voluntary conception control, to help parents plan their families and to help nations plan their growth. List available upon request outlines publications in the areas of birth control, religious support, marriage and family life, infertility, world population, public policy, research, and general information.

> 515 Madison Ave., New York, N. Y. 10022.

THE POPULATION COUNCIL. Pamphlets and materials. Demographic and biological research.

> 245 Park Ave., New York, N. Y. 10017.

POPULATION CRISIS COMMITTEE. Operates a campaign to activate the U. S. government in population control.

> 1730 K St., N. W., Washington, D. C. 20006.

*POPULATION POLICY PANEL, HUGH MOORE FUND. Bibliography, list of organizations, pamphlets available.

> 60 E. 42nd St., New York, N. Y. 10017.

*POPULATION REFERENCE BUREAU, INC. To educate the public about the population crisis. They publish *Population Bulletin, Population Profiles, World Data Sheet,* and *Clipsheet.*

> 1755 Mass. Ave., N. W., Washington, D. C. 20036.

UNITED NATIONS, BUREAU OF SOCIAL AFFAIRS. Statistical materials on world population trends.

> United Nations Bldg., New York, N. Y. 10017.

The following university-related programs are directly related to population problems:

CORNELL UNIVERSITY INTERNATIONAL POPULATION PROGRAM. Research in demography. Current emphasis on Latin America.
Dept. of Sociology, Cornell University, Ithaca, N. Y. 14850.

GEORGE WASHINGTON UNIVERSITY POPULATION RESEARCH PROJECT. Prepares and publishes series of booklets on the population problems of the world.
George Washington University, Washington, D. C. 20006.

GEORGETOWN UNIVERSITY CENTER FOR POPULATION RESEARCH. Conducts research in demography and the physiological aspects of reproduction.
Georgetown University, Washington, D. C. 20007.

HARVARD UNIVERSITY SCHOOL OF PUBLIC HEALTH CENTER FOR POPULATION STUDIES. Concerned with developing new knowledge through research with practical application of knowledge among population groups.
Harvard University, Cambridge, Mass. 02138.

MIAMI UNIVERSITY, SCRIPPS FOUNDATION FOR RESEARCH IN POPULATION PROBLEMS. Conducts research relating to world problems and to population study in the U. S.
Miami University, Oxford, Ohio 45056.

PRINCETON UNIVERSITY OFFICE OF POPULATION RESEARCH. List of publications by staff members available.
Princeton University, 5 Ivy Lane, Princeton, N. J. 08540.

UNIVERSITY OF CHICAGO POPULATION RESEARCH AND TRAINING CENTER. Conducts demographic research and training program for students.
935 E. 60th St., Chicago, Ill. 60637.

UNIVERSITY OF MICHIGAN POPULATION STUDIES CENTER. List of staff publications available.
University of Michigan, 527 E. Liberty St., Ann Arbor, Mich. 48104.

UNIVERSITY OF TEXAS, POPULATION RESEARCH CENTER. Conducts research in the U. S. and Latin America.
University of Texas, 217 Archway, Austin, Tex. 78712.

PERIODICALS AND JOURNALS

For an extensive list see BIBLIOGRAPHY ON POPULATION, Population Reference Bureau, 1755 Mass. Ave., N. W., Washington, D. C. 20036.

INTERNATIONAL PLANNED PARENTHOOD NEWS. 10 times
a year. $2.00. News, book reviews, articles and population prob-
lems throughout the world.

> International Planned Parenthood Federation, 18/20 Lower Regent
> St., London, S. W. I., England.

PLANNED PARENTHOOD NEWS. Q

> Planned Parenthood-World Population, 515 Madison Ave., New
> York, N. Y. 10022.

*POPULATION BULLETIN. BM $3.00, $.50 per copy. Major pub-
lication. Each issue devoted to analysis of some phase of population trends in the world.

POPULATION PROFILES. M $.25. Report on population develop-
ments.

> Population Reference Bureau, Inc., 1755 Mass. Ave., N.W., Wash-
> ington, D. C. 20036.

PRINTED MATERIALS

EXPANDING POPULATION IN A SHRINKING WORLD.
Excellent factual booklet. $.60.

*THIS CROWDED WORLD. Frederick Osborn. Outlines the basic
issues of the population explosion. $.25.

> Public Affairs Pamphlets, 381 Park Ave., S., New York, N. Y. 10016.

FOOD AND POPULATION. A packet of materials on the population explosion. $1.00.

> Division of Christian Social Concern, American Baptist Conven-
> tion, Valley Forge, Pa. 19481.

*INTERCOM: FOCUS ON WORLD POPULATION, Vol. 6, No.
1. An entire issue devoted to population problems. Contains
excellent listing of sources and agencies. $1.00.

> Foreign Policy Association, Inc., 345 E. 46th St., New York, N. Y.
> 10017.

*THE POPULATION BOMB. Pamphlet describes the extent and
effect of the population explosion. Free.

> Hugh Moore Fund, 60 E. 42nd St., New York, N. Y. 10017.

*WORLD POPULATION. January, 1967, issue of the *Annals* of the
American Academy of Political and Social Science. Excellent
resource. $2.50.

> 3937 Chestnut St., Philadelphia, Pa. 19104.

WORLD POPULATION DATA SHEET. Published annually
giving current population and related data for the major countries of the world. $.25.

> Population Reference Bureau, Inc., 1755 Mass. Ave., N. W., Wash-
> ington, D. C. 20036.

WORLD POPULATION PROBLEM. The population problem
viewed from a Catholic perspective. $.50.

> Family Life Bureau, U. S. Catholic Conference, 1312 Mass. Ave.,
> N. W., Washington, D. C. 20005.

WORLD POPULATION: PROSPECTS AND PROBLEMS. Describes population trends and projections. Discusses economics
of the population explosion. 25 pp. $.50.

> Chamber of Commerce of the U. S., 1615 H St., N. W., Washington,
> D. C. 20006.

AUDIO VISUALS

For an extensive listing of films, order *Guide to Films* from Planned
Parenthood-World Population, 515 Madison Ave., New York, N. Y.
10022.

*BOOMTIME. Color filmstrip. 59 frames. Script. Guide. $2.50 rental.
$7.00 purchase. Shows the new challenges for the church due
to the population growth, and mobility of its people. Art drawings.

THE SQUEEZE. B&W 10 min. $6.00 rental. An impressionistic
study of some of the problems of over-population. Tries to
motivate the audience to face this vital problem and to seek a
solution.

> Office for Audio Visuals, United Church of Christ, 1720 Chouteau
> Ave., St. Louis, Mo. 63103.

THE EARTH AND MANKIND. Six film series. 28 min. each.
B&W $8.00 rental each. Produced in 1960 by McGraw-Hill
Text-Film Division surveying the world population problem and
food supply. This series probes the population problem. Stanley
Burke, foreign correspondent and U. N. commentator, is the
narrator in a round-the-globe census survey which includes
these films:

*PEOPLE BY THE BILLIONS. An examination of the impli-
cations of the population explosion already under way.

MAN AND HIS RESOURCES. A study of the meaning of the
Universal Declaration of Human Rights in terms of the basic
raw materials of existence.

TO EACH A RIGHTFUL SHARE. An examination of man's
efforts to achieve a better life.

THE GLOBAL STRUGGLE FOR FOOD. A progress report
on efforts to expand world food production through water and
flood-control, agricultural advances, land-distribution, etc.

CAN THE EARTH PROVIDE? A view of the resources of
science to find new means of survival.

CHALLENGE TO MANKIND. Authorities from India, U. S.,

United Kingdom, Peru, and Canada express their views on the threat to mankind of overpopulation and tender some possible solutions.

SECRET HUNGER. 16 mm. 30 min. $7.50 rental. A picture of the struggle of people against want and hunger as a pattern of life due to overpopulation.

Contemporary Films, Inc., 267 W. 25th St., New York, N. Y. 10001.

*WORLD VIEW. 16 mm. B&W 30 min. Free loan. Explores problems resulting from huge growth of world population and explains the cause of the growth.

Librarian, United States Bureau of the Census, Dept. of Commerce, Washington, D. C. 20233.

OTHER HELPS

BIBLIOGRAPHY ON POPULATION. A superb 20-page bibliography on many phases of population. Lacks annotation. $.50.

Population Reference Bureau, Inc., 1755 Mass. Avve., N. W., Washington, D. C. 20036.

PUBLICATIONS ON WORLD POPULATION PROBLEMS. Single sheet. Compiled by the Hugh Moore Fund. Lacks annotation. Single copy free.

60 E. 42nd St., New York, N. Y. 10017.

PORNOGRAPHY

(See also Mass Communication and Morality)

BOOKS

THE BANNED BOOKS OF ENGLAND AND OTHER COUNTRIES. Alec Craig. George Allen & Unwin Ltd. 1962. OP

A study of books banned, why they were banned, and development in attitudes and laws related to obscenity. Contains little actual obscene or questionable material.

EROTIC IN LITERATURE. David Loth. Macfadden. 1961. $.60.

> A historical survey and contemporary analysis of pornography. Describes the extent, economics, and types of pornography as well as measures taken to control it. Some illustrative passages are erotic. Bibliography is helpful.

*FEDERAL CENSORSHIP. J. C. N. Paul and Murray L. Schwartz. The Free Press of Glencoe. 1961. $7.95.

> The author shows the use of federal control over the mail in regard to censorship, traces the development of censorship by the federal government, and discusses the future development. Excellent bibliography and appendix on court cases involving censorship.

*A HISTORY OF PORNOGRAPHY. H. M. Hyde. Farrar, Straus, and Giroux. 1965. $4.50.

> A non-judgmental history of pornography. Helpful background information. Material may be objectionable to some.

OBSCENITY AND THE LAW. Norman St. John-Stevas. Secker and Warburg. 1956. OP.

> A study of law and changing tastes. The author points out the intricate legal problems, and also those of literary taste and freedom of expression in literature. Historical. Helpful for background.

POISON PEDDLING ON AMERICA'S BOULEVARD. Bernard Brunsting. Van Kampen. 1953. OP.

> A description and denunciation of the sale of pornography by street merchants. While the book is somewhat dated the problem to which it speaks is current.

TO DEPRAVE AND CORRUPT. John Chandos, ed. Association. 1962. $3.75.

> Ten men and women—British, French, and American—discuss obscenity from a literary, legal, juridical, sociological, psychological, and religious perspective. They range in judgment from limited censorship to none at all.

ORGANIZATIONS AND SOURCES

CITIZENS FOR DECENT LITERATURE, INC. Publish a National Decency Report on the problem of obscenity and pornography.

> 18th Floor, Provident Tower, Cincinnati, Ohio 45202.

COMMISSION ON RESEARCH & SOCIAL ACTION, THE AMERICAN LUTHERAN CHURCH.

> 422 S. 5th St., Minneapolis, Minn. 55415.

GENERAL BOARD OF CHRISTIAN SOCIAL CONCERNS OF THE METHODIST CHURCH. Source lists and pamphlets available in quantity.

> 100 Maryland Ave., N. E., Washington, D. C. 20002.

INFORMATION SERVICE, NATIONAL COUNCIL OF CHURCHES. Material on censorship and obscenity.
475 Riverside Dr., New York, N. Y. 10027.

NATIONAL CATHOLIC OFFICE FOR MOTION PICTURES. Prepares and distributes a description and classification of home and foreign films.
453 Madison Ave., New York, N. Y. 10022.

NATIONAL OFFICE FOR DECENT LITERATURE. Established by the Roman Catholic bishops of the U. S. to review and evaluate comic books, magazines, and pocket size books. Evaluations available, $.75 a year.
33 E. Congress Parkway, Chicago, Ill. 60605.

OFFICE OF THE CLERK, SUPREME COURT OF THE UNITED STATES. Contact for copies of court decisions relating to censorship and obscenity.
Washington, D. C. 20543.

U. S. CATHOLIC CONFERENCE. Many materials on censorship, obscenity, and mass communication.
1312 Mass. Ave., N. W., Washington, D. C. 20005.

UNITED STATES POST OFFICE DEPT. Information on postal laws and regulations related to obscenity and censorship.
Washington, D. C. 20260.

PERIODICALS AND JOURNALS

THE NATIONAL DECENCY REPORTER. $5.00. Information on efforts to eliminate obscenity from American publications.
Citizens for Decent Literature, Inc., 3309 Carew Tower, Cincinnati, Ohio 45202.

PRINTED MATERIALS

BIBLE SPEAKS ON MORAL ISSUES, CHRISTIAN PRINCIPLES APPLIED TO MORAL PROBLEMS, and TEEN TALK ABOUT OBSCENE LITERATURE. Helpful, brief pamphlets. $.02 each.

CHRISTIANITY AND MORAL ISSUES. Booklet includes discussion of censorship and obscene literature. $1.00.

SALACIOUS MATERIAL: HOW TO COPE WITH IT. A packet of materials with suggested specific courses of action. $1.00.
Christian Life Commission, 206 Baptist Bldg., Dallas, Tex. 75201.

THE CHURCH LOOKS AT IMMORALITY IN PRINT AND ON SCREEN. A 14-page booklet outlining problems, setting forth positive suggestions, and providing discussion guides. Free.

Commission on Research and Social Action, American Lutheran Church, 422 S. 5th St., Minneapolis, Minn. 55415.

INFORMATION SERVICE, CENSORSHIP ISSUE. An appraisal of the problems of censorship and obscenity and a review of organizations working for decent literature. $.20.

A PLAN FOR PORNOGRAPHY CONTROL. $.20.

A PROBLEM FOR PARENTS. $.20.

A SICKNESS IN SOCIETY. A booklet by Ralph Cannon setting forth the nature of obscenity in American publications, mainly magazines. $.25.

Methodist General Board of Christian Social Concerns, 100 Maryland Ave., N. E., Washington, D. C. 20002.

*PORNOGRAPHY: ISSUES AND ANSWERS SERIES. Analyzes the extent and harm of pornography and offers suggested courses of action to cope with the problem. $.05.

Christian Life Commission, Southern Baptist Convention, 460 James Robertson Parkway, Nashville, Tenn. 37219.

AUDIO VISUALS

*THE ACCUSED. 16 mm. BW $6.00 rental. Loretta Young TV show. Shows fight made in one community to rid newsstands of obscene materials.

Cokesbury.

HOW FREE ARE YOU? 35 mm. filmstrip. Color. 75 frames. 33-1/3 rpm recording. $7.50 purchase. Covers many current problems, including pornography.

Service Dept. Methodist Church, 100 Maryland Ave., N. W., Washington, D. C. 20002.

POVERTY

(See also Economics, Daily Work, Labor, Leisure)

BOOKS

*CHRISTIAN CASE AGAINST POVERTY. Henry Clark. Association. 1965. $.75 paper.

> Written at the request of the National Council of Churches to awaken the conscience of the Christian concerning poverty in the world. Historically traces poverty and wealth through the years and concludes with a Christian approach to the subject. Well documented.

CHRISTIANITY AND THE AFFLUENT SOCIETY. Reginald H. Fuller and Brian K. Rice. Eerdmans. 1966. $3.95, $2.45 paper.

> Begins with consideration of biblical attitudes toward wealth and prosperity and offers a critique of the affluent society, its premises, goals, and achievements based on biblical insights.

CHURCH IN A SOCIETY OF ABUNDANCE. Arthur E. Walmsley, ed. Seabury. 1963. $3.95.

> A collection of relevant, vital articles on contemporary society and its demands upon the churches.

THE CHURCHES' WAR ON POVERTY. Lyle E. Schaller. Abingdon. 1967. $1.95 paper.

> Suggested guidelines for the participation of the churches in the Federal Anti-Poverty program. Somewhat objectionable to those believing in separation of church and state; practical helps for those who believe church and state should cooperate.

*NEED IS OUR NEIGHBOR. Byron Johnson. Friendship. 1966. $1.75 paper.

> Sets forth the many dilemmas of affluence and poverty facing individual Christians and the church. Presents an imperative for Christian action.

THE OTHER AMERICA: POVERTY IN THE UNITED STATES. Michael Harrington. Macmillan. 1962. $4.00. Penguin Books, 1964, $.95 paper.

> Focuses on poverty among industrial rejects, migrant workers, minorities and the aged.

POVERTY IN AFFLUENCE: THE SOCIAL, POLITICAL, AND ECONOMIC DIMENSIONS OF POVERTY IN THE UNITED STATES. Robert E. Will and Harold G. Vatter. Harcourt, Brace, and World. 1965. $2.45 paper.

> A technical and extensive study of poverty in America.

RICH MAN, POOR MAN. Herman P. Miller. Crowell. 1964. $4.95.

> Income distribution in the U. S. in relation to occupation, education, religion, race, age, health, and family.

THIS IS THE PUZZLE OF POVERTY. Jeanette Struchen. Friendship. 1966. $.85 paper.
> An over-all view of poverty with warm human-interest vignettes and pictures and graphs.

WEALTH AND WANT IN ONE WORLD. Muriel S. Webb, ed. Friendship. 1966. $1.95 paper.
> Vivid description of the peoples of the world as they struggle with the extremes of affluence and poverty.

ORGANIZATIONS AND SOURCES

AFL-CIO ANTI-POVERTY OFFICE. Materials and suggested programs of action to help eliminate poverty.
> 815—16th St., N. W., Washington, D. C. 20006.

BOARD OF SOCIAL MINISTRY, LUTHERAN CHURCH IN AMERICA. Materials on the responsibility of Christians and churches to deal with the problem of poverty.
> 231 Madison Ave., New York, N. Y. 10016.

DIVISION OF COMMUNITY SERVICES, EXECUTIVE COUNCIL, EPISCOPAL CHURCH.
> 815—2nd Ave., New York, N. Y. 10017.

DIVISION OF HUMAN RELATIONS AND ECONOMIC AFFAIRS, GENERAL BOARD OF CHRISTIAN SOCIAL CONCERNS OF THE METHODIST CHURCH. Bibliographies, pamphlets, and study guides on poverty.
> 100 Maryland Ave., N. E., Washington, D. C. 20002.

INTERRELIGIOUS COMMITTEE AGAINST POVERTY. Composed of representatives of the major Jewish, Catholic, and Protestant groups.
> Anti-Poverty Task Force, 110 Maryland Ave., N.E., Washington D. C. 20002.

NATIONAL CATHOLIC COORDINATING COMMITTEE ON ECONOMIC OPPORTUNITY.
> 1312 Massachusetts Ave., N. W., Washington, D. C. 20005.

*NATIONAL COUNCIL OF CHURCHES DEPT. OF CHURCH AND ECONOMIC LIFE. Material available on many aspects of poverty in America. Extensive source lists of books, pamphlets and films.
> 475 Riverside Dr., New York, N. Y. 10027.

*OFFICE OF ECONOMIC OPPORTUNITY. Material available on all aspects of poverty in the U. S.
> Washington, D. C. 20506.

*U. S. CATHOLIC CONFERENCE, DEPT. OF SOCIAL ACTION. Pamphlets and materials available on many aspects of poverty. Provides religious incentive to help.

    1312 Mass. Ave., N. W., Washington, D. C. 20005.

The following U. S. Government agencies also have materials and statistics on income and economics:

DEPT. OF AGRICULTURE, DEPT. OF HEALTH, EDUCATION, AND WELFARE, DEPT. OF COMMERCE, DEPT. OF LABOR, TREASURY DEPT.

    Washington, D. C.

PERIODICALS AND JOURNALS

See publications under Daily Work and Economics.

PRINTED MATERIALS

*ANTI-POVERTY ACTION GUIDES FOR THE LOCAL CHURCH. A set of ten guides outlining specific programs for the local church's war against poverty. $1.25 per set.

ONE-FIFTH OF THE NATION. Fact and action guide to poverty in the midst of plenty in the U. S. A. $.50.

    Office of Publication Services, National Council of Churches, 475 Riverside Dr., New York, N. Y. 10027.

*ANTI-POVERTY PACKET. Selected materials on poverty in America and the anti-poverty programs of government and church. $3.00.

    Church of the Brethren, Elgin, Ill. 60120.

CONCERN. Two special issues of this Methodist publication deal with "The Attack on Poverty" and "The Challenge of Affluence." $.50 for both.

    100 Maryland Ave., N. E., Washington, D. C. 20002.

EQUAL JUSTICE FOR THE POOR MAN, THE POOR AMONG US—CHALLENGE AND OPPORTUNITY, NEW OPPORTUNITIES FOR DEPRESSED AREAS. Concise, well-written pamphlets. $.25 each.

    Public Affairs Pamphlets, 381 Park Ave., S., New York, N. Y. 10016.

*POVERTY. Study packet of materials required to understand poverty and develop a plan of action. $2.00.

    Council of Christian Social Action, United Church of Christ, 289 Park Ave., S., New York, N. Y. 10010.

POVERTY IN THE UNITED STATES. A 304-page report prepared in 1964.

Committee on Education and Labor, House of Representatives, U. S. Congress, Washington, D. C. 20515.

PROFILES OF POVERTY. A vivid presentation of poverty in America. $.75.

American Association of University Women, 2401 Virginia Ave., N. W., Washington, D. C. 20037.

SOCIAL ACTION. The following issues of this publication of the United Church of Christ are devoted largely to a study of poverty: October, 1960; March, 1961; May, 1962; April, 1964; March, 1965. $.25 each.

289 Park Ave., S., New York, N. Y. 10010.

THERE SHALL BE NO POOR. Richard G. Hirsch. Deals with facts of poverty in America and what these facts demand. $.75.

Union of American Hebrew Congregations, 838—5th Ave., New York, N. Y. 10021.

SOCIAL PROGRESS. The following issues of this publication of the United Presbyterian Church in the U. S. A. are devoted largely to a study of poverty: February, 1963; November, 1963. $.25 each.

Witherspoon Bldg., Philadelphia, Pa. 19107.

AUDIO VISUALS

OEO FILM GUIDE. An extensive, annotated listing of films on poverty. Excellent source for audio-visual information.

Office of Economic Opportunity, Washington, D. C. 20506.

THE AFFLUENT SOCIETY. B&W 28½ min. Guide. $8.00 rental. A ride up the world's most luxurious street, New York's Park Avenue, which houses the Waldorf Astoria Hotel at one end and the Dept. of Welfare Relief Center at the other, to illustrate grinding poverty amid everyday luxury.

*HARVEST OF SHAME. B&W 54 min. Guide. $10.00 rental. ($8.00 to UCC). This film from CBS Reports reveals the plight of millions of migratory workers who harvest America's crops. Shows the degradation and exploitation of these men, women, and children, who are moved from state to state in trucks, live in crowded, unsanitary huts, and work long hours for little pay.

Office for Audio Visuals, United Church of Christ, 1505 Race St., Philadelphia, Pa. 19102.

THE CAPTIVE. 16 mm. Sound. 30 min. $8.00 rental. A stark portrayal of a family in Appalachia. Describes living conditions and problems faced by the people.

THE NEWCOMERS. 16 mm. Sound. (B&W) 30 min. $8.00 rental, postage extra. The influx of poor families to the inner city. Shows one aspect of poverty and the hopelessness of those caught in its grip.
Cokesbury.

CHILDREN WITHOUT. 16 mm. B&W 30 min. $5.00 rental. Documents the desperate circumstances under which the children of the inner city must grow up.

*HOW THINGS HIDE PEOPLE. Color filmstrip. Record. $7.50 purchase. Explores the problems faced by the middle-income person as he tries to understand and cope with the reality of poverty.

LIBERATE THE CAPTIVES. Color filmstrip. Recording. $7.50 purchase. Tells what a church and community can do to combat poverty.
American Baptist Films, Valley Forge, Pa. 19481.

P IS FOR POVERTY. 35 mm. 98-frame filmstrip. Record and script. Developed to arouse concern and action among churchmen. Includes "Action Guides for the Church's War on Poverty". $7.50.
Anti-Poverty Task Force, 475 Riverside Dr., New York, N. Y. 10027.

*SUPERFLUOUS PEOPLE. 16 mm. 55 min. $7.50 rental. Welfare presented as a material and moral problem. Shows many problems of the poor in the city.
AFL-CIO Film Dept., 815—16th St., N. W., Washington, D. C. 20006.

OTHER HELPS

POVERTY: A REVIEW AND ANNOTATED BIBLIOGRAPHY. Benjamin Schlesinger. University of Toronto. 1966. $5.00.
Extensive listing of books and resources for different aspects of poverty.

THE TYRANNY OF POVERTY. A selected bibliography of books, pamphlets, articles and memoranda on government and community action, employment, education, legal and social services, and economic and social problems. $.25.
The American Jewish Committee, Institute of Human Relations, 165 E. 56th St., New York, N. Y. 10022.

WORKING LIST OF CURRENT TITLES ON POVERTY. Selected books, pamphlets, articles, and films on poverty. $.10.
Office of Publication and Distribution, National Council of Churches, 475 Riverside Dr., New York, N. Y. 10027.

PROSTITUTION

(See also Sex, Venereal Disease)

BOOKS

CAST THE FIRST STONE. John M. Murtagh and Sara Harris. Pocket Books. 1963. $.35 paper.

> This is a portrayal of fifteen women who live in the weird world of prostitution. Their stories are told in a straightforward manner. It will help the reader to understand how prostitutes and pimps became the people they are today.

*CRIME IN AMERICA. Herbert A. Bloch, ed. Philosophical Library. 1961. $6.00.

> Chapter on the law and prostitution by a competent authority on crime.

*THE HISTORY OF PROSTITUTION. Vern L. Bullough. University Books, Inc. 1964. $7.50.

> A 304-page volume of history related primarily to western civilization. Done with good taste.

*PROSTITUTION AND MORALITY. Harry Benjamin and R. E. L. Masters. The Julian Press. 1964. $12.50.

> A definitive report (495 pages) on the prostitute in contemporary society with an analysis of the causes and effects of prostitution and its suppression.

PROSTITUTION IN EUROPE AND THE AMERICAS. Fernando Henriques. Citadel. 1965. $7.50.

> Part of a projected 3-volume study, this volume traces the development of prostitution from early Christianity to the present.

ORGANIZATIONS AND SOURCES

AMERICAN SOCIAL HEALTH ASSOCIATION. Research, public information and education dealing with commercialized prostitution and venereal disease. The only national voluntary agency which serves as a source of information and guidance in planning courses of action to suppress commercialized prostitution.

> 1790 Broadway, New York, N. Y. 10019.

PERIODICALS AND JOURNALS

SOCIAL HEALTH NEWS. M (except July, Aug.) $5.00. Free to persons with interest and activity in various fields of ASHA's program. Highlights ASHA program activities in fields of venereal disease and prostitution. Includes reviews of important literature in these fields and surveys other activities of importance.

American Social Health Assoc., 1790 Broadway, New York, N. Y. 10019.

PRINTED MATERIALS

GOOD LAWS—GOOD TOOLS. Discussion of the role of law in control of prostitution. Dated since written in 1952 but still helpful. $.15.

American Social Health Assoc., 1790 Broadway, New York, N. Y. 10019.

AUDIO VISUALS

None recommended.

RACE RELATIONS

(See also Citizenship, Economics, Extremism, Mental Health, Social Action and Welfare)

BOOKS

*THE BIBLE AND RACE. T. B. Maston. Broadman. 1959. $2.50.

Believing that the Bible is the standard, the author has set forth its teachings about God's intention for relations between the races. An examination of the basic scriptures used in racial discussions.

BLACK RELIGION. J. R. Washington. Beacon. 1964. $5.00. $2.45 paper.

A discussion of the nature of religion and church organization of the American Negro. Written by a Negro.

THE CHURCH IN THE RACIALLY CHANGING COMMU-

NITY. R. L. Wilson and J. H. Davis, eds. Abingdon. 1966.
$1.25 paper.

> A study of churches in communities undergoing change in the
> racial make-up of the population. Shows what has taken place,
> sketches current trends, and indicates possible responses by churches.

FREEDOM NOW: THE CIVIL RIGHTS STRUGGLE IN
AMERICA. Alan F. Westin, ed. Basic Books. 1964. $5.95.

> A detailed history of the civil rights movement—its tactics, leaders,
> and effect.

INTERMARRIAGE—INTERFAITH, INTERRACIAL, INTER-
ETHNIC. Albert I. Gordon. Beacon. 1964. $2.95 paper.

> The most complete survey available of the attitudes, problems, and
> possibilities surrounding intermarriage in America today.

MINORITIES IN AMERICAN SOCIETY. 2nd ed. Marden and
Meyer. American Book Co. 1962. $7.50.

> Deals from a sociological perspective with a number of minority
> groups in the United States.

THE NATURE OF PREJUDICE. Gordon W. Allport. Doubleday.
Abridged ed. 1954. $1.95 paper.

> An excellent book on prejudice by a noted scholar. Psychological
> and sociological in perspective. Includes a bibliography.

*THE NEGRO IN AMERICA. Talcott Parsons and Kenneth
Clark, eds. Houghton Mifflin. 1966. $9.50.

> An exhaustive, up-to-date, factual, objective look at the Negro in
> the U. S. Basic source book.

PASTOR AND THE RACE ISSUE. Daisuke Kitagawa. Seabury.
1965. $3.50.

> Intended for the professional leadership of the Christian churches.
> Its aim is to stimulate the churchmen "theologically" in the matter
> of race. It also takes seriously the disciplines of sociology, anthro-
> pology, psychology, and history.

THE PUERTO RICANS: STRANGERS—THEN NEIGHBORS.
Clarence Senior. Quadrangle Books. 1965. $1.45 paper.

> An examination of the patterns, history, and economic importance
> of Puerto Ricans.

PULPIT SPEAKS ON RACE. Alfred T. Davies, ed. Abingdon.
1965. $3.95.

> A collection of sermons on race by some of America's outstanding
> preachers. Helpful biblical, theological insights.

RACIAL AND CULTURAL MINORITIES. 3rd ed. G. E. Simp-
son and J. M. Yinger. Harper and Row. 1965. $8.75.

> A thorough sociology text on race relations. Deals mainly with the
> Negro and Jewish minorities.

*THE RACIAL PROBLEM IN CHRISTIAN PERSPECTIVE.
Kyle Haselden. Harper and Brothers. 1959. $1.45 paper.

> Discusses the moral commitment of Christians on racial questions, the damaging effects of prejudice and discrimination on both the victim and the guilty party, causes of the problem, and ways in which Christian faith and action can help to solve it.

RACISM: A WORLD ISSUE. Edmund D. Soper. Abingdon. 1947. OP.

> A thorough discussion of racism in our world. While dated, this is still a helpful volume and the only work of its kind.

*RACISM AND THE CHRISTIAN UNDERSTANDING OF MAN. George D. Kelsey. Scribners. 1965. $2.95 paper.

> A book on race from a Christian perspective by a Negro. Indicates racism is a religion which contradicts the Christian faith.

SEGREGATION AND DESEGREGATION. T. B. Maston. Macmillan. 1959. $3.50.

> This book contains a study of the factors which led to the Supreme Court decision in 1954 on segregation and the public schools and of the effects of the decision. Also there is a discussion of the relation of the churches to the segregation problem.

THE UNSILENT SOUTH: PROPHETIC PREACHING IN RACIAL CRISIS. Donald W. Shriver, Jr., ed. John Knox. 1965. $2.25 paper.

> A volume of sermons on race from southern preachers. Indicates the South has not been silent on race and provides helpful material from a Christian perspective on race.

ORGANIZATIONS AND SOURCES

Organizations dealing in a general and constructive way with race relations:

AFL-CIO DEPT. OF CIVIL RIGHTS. Materials favoring civil rights movement and encouraging the support of labor.

> 815—16th St., N. W., Washington D. C. 20006.

AMERICAN CIVIL LIBERTIES UNION. Works actively to promote many aspects of civil liberty, including areas related to race. Materials available.

> 156 Fifth Ave., New York, N. Y. 10010.

*ANTI-DEFAMATION LEAGUE OF B'NAI B'RITH. Numerous pamphlets, books, films, and resource guides.

> 315 Lexington Ave., New York, N. Y. 10016.

*CENTER FOR THE STUDY OF DEMOCRATIC INSTITUTIONS. Many books and booklets available favoring civil rights, better race relations, and elimination of prejudice. Write for list of materials.

> Box 4068, Santa Barbara, Cal. 93103.

CHRISTIAN LIFE COMMISSION, SOUTHERN BAPTIST CONVENTION. A large amount of material available on many aspects of race. Write for list.
460 James Robertson Parkway, Nashville, Tenn. 37219.

*COMMISSION ON RELIGION AND RACE, DEPT. OF SOCIAL JUSTICE, NATIONAL COUNCIL OF CHURCHES. Several sample articles and Commission reports favoring better race relations, desegregation, and civil rights are available. Also material from National Conference on Race.
475 Riverside Dr., New York, N. Y. 10027.

COMMITTEE FOR RACIAL JUSTICE NOW, UNITED CHURCH OF CHRIST. A large supply of sample materials including two bibliographies. Also, there are a large number of tracts, article reprints, etc. available at various costs.
289 Park Ave., S., New York, N. Y. 10010.

COMMITTEE OF SOUTHERN CHURCHMEN. Work for racial justice and publish *Katallagete,* a magazine, $2 for 4 issues.
1207 18th Ave. South, Nashville, Tenn. 37212.

EPISCOPAL SOCIETY FOR CULTURAL AND RACIAL UNITY. Publishes bimonthly Newsletter. Will send free samples, plus a large supply of material from which to order.
5 Forsyth St., N. W., Atlanta, Ga. 30303.

LUTHERAN HUMAN RELATIONS ASSOCIATION OF AMERICA, VALPARAISO UNIVERSITY. Publishes *Vanguard* and *Chapter Bulletin* monthly. Several sample items available and other items for sale at various prices. Helpful in providing needed literature.
Valparaiso, Ind. 46383.

METHODIST GENERAL BOARD OF CHRISTIAN SOCIAL CONCERNS. Specialized study in race relations.
100 Maryland Ave., N. E., Washington, D. C. 20002.

NATIONAL CATHOLIC CONFERENCE FOR INTERRACIAL JUSTICE. Education and action programs to help resolve race relation conflicts.
1307 S. Wabash Ave., Chicago, Ill. 60605.

NATIONAL INSTITUTE ON RELIGION AND RACE. Conducts programs and conferences, publishes a newsletter, and prints material on race. Devoted to interreligious cooperation aiding the civil rights movement.
3052 Sutherland Ave., Indianapolis, Ind. 46205.

PRESBYTERIAN INTERRACIAL COUNCIL. Promotes program of racial justice and reconciliation.
1570 Chambers Rd., St. Louis, Mo. 63136.

Organizations devoted almost exclusively to promoting civil rights:

A. PHILIP RANDOLPH INSTITUTE. Founded in 1964 to urge the full participation of the labor movement, religious groups, liberals and intellectuals in the day-to-day work of the civil rights movement.
217 W. 125th St., New York, N. Y. 10027.

CIVIL RIGHTS DIVISION, U. S. DEPARTMENT OF JUSTICE. Some sample materials available on legal aspects of civil rights movement.
Washington, D. C. 20530.

CONGRESS OF RACIAL EQUALITY (CORE). Works to eliminate all forms of racial discrimination through nonviolent means.
200 W. 135th St., New York, N. Y. 10030.

LEADERSHIP CONFERENCE ON CIVIL RIGHTS. A wealth of sample materials available defending and guiding the civil rights movement.
2027 Mass. Ave., N. W., Washington, D. C. 20036.

*NATIONAL ASSOCIATION FOR THE ADVANCEMENT OF COLORED PEOPLE (NAACP). Work is largely legal but prints a mass of material on all aspects of race relations and civil rights. An excellent bibliography of civil rights is available free of charge.
20 W. 40th St., New York, N. Y. 10018.

NATIONAL COMMITTEE AGAINST DISCRIMINATION IN HOUSING. Summary of statistics and ordinances related to fair housing available.
323 Lexington Ave., New York, N. Y. 10016.

NATIONAL URBAN LEAGUE. Concentrates on areas of housing, employment, education, etc. Local chapters have up-to-date information on local and national conditions.
14 E. 48th St., New York, N. Y. 10017.

PENNSYLVANIA HUMAN RELATIONS COMMISSION. A large number of excellent materials related to better human relations. Helpful action guides and lists of sources—books, films, filmstrips—on race.
1401 Labor and Industry Bldg., Harrisburg, Pa. 17120.

SOUTHERN CHRISTIAN LEADERSHIP CONFERENCE.

Pamphlets and brochures available. Works according to non-violent philosophy to achieve full citizenship rights for the Negro.
334 Auburn Ave., N. E., Atlanta, Ga. 30303.

*SOUTHERN REGIONAL COUNCIL, INC. Several free booklets, a bibliography, and a large supply of material at various prices available. Education, economics, justice, housing, and politics in relation to the Negro researched and reported. Write for list of special reports.
5 Forsyth St., N. W., Atlanta, Ga. 30303.

*U. S. COMMISSION ON CIVIL RIGHTS. Several sample tracts and catalog of publications. Works to implement civil rights ideals and legislation in the U. S.
1701 Pennsylvania Ave., N. W., Washington, D. C. 20006.

Anti-civil rights organizations:
AMERICAN NAZI PARTY NATIONAL HEADQUARTERS. Racist in tone, anti-Negro and anti-civil rights. Publications and demonstrations are main activities.
Box 5505, Arlington, Va. 22205.

ASSOCIATION OF CITIZENS' COUNCILS. Many tracts, pamphlets, and reports available defending segregation.
Box 886, Greenwood, Miss. 38930.

ASSOCIATION OF CITIZENS' COUNCILS OF LOUISIANA. Works to defend segregation and defeat objectives of civil rights movement.
Homer, La. 71040.

CITIZENS' COUNCILS OF AMERICA. Many free materials available describing the segregationist position.
315-325 Plaza Bldg., Jackson, Miss. 39201.

KU KLUX KLAN, NATIONAL KNIGHTS OF KKK, INC. Various booklets and tracts available explaining their position, symbols, etc. Strongly against civil rights movement.
Box 657, Tucker, Ga. 30084.

Organizations related to Indian affairs:
AMERICAN INDIAN HISTORICAL SOCIETY. Publishes The Indian Historian, Newservice Bulletin for Indian Newspapers, and scholarly materials on the Indian in America. Write for list of source materials.
1451 Masonic Ave., San Francisco, Cal. 94117.

ASSOCIATION ON AMERICAN INDIAN AFFAIRS, INC. Has available excellent bibliography on Indians and Indian affairs. Publishes bimonthly Indian Affairs Newsletter.
432 Park Ave., S., New York, N. Y. 10016.

BUREAU OF AMERICAN ETHNOLOGY. Extensive reference lists on Indian history, culture, and traditions. Write for list of materials available at nominal prices.

Smithsonian Office of Anthropology, 10th and Constitution Ave., Washington, D. C. 20560.

*BUREAU OF INDIAN AFFAIRS, U. S. DEPT. OF THE INTERIOR. Booklets and other materials on the American Indian.
Washington, D. C. 20240.

INDIAN RIGHTS ASSOCIATION. Publishes *Indian Truth* quarterly. Works to help improve the living standards of the American Indian. Map of Indian locations available.

1505 Race St., Philadelphia, Pa. 19102.

Organizations related to Latin American Affairs:

AMERICAN G.I. FORUM. Action and educational organization.

621 Gabaldon Rd., N. E., Albuquerque, N. M.

LEAGUE OF UNITED LATIN-AMERICAN CITIZENS. Works for improved conditions.

800 S. Van Ness Ave., San Francisco, Cal.

In addition most of the organizations listed in the appendix have materials related to race.

PERIODICALS AND JOURNALS

THE CITIZEN. M $3.00. An example of a segregationist, anti-civil rights publication.

Citizens' Councils of America, 315-325 Plaza Bldg., Jackson, Miss. 39201.

COMMUNITY. M $2.00. Devoted to news related to race relations. Strongly opposed to segregation and in favor of civil rights.

Friendship House, 4233 S. Indiana Ave., Chicago, Ill. 60653.

FREEDOMWAYS. Q $3.50. Articles by Negro scholars, poets, and artists on topical questions of the Negro freedom movement. Concerned with Africa, Latin America, and the U.S.

799 Broadway, New York, N. Y. 10003.

INDIAN AFFAIRS. BM $3.00 for 5 issues. Newsletter of Association on American Indian Affairs, Inc. News about Indians in America and laws and programs related to them.

432 Park Ave., S., New York, N. Y. 10016.

*INTERRACIAL NEWS SERVICE. BM $2.50 for 2 years. Articles, statistics, and suggested reading related to race relations.

Dept. of Religion and Race, National Council of Churches, 475 Riverside Dr., New York, N. Y. 10027.

INTERRACIAL REVIEW. M $4.00. Urges better race relations. Contains articles and study papers.

    Catholic Interracial Council of New York, 55 Liberty St., Rm. 2204, New York, N. Y. 10005.

JOURNAL OF NEGRO EDUCATION. Q $4.00, $1.50 per copy. Promotes the collecting of information and the conducting of investigations concerning the education, life, and welfare of Negroes and other minority groups. Stresses critical studies.

    Howard University, Washington, D. C. 20001.

JOURNAL OF NEGRO HISTORY. Q $5.00. $1.50 per copy. Treats definitively history of the Negro. Articles come from scholars and are largely concerned with the past and the extent to which that past has determined his present status.

    The Association for the Study of Negro Life and History, Inc., 1538 Ninth St., N. W., Washington, D. C. 20001.

*NEWSLETTER: NATIONAL INSTITUTE ON RELIGION AND RACE. BW $3.00. Information on civil rights movement with emphasis on roles of religious groups and particularly interreligious cooperation.

    3052 Sutherland Ave., Indianapolis, Ind. 46205.

SOUTHERN EDUCATION REPORT. BM $2.00. Supurb source of information on Negro education in the South.

    Southern Education Reporting Service, P.O. Box 6156, Nashville, Tenn. 37212.

PRINTED MATERIALS

*ACTION GUIDE FOR RACIAL JUSTICE NOW. Four booklets on (1) employment, (2) housing, (3) inclusiveness in churches, and (4) voter registration. Each sets forth suggestions for church involvement in these areas and supplies resource suggestions for further study. $.25.

*MARRIAGE ACROSS RACIAL LINES. A packet of materials for thought and discussion. $1.00.

    Council for Christian Social Action, United Church of Christ, 289 Park Ave., S., New York, N. Y. 10010.

*A CHRISTIAN APPROACH TO QUESTIONS OF INTERRACIAL MARRIAGE. Provides a basis for a rational, responsible approach to a highly emotional subject. $.10.

ON CIVIL DISOBEDIENCE. Discussion of civil disobedience within context of (1) the Christian ethic, (2) the American federal system of government. $.40.

    Service Dept. Methodist Church, 100 Maryland Ave., N. E., Washington, D. C. 20002.

A CHRISTIAN VIEW ON SEGREGATION and A JEWISH VIEW ON SEGREGATION. Two statements which illustrate the segregationist stance on race. Single copies free.

> Citizen's Councils, 207 W. Market St., Greenwood, Miss. 38930.

CHRISTIANITY AND RACE RELATIONS. Sermons and addresses from two national conferences on race. $.50.

*INTERRACIAL MARRIAGE, IS SEGREGATION CHRISTIAN? and BIBLE SPEAKS ON RACE. Three of many pamphlets on race. Deal with explosive topics in reasonable biblical approach. $.02 each.

*RACE RELATIONS: ISSUES AND ANSWERS SERIES. Problem areas in race and what Christians ought to be doing. $.05.

> Christian Life Commission, Southern Baptist Convention, 460 James Robertson Parkway, Nashville, Tenn. 37219.

*THE CHURCH SPEAKS ON CIVIL DISOBEDIENCE ($4.50 per 100) and THE CIVIL RIGHTS MOVEMENT IN THE LIGHT OF CHRISTIAN TEACHING ($6.50 per 100 and single copies free). Two studies related to the questions: "Is civil disobedience justified?" and "Should churches become actively involved in social issues, such as race?"

> Board of Christian Education, Presbyterian Church, U. S., Box 1176, Richmond, Va. 23209.

THE CHURCHES AND FAIR EMPLOYMENT PRACTICES. $1.00.

THE CHURCHES AND NON-SEGREGATED HOUSING, $2.00.

THE CHURCHES AND THE RIGHT TO VOTE. $1.00.

RACIAL INTEGRATION IN THE CHURCHES. $3.00.

SOCIAL ACTIVITIES ACROSS RACIAL AND CULTURAL LINES. $1.00.

Each of these packets is made up of pertinent literature on race relations from denominations and organizations in the intergroup relations field.

> Commission on Racial and Cultural Relations, National Council of Churches, 475 Riverside Dr., New York, N. Y. 10027.

CIVIL RIGHTS. The facts about the civil rights movement from 1960-1966. Over 402 pages of excellent material presented in news format. $3.95.

> Facts on File, 119 W. 57th St., New York, N. Y. 10019.

A CONGRESSIONAL GUIDE FOR HUMAN RELATIONS. A practical guide to be used for study by a local congregation. Though Lutheran oriented, it is helpful for all.

> Commission on Research and Social Action, The American Lutheran Church, 422 S. 5th St., Minneapolis, Minn. 55415.

THE ECONOMIC STATUS OF NEGROES. A 23-page factual booklet complete with charts. $.25.

THE PRICE WE PAY FOR DISCRIMINATION. A compilation of reputable statements indicating the high price of discrimination. $.75.

> Southern Regional Council, 5 Forsyth St., N. W., Atlanta, Ga. 30303.

EPITAPH FOR JIM CROW. Examines the historical, sociological, psychological and political forces which shape intergroup relations in the U.S., and traces the development of race relations from the nineteenth to the present century. $.75.

RACE AND INTELLIGENCE. Melvin Tumin, ed. An examination by four social scientists of the charge that Negroes have a lower intelligence than whites. $.75, paper.

> Anti-Defamation League of B'nai B'rith, 315 Lexington Ave., New York, N. Y. 10016.

FAIR HOUSING HANDBOOK. A manual of action written for those working to create and maintain inclusive communities. List of resources. $.50.

KIT OF SELECTED ITEMS. Pamphlets and booklets on discrimination in housing. $1.00.

> National Committee Against Discrimination in Housing, 323 Lexington Ave., New York, N. Y. 10016.

INTERRACIAL MARRIAGE? Proceedings of the 1958 Valparaiso University Institute on Human Relations, Valparaiso, Indiana, July 25-27. $1.00.

> Lutheran Human Relations Assoc. of America, Valparaiso University, Valparaiso, Ind. 46383.

THE MYTHS OF RACIAL INTEGRATION. Mrs. Naomi Levine. This pamphlet answers some of the imaginary fears and myths raised during group discussions on integration. $.50.

> American Jewish Congress, 15 E. 84th St., New York, N. Y. 10028.

*THE NEGRO IN AMERICA. Seeks to show the place of the Negro in American life in a concise fashion. $.25.

*THE RACES OF MANKIND. Written by two noted anthropologists, this pamphlet concisely presents the races of the world, their relation, and comparison. $.25.

> Public Affairs Pamphlets, 381 Park Ave., S., New York, N. Y. 10016.

THE NEGRO FAMILY. A 78-page booklet with many charts. Sets forth the state of the Negro family and compares the plight of the Negro with other Americans. $.45.

RACIAL ISOLATION IN THE PUBLIC SCHOOLS. A report of the U.S. Commission on Civil Rights, 1967. $1.00.

> Dept. of Public Documents, U. S. Govt. Printing Office, Washington, D. C. 20402.

THE RACE QUESTION IN MODERN SCIENCE. Series.
UNESCO has called upon outstanding anthropolgists, sociologists, biologists and psychologists of international reputation to prepare a series of publications, each dealing with a different aspect of the race question.
Titles include:
RACE AND BIOLOGY: L. C. Dunn. 46 pp. $.60.
RACE AND CULTURE. Michel Leiris. 44 pp. $.60.
RACE AND HISTORY. Claude Levi-Strauss. 40 pp. $.30.
RACE AND PSYCHOLOGY. Otto Klineberg. 36 pp. $.60.
RACE AND SOCIETY. Kenneth L. Little. 56 pp. $.60.
RACE RELATIONS AND MENTAL HEALTH. Marie Jahoda. 1960. 48 pp. $.50.
RACE MIXTURE. Harry L. Shapiro. 50 pp. $.60.
RACIAL MYTHS. Juan Comas. 49 pp. $.60.
THE ROOTS OF PREJUDICE. Arnold Rose. 35 pp. $.30.
UNESCO Publications Center, 317 E. 34th St., New York, N. Y. 10016.

*RACE RELATIONS PACKET. Selected materials on the Bible and race, prejudice, nonviolent resistance, and related subjects. $3.00.
Church of the Brethren, Elgin, Ill. 60120.

*SENSE AND NONSENSE ABOUT RACE. Ethel J. Alpenfels. 1957. 64 pp. $.75 paper. An anthropologist presents facts that explode racial myths and superstitions. Excellent bibliography. Highly recommended. For adults and youth.

THE STORY OF THE AMERICAN NEGRO. Ina Corinne Brown. 1957. $1.50 paper. Covers a 300-year period of history—from Negro civilizations of Africa through the changing social and economic patterns of the Negro in American life. For adults and youth.
Friendship Press, 475 Riverside Dr., New York, N. Y. 10027.

WHAT CHRISTIANS CAN DO ABOUT RACE RELATIONS. A pamphlet with specific, practical suggestions. $.02.
Christian Life Commission, 206 Baptist Bldg., Dallas, Texas, 75201.

AUDIO VISUALS

Excellent sources for films and filmstrips (write for catalogues):
AMERICAN JEWISH CONGESS.
15 E. 84th St., New York, N. Y. 10028.
ANTI-DEFAMATION LEAGUE OF B'NAI B'RITH.
315 Lexington Ave., New York, N. Y. 10016.
FELLOWSHIP OF RECONCILIATION.
Box 271, Nyack, N. Y. 10970.

NATIONAL CONFERENCE OF CHRISTIANS AND JEWS.
43 W. 57th St., New York, N. Y. 10019.

NATIONAL URBAN LEAGUE.
14 E. 48th St., New York, N. Y. 10017.

ALL THE WAY HOME. 16 mm. B&W 28 min. $3.50 rental. What happens in a typical suburban community when a Negro couple comes to look at a house marked "for sale?" This is a fictionalized drama that explodes the myth of "falling property values" and explores the human resources that can ease the transition to integrated neighborhoods.

BOUNDARY LINES. 16 mm. Color. 10 min. $2.50 rental. What separates people from each other? This highly stylized cartoon film with music provides a stimulating basis for a discussion of the question of prejudice and its origins.

*BROTHERHOOD OF MAN. 16 mm. Color. 15 min. $2.50 rental. Based on the pamphlet, *The Races of Mankind,* this animated cartoon outlines the basic scientific facts about racial and individual differences.
Audio-Visual Dept., Fellowship of Reconciliation, Box 271, Nyack N. Y. 10970.

BIBLICAL INSIGHT ON RACE. Tape of address by T. B. Maston 1962. Free loan.
Campus Tape Service, Broadman Films Dept., Baptist S. S. Board 127 Ninth Ave., N., Nashville, Tenn. 37203.

COLOR OF MAN. 16 mm. Color. 10 min. $3.00 rental. Produced by the University of California, this film presents a scientific explanation for the different colors of man's skin.

NO HIDING PLACE. 16 mm. B&W 50 min. $7.50 rental. Presents work of blockbusters who exploit racial fears in changing neighborhoods for personal profit. Shows how to develop community action to prevent chaos.
AFL-CIO Film Library, 815—16th St., N. W., Washington, D. C 20006.

CRESCENDO. 35 mm. Color filmstrip. 70 frames. 33-1/3 rpm recording. $7.50 purchase. Traces the Negro protest from its earliest beginnings to its present rising volume and varied expressions.
Service Center, 7820 Reading Rd., Cincinnati, Ohio 45237.

*MIXED MARRIAGES. 16 mm. B&W 20 min. $8.00 rental. Light is thrown on one of the most emotionally charged questions of the day—miscegenation. Helpful to those who ask the question "Would you want your daughter to marry a . . .?" and to those who don't ask the question.

*PROPERTY VALUES AND RACE. 16 mm. B&W 24 min. $8.00 rental. Based on careful and objective research, this film explores a widely held myth that property values always drop when a nonwhite family moves into a white neighborhood.

WE ARE ALL BROTHERS. 35 mm. Color filmstrip. Script. 61 frames. $2.50 rental. $3.50 purchase. A series of humorous stick drawings which show the basic similarity of the races of mankind, proving unquestionably that physically as well as spiritually all men are brothers.

  Office for Audio Visuals, United Church of Christ, 1720 Chouteau Ave., St. Louis, Mo. 63103.

*NO MAN IS AN ISLAND. 16 mm. B&W 28 min. $6.50 rental. Human relations is the theme of this film in which two friends, one white, one Negro, find their friendship tested by the prejudices of a community. An award-winning film. Highly recommended for young people and adults for discussion of race relations and integration.

  Augsburg Publishing House, Films Dept., 57 E. Main St., Columbus, Ohio 43215.

*OUR RACE PROBLEMS. 2 part film. B&W 29 min. each. $5.40 rental each.

  Part 1—Presents two points of view concerning the race problem in America. Mr. Harry Ashmore, editor of the *Arkansas Gazette,* Little Rock, outlines the liberal position; Mr. William Simmons, editor of *Citizen's Council* newspaper, Jackson, Mississippi, explains the conservative viewpoint.

  Part 2—Continues the discussion of the race problem in America. Dr. Benjamin Mays. Pres. of Morehouse College, Atlanta, Georgia, and Mr. Charles Burton, Assistant County Agent, Greenville, Mississippi, present the Negro point of view concerning many aspects of racial prejudice.

THE WHITE SOUTH: TWO VIEWS. 16 mm. Sound. B&W 50 min. $8.15 rental. Juxtaposes the Southern conservative viewpoint with that of the Southern liberal regarding racial relations. Interviews noted persons holding different views.

  Audio Visual Center, Indiana University, Bloomington, Ind. 47405.

WALK IN MY SHOES. 16 mm. B&W 42 min. $5.00 rental. A documentary exploring the innermost feelings of the Negro as he reacts to prejudice and discrimination in America. The film endeavors to project what it is like to "walk in the shoes" of the Negro—whether as a professional in Chicago or a laborer in New York.

  Southern Office, Anti-Defamation League, 41 Exchange Pl., S. E., Atlanta, Ga. 30303.

OTHER HELPS

ANNOTATED LISTING OF SEGREGATIONIST MATERIALS
are found in issues of *The Citizen,* usually in the January issue.
    The Citizen, 315-325 Plaza Bldg., Jackson, Miss. 39201.

BIBLIOGRAPHY ON INDIANS. An extensive, annotated bibliography on the American Indians.
    Association on American Indian Affairs, Inc., 432 Park Ave., S., New York, N. Y. 10016.

THE NEGRO IN AMERICA: A BIBLIOGRAPHY. Elizabeth W. Miller, comp. Harvard University Press. 1966. $2.95 paper. An annotated bibliography divided topically. Excellent resources.

THE NEGRO IN THE UNITED STATES: A RESEARCH GUIDE. Erwin K. Welsch. Indiana University Press. 1965. $1.85 paper. A reliable research tool for extensive study.

PUBLICATIONS. Annotated listing of resources on race relations.
    Commission on Racial and Cultural Relations, National Council of Churches, 475 Riverside Dr., New York, N. Y. 10027.

READINGS AND REFERENCES IN INTERGROUP RELATIONS. Annotated listings of books and periodicals. Excellent.
    National Association of Intergroup Relations Officials, 2027 Mass. Ave., N. W., Washington, D. C. 20036.

RESEARCH ANNUAL ON INTERGROUP RELATIONS. Melvin Tumin, ed. Frederick Praeger, Inc. $1.95, paper. Abstracts of articles and reports on research projects in many areas of intergroup relations, foreign and home.

RESOURCE UNIT ON CIVIL RIGHTS AND CIVIL LIBERTIES. Subject discussion, learning activities, list of audio-visual materials and an extensive bibliography. For teachers of elementary through senior high school grades. $.35.

RESOURCE UNIT ON PREJUDICE AND DISCRIMINATION. Subject outline, learning activities, list of audio-visual materials and an extensive bibliography. For first through twelfth grade teachers. $.35.
    Anti-Defamation League of B'nai B'rith, 315 Lexington Ave., New York, N. Y. 10016.

SEX

(See also Decision Making, Family, Homosexuality, Planned Parenthood, Prostitution, Unwed Parents, Venereal Disease)

BOOKS

AMERICAN SEX REVOLUTION. Pitirim Sorokin. Sargent. 1956. $3.50.

> A somewhat dated work that analyzes the changes in America regarding sex. It holds out the hope that America will move through the era of anarchy and establish a sane sex order.

THE ETHICS OF SEX. Helmut Thielicke. Harper & Row. 1964. $4.95.

> An exhaustive study (338 pages) of sex from a Christian theological perspective. Contains practical application of basic insights. Technical, yet readable.

LOVE AND THE FACTS OF LIFE. Evelyn M. Duvall. Association. 1963. $4.95.

> One of the very best introductions to sex for young teenagers. For reading by young people.

THE GREAT SEX SWINDLE. John W. Drakeford. Broadman. 1966. $2.75.

> An examination and refutation of current arguments favoring free love. Sets forth pro and con arguments related to sexual discipline and laxity.

PREMARITAL SEX IN A CHANGING SOCIETY. Robert R. Bell. Prentice-Hall. 1966. $4.95, $1.95 paper.

> A sociological study of trends and arguments in relation to premarital sex| Discusses forces which have influenceed premarital sexual values and behavior. Helpful for understanding current situation.

*SEX AND LOVE IN THE BIBLE. William G. Cole. Brown Books. 1959. $6.50.

> An outstanding work on the biblical understanding of sex. Probably the best reference book for pastors and counselors who wish to shed biblical light on modern sexual discussions.

SEXUAL ETHICS. A CHRISTIAN VIEW. Sherwin Bailey. Macmillan. 1963. $1.45.

> Contains sections on history, guiding principles, and specific problems. Helpful to average reader.

*TEACHING ABOUT SEX: A CHRISTIAN APPROACH. John Howell. Broadman. 1967. $3.95.

> Practical suggestions for sex education from a Christian point of view within the home and church.

WHAT CHRISTIANITY SAYS ABOUT SEX, LOVE AND
MARRIAGE. Roland H. Bainton. Association. 1957. $.75 paper.
>By a renowned historian, a well-written historical approach. Provides
helpful insight into background of current struggle over sex
standards.

*WHAT TO TELL YOUR CHILDREN ABOUT SEX. Child
Study Association Staff. Pocket Books, Inc. 1964. $.50 paper.
>Each stage of child development—infancy through adolescence—
is covered in separate sections in question-and-answer form.

*WHY WAIT TILL MARRIAGE? Evelyn M. Duvall. Association.
1965. $2.95.
>Sets forth for young people in a clear way the reasons for waiting
until marriage to have sexual intercourse.

For books on sex and the New Morality see the section on Decision
Making.

ORGANIZATIONS AND SOURCES

AMERICAN ASSOCIATION FOR HEALTH, PHYSICAL EDU-
CATION AND RECREATION, NATIONAL EDUCATION
ASSOCIATION. Sex education programs, mainly for schools,
available. Write for list of pamphlets on sex education.
>1201—16th St., N. W., Washington, D. C. 20036.

AMERICAN MEDICAL ASSOCIATION. Sex education pamphlets available.
>535 N. Dearborn St., Chicago, Ill. 60610.

*AMERICAN SOCIAL HEALTH ASSOCIATION. A number of
helpful pamphlets and booklets on sex education. Write for list.
>1790 Broadway, New York, N. Y. 10019.

*CHILD STUDY ASSOCIATION OF AMERICA. Pamphlets and
reading list on sex education for children.
>9 E. 89th St., New York, N. Y. 10028.

*FAMILY LIFE PUBLICATIONS, INC. Extensive materials for
sex education. Write for listing of counseling aids: inventories,
checklists, and prediction schedules. Excellent for persons involved in sex education and marriage counseling, especially Sex
Knowledge Inventories, Forms X and Y.
>Box 6725, College Station, Durham, N. C. 27708.

GROUP FOR THE ADVANCEMENT OF PSYCHIATRY. Research and publications in sex.
>104 E. 25th St., New York, N. Y. 10010.

GUIDANCE ASSOCIATES. Materials, filmstrips, and records for
youth on sex.
>Pleasantville, New York 10570.

SCIENCE RESEARCH ASSOCIATES. Pamphlets and bibliographies available.

> 259 E. Erie St., Chicago, Ill. 60611.

*SEX INFORMATION AND EDUCATION COUNCIL OF THE U.S. (SIECUS). Lists of materials available are found in *SIECUS Newsletter* published quarterly. Discussion guides available at $.50 each on sex education, homosexuality, and masturbation.

> 1855 Broadway, New York, N. Y. 10023.

SOCIETY FOR THE SCIENTIFIC STUDY OF SEX, INC. A medical society to disseminate information in terms of lectures, seminars, and an annual conference. They publish a *Journal of Sex Research*.

> 12 E. 41st St., New York, N. Y. 10017.

The following church-related organizations also have many helpful materials available:

BOARD OF CHRISTIAN EDUCATION, THE PRESBYTERIAN CHURCH, U.S.

> Box 1176, Richmond, Va. 23209.

CHRISTIAN LIFE COMMISSION, SOUTHERN BAPTIST CONVENTION.

> 460 James Robertson Parkway, Nashville, Tenn. 37219.

COMMISSION ON RESEARCH AND SOCIAL ACTION, THE AMERICAN LUTHERAN CHURCH.

> 422 S. 5th St., Minneapolis, Minn. 55415.

CONCORDIA TRACT MISSION.

> Box 201, St. Louis, Mo. 63166.

DEPT. OF THE CHRISTIAN FAMILY, BOARD OF EDUCATION, THE METHODIST CHURCH.

> Box 871, Nashville, Tenn. 37202.

FAMILY LIFE BUREAU, U.S. CATHOLIC CONFERENCE.

> 1312 Mass. Ave., N. W., Washington, D. C. 20005.

DEPT. OF MARRIAGE AND FAMILY, NATIONAL COUNCIL OF CHURCHES

> 475 Riverside Dr., New York, N. Y. 10027.

PERIODICALS AND JOURNALS

AMERICAN JOURNAL OF PSYCHIATRY. M $14.00, $1.50 per copy. A professional journal which often contains articles and reviews of material related to sex from a psychological point of view.

> American Psychiatric Assoc., 500 Fifth Ave., New York, N. Y. 10036.

THE JOURNAL OF SEX RESEARCH. Q $10.00. Publication of Society for the Scientific Study of Sex, Inc. Research reports, largely from medical point of view.

> Suite 1104, 12 E. 41st St., New York, N. Y. 10017.

*SIECUS NEWSLETTER. Q $2.00. Includes lists of current material available, recent books, and magazine articles.

> Sex Information and Education Council of the U. S., 1855 Broadway, New York, N. Y. 10023.

PRINTED MATERIALS

THE BIBLE SPEAKS ON SEX, TEEN TALK ABOUT PETTING, AND TEEN TALK ABOUT GOING STEADY. Attractive pamphlets for youth from a Christian viewpoint. $.02 each.

> Christian Life Commission, 206 Baptist Bldg., Dallas, Tex. 75201.

BOYS WANT TO KNOW. Briefly describes the physiological changes of boys 13 and over. $.15.

THE GIFT OF LIFE. Explains the biological facts of life. $.25.

GIRLS WANT TO KNOW. Contains facts about growing up and the biology of puberty. $.15.

KNOW YOUR DAUGHTER. For parents of girls 10-13. $.15.

KNOW YOUR SON. For parents of boys 10-13. $.15.

LET'S TELL THE WHOLE STORY ABOUT SEX. Candidly interprets the major aspects of sex education. $.20.

PARENTS TELL YOUR CHILDREN. Suggestions on answering questions asked by children between the ages of 6 and 10. $.15.

YOUR CHILD'S QUESTIONS—HOW TO ANSWER THEM. Suggestions on answering questions asked by children between the ages of 3 and 6. $.15.

> American Social Health Association, 1790 Broadway, New York, N. Y. 10019.

CATHOLIC PARENT'S GUIDE: SEX EDUCATION. A thorough, practical guide on sex education from a Catholic viewpoint. $2.95.

> Family Life Bureau, U. S. Catholic Conference, 1312 Mass. Ave., N.W., Washington, D. C. 20005.

*CHRISTIAN STUDENT AND SEX. A valuable guide to serious study. Contains annotated list of basic sources and outline of study. $.25.

United Campus Christian Fellowship Publications Office, 1720 Chouteau Ave., St. Louis, Mo. 63103.

FACTS OF LIFE FOR CHILDREN. Excellent guidance from a secular viewpoint. $.75.
> Publications Dept., Child Study Assoc. of America, 9 E. 89th St., New York, N. Y. 10028.

*SEX AND OUR SOCIETY. Pamphlet providing brief overview of sex in America. A constructive, rational approach. $.25.
> Public Affairs Pamphlets, 381 Park Ave., S., New York, N. Y. 10016.

*SEX AND THE WHOLE PERSON. Helpful resource for teachers, counselors, and pastors seeking ways to help youth in the area of sex and Christian living. Leader's Guide, $1.00. Student's Book, $.60.
> Service Dept. Methodist Church, 100 Maryland Ave., N. E., Washington, D. C. 20002.

SEX EDUCATION BOOKLETS. Seven booklets providing sex education from 8 to adult. Written to specific age levels, attractive, from a Christian point of view. $2.00.

WHY LOVE ASKS YOU TO WAIT. A positive statement on love, sex, and premarital chastity. $.25.
> Concordia, 3558 S. Jefferson Ave., St. Louis, Mo. 63118.

*SEXUAL INTEGRITY IN MODERN SOCIETY. A superb study guide from a Christian viewpoint on many aspects of sex: biblical view, premarital sexual intercourse, sex in marriage, birth control, lustful looking, artificial insemination, abortion, masturbation, and homosexuality. $.10.
> Commission on Research and Social Action, The American Lutheran Church, 422 S. 5th St., Minneapolis, Minn. 55415.

SENSE AND NONSENSE ABOUT SEX. Evelyn M. and Sylvanus M. Duvall. Another helpful work by the Duvall's geared to the level of the teenager. Reflection Book. $.50. Available in many book stores.
> Association Press, 291 Broadway, New York, N. Y. 10007.

SIECUS DISCUSSION GUIDE: MASTURBATION. A guide for group leaders or individuals. Excellent material on a seldom-discussed subject. $.50.
> SIECUS, 1855 Broadway, New York, N. Y. 10023.

AUDIO VISUALS

*A BASIS FOR SEX MORALITY SERIES. Six filmstrips, basically secular in approach. Color. Script. Guide. 33-1/3 rpm records.

Approximately 18 min. each. $3.50 rental each. $10.00 purchase each. Complete set $45.90.

LOVE, FRIENDSHIP AND MARRIAGE. 60 frames. The importance of personal relationships to physical, mental and spiritual health. How the man-woman relationship leads to mature self-hood or to personal ruination. Today's confused thinking on sex morality. Double standards. The debasing of sex through commercialization. Problems and opportunities in new-found freedoms.

THE NATURE OF SEX. 52 frames. Growing divorce rates. Increased pre-marital promiscuity. New sexual freedoms. The need for understanding and the true and deeper dimensions of sex. "Love" defined. The meaning of "oneness" in marriage in both biblical and contemporary terms. The purposes of marriage.

MAN-WOMAN RELATIONSHIP, THE. 54 frames. The growth of sexual activities through successive periods of life. Dangers and symptoms of arrested development.

PRE-MARITAL RELATIONSHIPS. 54 frames. "Erotic" feelings and "sexual" feelings defined. Chastity. Responsibility to self, lover and society. Reasons why sexual intercourse should wait for marriage.

RATIONALIZING SEX BEHAVIOR. 45 frames. Arguments used to rationalize illicit pre-marital sex behavior, and why abstinence is the wiser choice. The exclusivity of genuine love.

GUIDELINES FOR SEX BEHAVIOR. 58 frames. The problem of erotic activity before marriage. Guidelines for evaluating sexual behavior. Plotting a course through friendship, engagement and marriage. The importance of a happy marriage.

Office for Audio Visuals, United Church of Christ, 1720 Chouteau Ave., St. Louis, Mo. 63103.

BIBLICAL INSIGHT ON SEX AND MARRIAGE. Tape of address by T. B. Maston. 1962. Free loan.

Campus Tape Service, Broadman Films Dept., Baptist S. S. Board, 127 Ninth Ave., N., Nashville, Tenn. 37203.

FROM GENERATION TO GENERATION. Color. 30 min. $10.00 rental. Charming scenes of nature and family life provide setting for story. Illustrated by animated diagrams of human reproduction. Starts with ovum, continues with menstrual cycle, formation and growth of embryo, labor, and birth of child, and returns to scenes of nature and family life.

Cokesbury.

*HUMAN REPRODUCTION. B&W 23 min. $5.00 rental. Clear account of reproductive anatomy and process of normal human birth. Models and animated drawings describe reproductive organs of men and women. Shows the normality of reproduction and importance of knowledge of these facts as preparation for successful marriage and parenthood.

Audio Visual Center, Indiana University, Bloomington, Ind. 47405.

LET'S TELL THE WHOLE STORY ABOUT SEX. Four recorded conversations between parents and youth. 33-⅓ rpm. $1.50. Script $.20. For adults. HOW BABIES ARE BORN, MENSTRUATION, PROBLEMS OF GROWING BOYS, THE MARRIAGE UNION.

American Social Health Assoc., 1790 Broadway, New York, N. Y. 10019.

SEX: A MORAL DILEMMA FOR TEENAGERS. 2 full color filmstrips, 2 12″ lp records. $29.95 purchase. Part I, 89 frames, 16 min. Part II, 81 frames, 15 min. This sound filmstrip examines the many faces of sexual experimentation in the light of a morality which has substance in the eyes of today's youth. It offers answers to pressing questions in terms acceptable to youth. Especially helpful to stimulate discussion.

Guidance Associates. Pleasantville, N. Y. 10570.

SEX AND LOVE FOR CHRISTIAN TEENS. Two filmstrips. WHAT YOU THINK ABOUT SEX, 46 frames; WHAT YOU DO ABOUT SEX, 45 frames. Color. Script. Guide. Record. Produced by Family Films, 1966. $6.50 purchase each filmstrip. $10.00 each filmstrip with record. $16.50 for set. This set does a fairly complete job of introducing the Christian view of sex and raising relevant issues. The emphases on sex as part of the total person, self respect and responsibility and necessity to make decisions and set standards of behavior in light of one's beliefs are good.

T.E.A. Film Library, 4006 Live Oak St., Dallas, Tex. 75204.

SEX MORALITY TEACHING RECORD KIT. Familiarizes with today's sexual revolution and provides guides to programs. Designed mainly to help adults understand youth's views on sex. $10.00.

Bureau of Communications, National Board, YWCA, 600 Lexington Ave., New York, N. Y. 10022.

THE STORY OF MENSTRUATION. 16 mm. Color. Sound. Animated. 10 min. Free on short term loan. An educational film to help young girls approach adolescence with confidence and understanding.

THE STORY OF MENSTRUATION. 35 mm. Technicolor filmstrip. 10 min. $3.00 purchase. This animated Walt Disney Production tastefully explains a natural biological function and helps girls become confident and well-adjusted young women.

It is excellent for use in fifth grades through high school, and
by parents and adult women's groups.

Association Films.

OTHER HELPS

BOOKS FOR SELF-HELP IN SEX EDUCATION. Annotated
list of books on sex for the unmarried and married. Single
copy free.

Family Life Publications, Box 6725 College Station, Durham, N. C
27708.

RECOMMENDED READING ON SEX EDUCATION. Broad
descriptive list of books and pamphlets as helpful guides in sex
education. 16 pp. $.25.

Publications Dept., Child Study Assoc. of America, 9 E. 89th St
New York, N. Y. 10028.

SOCIAL ACTION AND WELFARE

BOOKS

CHRIST AND CULTURE. H. Richard Niebuhr. Harper. 1956
$1.60 paper.

A careful, scholarly analysis of the relation of Christians and
churches to the world from both a historical and contemporary
perspective.

CHRISTIAN ETHICS AND SOCIAL POLICY. John C. Bennett
Scribners. 1946. $2.95.

Simply written critique of four social strategies and a presentation
of a fifth. An introductory book on basic Christian social ethics.

'CHRISTIAN SOCIAL ETHICS. Albert Rasmussen. Prentice-Hall
1956. $7.95.

A basic work that seeks to utilize the influence of the Christian in his
culture—vocation, politics, reconciliation. Readable and practical

CHRISTIAN SOCIAL ETHICS IN A CHANGING WORLD.
John C. Bennett, ed. Association. 1966. $5.50.

A symposium by outstanding churchmen concerned with rethinking Christian social responsibilities. Includes such leaders as Roger Shinn, Walter Muelder, Roger Mehl, and John Bennett with their views on the theological basis of Christian social ethics.

*THE CHURCH AND SOCIAL RESPONSIBILITY. J. Richard Spann. Abingdon. 1953. $2.75.

Useful for general survey of relation of the churches to social action. Specific suggestions for applying the gospel to present-day problems.

COMMUNITY POWER STRUCTURE. Floyd Hunter. Anchor. 1964. $1.45 paper.

How to size up a community for effective social action. Practical for any group entering action to alter a community.

INASMUCH: CHRISTIAN RESPONSIBILITY IN THE 20TH CENTURY. David O. Moberg. Eerdmans. 1965. $2.25 paper.

Designed for Christian ministers and laymen as a starting point for study, thought, discussion, prayer, and work in the subject of Christian social responsibility. Should stimulate effective action on matters related to the church's mission in society.

THE RESPONSIBLE CHRISTIAN. A PROTESTANT INTER-PRETATION. Victor Obenhaus. University of Chicago Press. 1957. $4.00.

A discussion of the inseparable relation between Christianity and some of the critical social decisions of this generation.

TO CHANGE THE WORLD. Ross Coggins. Broadman. 1964. $1.50.

A brief, practical book emphasizing the Christian's responsibility to change the world through both evangelism and social action.

UNDER ORDERS: THE CHURCHES AND PUBLIC AFFAIRS.
Roswell P. Barnes. Doubleday. 1961. $2.95, $1.00 paper.

By a World Council of Churches executive. Call to and rationale for church involvement in social action. Shows different ways churches can influence the community.

WHERE TO GO FOR HELP. Wayne Oates. Westminster. 1957. $2.50.

Practical suggestions of sources of help for many personal problems and community issues.

The following books discuss various social issues and problems from religious perspective and indicate the challenge and response for which these issues call:

ASPECTS OF CHRISTIAN SOCIAL ETHICS. Carl F. H. Henry. Eardman. 1964. $3.95.

BELIEVE AND BEHAVE. Foy Valentine. Broadman. 1964. $1.50.

BIBLICAL FAITH AND SOCIAL ETHICS. E. Clinton Gardner Harper. 1960. $5.50.

CHRISTIAN FAITH AND SOCIAL ACTION. John A. Hutchison ed. Scribners. 1953. OP.

THE CHRISTIAN LIFE. Waldo Beach. CLC Press. 1966. $2.95 paper.

CHRISTIANITY AND WORLD ISSUES. T. B. Maston. Macmillan. 1957. $5.95.

CRISES IN MORALITY. C. W. Scudder, ed. Broadman. 1964 $3.50.

TANGLED WORLD. Roger Shinn. Scribners. 1965. $1.00 paper.

HOW TO DEAL WITH CONTROVERSIAL ISSUES. William M. Pinson, Jr. Broadman. 1966. $1.50.

The following books discuss various social issues and problems from a generally secular perspective; they are representative of many similar works:

CONTEMPORARY MORAL ISSUES. Harry K. Girvetz, ed Wadsworth. 1965. $3.95 paper.

CONTEMPORARY SOCIAL PROBLEMS. 2nd ed. Merton and Nisbet. Harcourt, Brace, and World. 1966. $8.95.

SOCIAL CONTROVERSY. Peterson and Matza, eds. Wadsworth 1963. $3.95 paper.

SOCIAL PROBLEMS. Cole and Miller. McKay. 1963. $6.00.

THE SOCIOLOGY OF SOCIAL PROBLEMS. 3rd ed. Horton and Leslie. Appleton-Century Crofts. 1965. $7.50.

ORGANIZATIONS AND SOURCES

NATIONAL CONFERENCE ON SOCIAL WELFARE. Publish a wealth of material of interest to social workers, agency administrators, agency board members, health and welfare councils community planners, government officials, public relations specialists, businessmen, educators, civic leaders, and allied professions: religion, law, medicine, psychiatry, psychology, sociology 104 E. 25th St., New York, N. Y. 10010.

NATIONAL SOCIAL WELFARE ASSEMBLY, INC. Central national planning and coordinating agency for the social wel fare field. Publications list available. They publish *The Assembly Letter* reporting current activities and *Service Directory of National Organizations* listing the purposes, programs, services and organizational structures for the 77 major national health, welfare and recreational agencies.

> 345 E. 46th St., New York, N. Y. 10017.

THE SALVATION ARMY. Many pamphlets, booklets, reprints and rental films.

> 120 W. 14th St., New York, N. Y. 10011.

In addition the church-related agencies and organizations listed in the appendix are directly concerned with social action.

PERIODICALS AND JOURNALS

THE ASSEMBLY LETTER. 8 issues per year. $1.50. Reports current activities of National Social Welfare Assembly, Inc.

> 345 E. 46th St., New York, N. Y. 10017.

PUBLIC WELFARE. Q $6.00. Publication focused on administration and program services in the public welfare field at Federal, state and local levels.

> Publications Dept., American Public Welfare Assoc., 1313 E. 60th St., Chicago, Ill. 60637.

In addition see the listing in the appendix of publications which deal with social issues and action. Note especially the following:

CHRISTIAN FAITH IN ACTION
CONCERN
CONCERN FOR CHRISTIAN CITIZENS
INFORMATION SERVICE, INC.
LIGHT
SOCIAL ACTION
SOCIAL PROGRESS

PRINTED MATERIALS

BASES FOR LUTHERAN SOCIAL ACTION. A biblical and theological discussion. 35 pp. 1965. $.13.

CONGREGATIONS ALERT FOR SOCIAL ACTION. Suggested for local church social action. $.03.

> Commission on Research and Social Action, American Lutheran Church, 422 S. 5th St., Minneapolis, Minn. 55415.

CHRISTIAN ACTION AND COMMUNITY SERVICE. A practical manual on how to organize the church for effective service in area of social action. $.60.

A RESOURCE GUIDE ON CHRISTIAN ACTION AND COM-
MUNITY SERVICE. Guide for planning church action on
social problems. $.10.
> Christian Board of Publications, Box 179, Beaumont and Pine Blvd.,
> St. Louis, Mo. 63166.

THE CHURCH AND SOCIAL WELFARE. H. M. Miller. A brief
pamphlet analyzing the relation of churches and welfare programs. $.10.

COMPASSION AND COMMUNITY. H. M. Miller. Includes historical perspective, current trends and problems, outline of continuing responsibilities, and practical suggestions for the church's
approach. $2.00.

*SOCIAL CHANGE AND MORAL VALUES. The how of social
change and a discussion of the role of the churches. Pamphlet
$4.00 per 100. Booklet, $.50.
> Service Dept., Methodist Church, 100 Maryland Ave., N. E., Wash-
> ington, D. C. 20002.

*THE CHURCH AND THE COMMUNITY. A resource booklet
for a church study group on social action. $1.00. Discussion
Guide, $.50. Prepared by Dept. of Social Education and Action,
United Presbyterian Church.
> Westminster Book Store, Witherspoon Bldg., Philadelphia, Pa.
> 19107.

DISCOVERING YOUR COMMUNITY. A step-by-step guide for
analyzing a community.

THE RESPONSIBILITY OF THE CHURCH IN THE WORLD.
George Chauncey. A paper developing the theme of church involvement in action to change the world.

THE ROLE OF THE MINISTER IN CHRISTIAN ACTION.
In practical way outlines the role of minister in dealing with
social issues.

*THE THEOLOGICAL BASIS FOR CHRISTIAN SOCIAL AC-
TION. The Church Speaks series. Single copy free. $7.50 per
100.

THEOLOGY OF CHRISTIAN ACTION. Basic theological pre-
suppositions for Christian social action.
> Division of Christian Action, Presbyterian Church, U. S., Box
> 1176, Richmond, Va. 23209.

FOR THE WORLD. Colin W. Williams. A look at current critical
issues calling for action.

THE SOCIAL MINISTRY OF THE LOCAL CHURCH. Muriel
S. Webb. $.30.
> Dept. of Publication Services, National Council of Churches, 475
> Riverside Dr., New York, N. Y. 10027.

A MANUAL FOR CHRISTIAN SOCIAL ACTION. A guide for the local church. $.35.

TOOL CHEST. Contains above manual and other materials for social action committees. $1.00.

> Council for Christian Social Action, United Church of Christ, 289 Park Ave., S., New York, N. Y. 10010.

SERVICE DIRECTORY OF NATIONAL ORGANIZATIONS. Outlines purposes, programs, services, organizational structures for the 77 major national health, welfare and recreational agencies, governmental and voluntary. Tells where and how to apply for services. $2.25.

> National Social Welfare Assembly, 345 E. 46th St., New York, N. Y. 10017.

*SOCIAL EDUCATION AND ACTION PACKET; SOCIAL WELFARE PACKET. Selected materials on the Christian basis, goals, and methods of social action, on the church's influence on the community, and on action programs for the local church. $3.00 each.

> Church of the Brethren, Elgin, Ill. 60120.

AUDIO VISUALS

*CALL FOR THE QUESTION. Filmstrip with 33-⅓ rpm record. Script. 53 frames. $10.00 purchase. On the synagogue and social action with recorded narration.

> Union of American Hebrew Congregations, 838 Fifth Ave., New York, N. Y. 10021.

THE WORD MADE DEED. Filmstrip with recorded narration. 15 min. Sets forth effective methods for applying the Christian faith to life in community action. $7.50 purchase.

THEOLOGICAL BASIS FOR CHRISTIAN ACTION and THE LOCAL CHURCH AND THE WORLD. Tapes by Waldo Beach. $2.50 each.

> Division of Christian Action, Presbyterian Church, U. S., Box 1176, Richmond, Va. 23209; or from TRAV, Presbyterian Church, U. S., 341 Ponce de Leon Ave., N. E., Atlanta, Ga. 30308.

THE FACTORS THAT CONFRONT US. 35 mm. Color filmstrip with 33-⅓ rpm recording. 79 frames. 15 min. $3.50 purchase for filmstrip with script. $5.00 with record. Sets forth chief social issues.

> Audio Visual Services, Room 1331, 475 Riverside Dr., New York, N. Y. 10027.

HANGMAN. Color. 12 min. $12.50 rental. 1964. An eloquent film which pierces to the conscience of humankind. Man has no choice but to speak out against all injustice, or he is doomed. Involvement as an individual moral responsibility is one of today's problems.

Contemporary Films, Inc., 267 W. 25th St., New York, N. Y. 10001.

I DON'T WANT TO GET INVOLVED. 16 mm. Color. 30 min. $15.00 rental. Deals in a dramatic way with apathy and the question of how to awaken concern for others.

Family Films, 5823 Santa Monica Blvd., Hollywood, Cal. 90038.

*SOCIAL CHANGE AND MORAL VALUES. 35 mm. Color filmstrip with 33-⅓ rpm record. 63 frames. 10 min. $10.00 sale. Outlines the changing world and suggests positive responses to help direct the change toward good ends.

WHAT HAPPENED TO HANNAH? 35 mm. Color filmstrip with 33-⅓ rpm recording. Script. Guide. 86 frames. $10.00 purchase. Hannah, a member of a local congregation, has needs which awaken the church to opportunities and responsibilities of ministry in the community.

Service Dept., Methodist Church, 100 Maryland Ave., N. E., Washington, D. C. 20002.

THIS IS THE MARK. 35 mm. Filmstrip. 20 min. $3.50 purchase. Outlines areas of social ministry.

Lutheran Church Supply Stores, 2900 Queen Lane, Philadelphia, Pa. 19129.

A TRAIN OF ACTION. 16 mm. Color. 28 min. $12.00 rental. Shows how a group can organize for effective action in a community.

*WORLD ON FIRE. 16 mm. B&W 30 min. $10.00 rental. Guide, $.10. A church council wrestles with racial tension, growing immorality, population explosion and other issues of our changing times.

Office for Audio Visuals, United Church of Christ, 1720 Chouteau Ave., St. Louis, Mo. 63103.

OTHER HELPS

SELECTED BIBLIOGRAPHIES ON SOCIAL WELFARE.

National Conference on Social Welfare, 22 W. Gay St., Columbus, Ohio 43215.

TOBACCO

(See also Alcohol, Narcotics)

BOOKS

CONSUMERS UNION REPORT ON SMOKING AND THE
PUBLIC INTEREST. Editors of Consumer Report. Consumers
Union. 1963. $1.50 paper.

> A thorough review of the medical evidence relating cigarette
> smoking to disease, a report on industry activities in connection
> with the problem, and a survey of possible steps in a program to
> deal with it.

DYING TO SMOKE. Robert Osborn and Fred Benton. Houghton.
1964. $4.95.

> A rather unusual "cartoon presentation" that graphically depicts
> what smoking does to a person's health.

HOW TO STOP SMOKING. Herbert Brean. Vanguard. 1958.
$3.50. Pocket Books, 1963, $.35 paper.

> An easy-to-read book intended for chain-smokers. Analyzes the whys
> of smoking and suggests helpful day-by-day advice that can lead to
> an end to the habit.

SMOKE SCREEN: TOBACCO AND THE PUBLIC WELFARE.
Maurine Neuberger. Prentice-Hall. 1963. $3.95.

> Treats tobacco problem from public and social perspective as well
> as personal; rather unique in this respect.

*SMOKING AND HEALTH. U.S. Surgeon General Advisory Com-
mittee. Supt. of Documents, U.S. Govt. Printing Office. $1.25.

> The definitive work in the field of smoking. Thorough and technical
> in its approach. Almost 400 pages of reports, charts, evidence, and
> conclusions linking smoking with serious health problems.

SMOKING AND YOUR LIFE. Alton Ochsner. Messner. 1964.
$3.00.

> The author is former president of the American College of Surgeons
> of the American Association for Thoractic Surgery. Presents medical
> evidence against smoking.

*TOBACCO AND AMERICANS. Robert K. Heimann. McGraw-
Hill. 1960. OP.

> A historical sketch of the evolution of the tobacco business. Very
> pro-tobacco in its approach.

*YOUNG PEOPLE AND SMOKING. Arthur H. Cain. The John
Day Co. 1965. $3.50.

> Presents the facts on smoking to young people in a concise manner.
> Leaves it to the youth to make his own decision after reading the
> various facts and opinions.

ORGANIZATIONS AND SOURCES

AMERICAN CANCER SOCIETY, INC. Research and published reports on harm of tobacco.
>521 W. 57th St., New York, N. Y. 10019.

AMERICAN HEART ASSOCIATION. Reports and pamphlets on relation of heart disease and tobacco.
>44 E. 23rd St., New York, N. Y. 10010.

AMERICAN MEDICAL ASSOCIATION. Medical reports on harmful effects of tobacco.
>535 N. Dearborn St., Chicago, Ill. 60610.

AMERICAN TEMPERANCE SOCIETY. Several small, well-done pamphlets, two periodicals *Smoke Signals* and *The Winner,* and filmstrips.
>6840 Eastern Ave., N.W., Washington, D. C. 20012.

THE CHRISTIAN LIFE COMMISSION OF THE BAPTIST GENERAL CONVENTION OF TEXAS.
>206 Baptist Bldg., Dallas, Tex. 75201.

DIVISION OF ALCOHOL PROBLEMS AND GENERAL WELFARE, GENERAL BOARD OF CHRISTIAN SOCIAL CONCERNS OF THE METHODIST CHURCH.
>100 Maryland Ave., N. E., Washington, D. C. 20002.

TOBACCO INSTITUTE. Research into tobacco and health. Publishes periodicals. Generally pro-tobacco.
>1735 K St., N. W., Washington, D. C. 20006.

PERIODICALS AND JOURNALS

LISTEN. M $3.00. Colorful, attractive journal dealing with tobacco, alcohol, and narcotics.

SMOKE SIGNALS. M $1.00. To help interpret in a popularized way the extensive tobacco research of today and encourage healthful living in the light of current findings.

THE WINNER. M except summer. $1.00. Facts on tobacco written for grade school children.
>American Temperance Society, 6840 Eastern Ave., N. W., Washington, D. C. 20012.

MEDICAL BULLETIN ON TOBACCO. 4 times a yr. free on request. Published by the American Public Health Assoc., American Heart Assoc., American Cancer Society, and the National Tuberculosis Assoc. for physicians.
>Room 1410, 1740 Broadway, New York, N. Y. 10019.

PRINTED MATERIALS

*CIGARETTE SMOKING AND CANCER. The close relation between the two is set out.

TO SMOKE OR NOT TO SMOKE. Pamphlet. Single copy free.

> The American Cancer Society, Inc., 521 W. 57th St., New York, N. Y. 10019.

*CIGARETTES AND HEALTH, IT'S NOT TOO LATE TO STOP SMOKING CIGARETTES, and **SMOKING—THE GREAT DILEMMA.** Pamphlets from secular viewpoint. Warning about the danger of smoking and offering suggestions on how to stop. $.25.

> Public Affairs Pamphlets, 381 Park Ave., S., New York, N. Y. 10016.

CONSUMER REPORTS. Jan. 1960. Comprehensive and unbiased study on cigarette smoking. Reports contain information and graphs on laboratory tests. $.60.

> Consumers Union, 256 Washington St., Mt. Vernon, N. Y. 10550.

MIND IF I SMOKE? Harold Shryock, M.D. Medical facts about smoking in relation to lung cancer, heart disease, blood pressure, and the best ways to stop smoking. 140 pp. $.75.

> American Temperance Society, 6840 Eastern Ave., N. W., Washington, D. C. 20012.

SMOKING AND HEALTH. Report of the Advisory Committee to the Surgeon General of the Public Health Service, 1964. $1.25.

*NO SMOKING. Five pamphlets especially for young people, against smoking. $.65.

> Supt. of Documents, U. S. Government Printing Office, Washington, D. C. 20402.

*SMOKING AND HEART DISEASE. Medical report on relation of tobacco to heart disease. Single copy free.

> American Heart Association, 44 E. 23rd St., New York, N. Y. 10010.

WE PREFER NOT TO SMOKE. A pamphlet which is an actual letter from a doctor to his children telling why he and his wife do not smoke. $.02.

> Christian Life Commission, 206 Baptist Bldg., Dallas, Tex. 75201.

AUDIO VISUALS

HOW TO STOP SMOKING. Filmstrip. $3.50 purchase. Gives concrete suggestions in a step-by-step program for those really anxious to stop. Proved by experience to be effective.

WHY DO SO MANY DOCTORS SMOKE? Filmstrip. $3.50 purchase. Applicable to general public, giving the psychological, physical and social reasons underlying the smoking habit. Tape with narration for both filmstrips $4.25.

> American Temperance Society, 6840 Eastern Ave., N. W., Washington, D. C. 20012.

*IS SMOKING WORTH IT? 16 mm. Color. Sound. 20 min. Free. Emphasizes the reasons for quitting and never beginning smoking.

*TO SMOKE OR NOT TO SMOKE. 35 mm. Color filmstrip. 33-⅓ rpm record. Free. Medical facts on danger of tobacco.

> Order from nearest American Cancer Society division.

*TOBACCO AND ALCOHOL. 2 full-color filmstrips. 2 12" lp records. $29.95 purchase. Part I, 76 frames, 13 min. Part II, 78 frames, 13 min. Structured to dramatize the real dangers inherent in smoking and drinking. Excellent factual presentation.

> Guidance Associates. Pleasantville, N. Y. 10570.

TOBACCO AND THE HUMAN BODY. 16 mm. B&W Sound. $4.00 rental. Produced by Encyclopedia Britannica Films. Provides medical facts on effect of tobacco.

> Cokesbury.

TOBACCO AND YOUR HEALTH. Color filmstrip with record and guide. 46 frames. 14 min. $9.50 purchase. Illustrates potential dangers to the individual. Psychological reasons underlying the attraction of smoking to teenagers; social and economic implications.

> Society for Visual Education, Inc., 1345 Diversey Parkway, Chicago, Ill. 60614.

*UP IN SMOKE. 16 mm. Color. 23 min. $7.50 rental. Weekly $22.50. This film realistically depicts the advertising and sales promotion campaigns tobacco companies stage to reach every man, woman and child in the country.

> Association Films.

UNITED NATIONS

(See also International Affairs, War-Peace)

BOOKS

*THE FIRST BOOK OF THE UNITED NATIONS. Edna Epstein. Watts. 1960. $1.00 paper.

> A clear, simple explanation of the U. N. Written for young people but helpful for all ages.

HOW UNITED NATIONS DECISIONS ARE MADE. John G. Hadwen and Johan Kaufmann. Oceana. 1961. $3.75.

> Describes the way United Nations diplomacy is carried out.

THE QUEST FOR PEACE. Andrew W. Cordier and Wilder Foote, eds. Columbia. 1965. $7.95.

> A personal tribute to Dag Hammarskjold and an analysis of the U. N. by men like U Thant, Adlai Stevenson, Ralph Bunche, etc.

*THE UNITED NATIONS AND HOW IT WORKS. David Cushman Coyle. Columbia University Press. 1965. $6.00, $.60 paper.

> The work, problems, aims, and achievements of the U. N. A comprehensive, useful source book.

THE UNITED NATIONS—DESIGN FOR PEACE. Stephen S. Fenichell. Holt, Rinehart, and Winston. 1960. $1.65 paper.

> A behind-the-scenes study of how the U. N. works in all parts of the world to remove the causes of war.

*UNITED NATIONS: STRUCTURE FOR PEACE. Ernest A. Gross. Harper. 1962. $1.95.

> Sponsored by the Council on Foreign Relations. Appraises the organization and record of the U. N. especially from the viewpoint of the U. S. Suggests ways in which the U. N. can be more effectively employed to promote the peace.

VEST POCKET HANDBOOK ON THE UNITED NATIONS. Bradford Chambers. Follett. $1.95.

> All the facts easy to find on the U. N., its specialized agencies and the U. N. missions. 357 pp.

WORLD UNDERSTANDING: A SELECTED BIBLIOGRAPHY. U.N. Association for the U.S.A., Inc. Oceana. $7.50.

> Annotated compilations of materials for teaching and learning about the U. N. organized into topical categories and graded. 288 pp.

ORGANIZATIONS AND SOURCES

AMERICAN ASSOCIATION FOR THE U. N. Kits and pamphlets on many phases of U. N. Write for list of resources.
345 E. 46th St., New York, N. Y. 10017.

*THE CHURCH CENTER FOR THE UNITED NATIONS. Center for church groups having offices related to U.N. For source of materials with religious perspective write the specific denominations.
>   777 U. N. Plaza, New York, N. Y. 10017.

COMMISSION TO STUDY THE ORGANIZATION OF PEACE. Prepares and distributes reports on the function of the U. N.
>   866 U. N. Plaza, New York, N. Y. 10017.

DEPT. OF INTERNATIONAL AFFAIRS, THE NATIONAL COUNCIL OF CHURCHES. Urges support of U. N. and publishes information on the organization.
>   475 Riverside Dr., New York, N. Y. 10027.

LEAGUE OF WOMEN VOTERS. Tape recordings and materials available on U. N.; write for list of resources.
>   1026—17th St., N. W., Washington, D. C. 20036.

*UNITED NATIONS ASOCIATION OF THE U.S.A. Publications list available. Excellent materials describe work of U. N. and urge support. They publish *Spectrum,* a journal of opinion on controversial issues and *United Nations Leaders Guide* for individual and community action.
>   345 E. 46th St., New York, N. Y. 10017.

*UNITED NATIONS, SALES SECTION, PUBLISHING SERVICE. Catalogs and book lists available.
>   New York, N. Y. 10017.

Several organizations in the United States are highly critical of the U.N. Examples of materials from such organizations can be obtained from:

AMERICA'S FUTURE, INC., 542 Main St., New Rochelle, N. Y. 10801.

CHRISTIAN CRUSADE, Box 977, Tulsa, Okla. 74102.

CHRISTIAN FREEDOM FOUNDATION, 250 W. 57th St., New York, N. Y. 10019.

PERIODICALS AND JOURNALS

COVERING THE U. N. W $3.00. Free to newspapers. News briefs of economic and social activities of U. N.
>   Room 807, 345 E. 46th St., New York, N. Y. 10017.

*UN MONTHLY CHRONICLE. M $6.00, $.50 per copy. Designed

to advance public understanding of the work of the U. N. by providing an objective, comprehensive and documented account of the organization's activities as well as information on its related agencies.

United Nations, Sales Section, Publishing Service, New York, N. Y. 10017.

UNICEF NEWS. M Free. Selection of information, feature material and news on the needs of children and youth in the developing countries and the opportunities for action, including the work of UNICEF.

UNICEF Public Information Div., United Nations, New York, N Y. 10017.

UNITED NATIONS LEADERS GUIDE. A $.25. Helps for individual and community action.

United Nations Association of the U. S. A., 345 E. 46th St., New York, N. Y. 10017.

*WORLD VIEW. M $4.00, $.40 per copy. World affairs in general discussed with information on U.N. activities.

Council on Religion and International Affairs, 170 E. 64th St., New York, N. Y. 10021.

PRINTED MATERIALS

*A CHRISTIAN'S PRIMER OF THE UNITED NATIONS. General information to help understand organization and function of the U.N. $.75.

Woman's Division of Christian Service, Board of Missions, Methodist Church, 7820 Reading Rd., Cincinnati, Ohio 45237.

A PICTORIAL BOOKLET OF THE UNITED NATIONS. 24 pp. $.75.
BASIC FACTS ABOUT THE UNITED NATIONS. 47 pp. $.25.
CHARTER OF THE UNITED NATIONS. 96 pp. $.10.
*UNITED NATIONS: WHAT YOU SHOULD KNOW ABOUT IT. 52 pp. $.35. The above contain facts and pictures of the U. N.
YEARBOOK OF THE UNITED NATIONS. Published annually. Describes work of U. N. and provides significant information on member nations. $21.75 plus postage.

Sales Section, United Nations, New York, N. Y. 10017.

*QUESTIONS AND ANSWERS ON THE U. N. Source material in question and answer form. 58 pp. $.25.
THE UNITED NATIONS AND ITS RELATED AGENCIES. Six panel folders describe role of U. N. and specialized agencies. $.10.
UNITED NATIONS: PIETY, MYTH, AND TRUTH. An appraisal of the U. N. in answer to current criticisms. 185 pp. $.85.

*THE UNITED NATIONS: WHAT IT IS . . . WHAT IT DOES
. . . HOW IT WORKS. 32 pp. $.15.
>U. N. Association of the U. S. A., 345 E. 46th St., New York,
N. Y. 10017.

AUDIO VISUALS

*INTERCOM—DIRECTORY OF WORLD AFFAIRS FILMS. A
full listing of film resources in the world affairs and U. N. fields.
Includes descriptions of films and how they can be secured. $1.00.
>U. N. Association of the U. S. A., 345 E. 46th St., New York,
N. Y. 10017.

LIST OF FILMS ON UNICEF. Available from U. S. Committee
for UNICEF, Box 1618, Church St. Station, New York, N. Y.
10008.

*List of United Nations films available from Film Distribution Officer,
United Nations, New York, N. Y. 10017. The following are
available in 16 mm. sound versions:
THE UNITED NATIONS: ITS CHARTER AND ORGANI-
ZATION. A series of 7 films on the U.N.: THE CHARTER,
THE GENERAL ASSEMBLY, THE TRUSTEESHIP COUN-
CIL AND SYSTEMS, THE ECONOMIC AND SOCIAL
COUNCIL, THE SECURITY COUNCIL, THE INTERNA-
TIONAL COURT OF JUSTICE, and THE WORLD
METEOROLOGICAL ORGANIZATION. All approximately
15 min. $5.00 rental.

THE CHRISTIAN AND THE UNITED NATIONS. Tape 36 min.
Free loan. Dag Hammarskjold speaking. Presents reasons for
and ways to support U. N.
>Reigner Recordings Library, Audio-Visual Center, Union Theologi-
cal Seminary, Richmond, Va. 23227.

FATE OF A CHILD. 16 mm. B&W 17 min. $6.00 rental. Urgent
needs of less-developed Latin American nations presented. Shows
U. N. programs effectively at work.
>Cokesbury.

FOR THE HEALING OF THE NATIONS. Filmstrip with record.
$5.00 purchase only. Describes the history and purposes of the
Church Center for the United Nations.
>Service Dept., Methodist Church, 100 Maryland Ave., N.E., Wash-
ington, D. C. 20002.

THE PEOPLE'S CHARTER. 16 mm. B&W 17 min. $2.90 rental.
Documentary on conception and early days of the U. N.

*WORKSHOP FOR PEACE. 16 mm. 24 min. $3.65 rental. The story of the U. N. headquarters.
     Audio Visual Center, Indiana University, Bloomington, Ind. 47405.

UNWED PARENTS—ADOPTION

(See also Family, Sex)

BOOKS

ADOPTED FAMILY. Florence Rondell and Ruth Michaels. Crown Publishers. 1965. $3.95.
     Two volumes, one for the parents and one for the adopted child. Helpful for the family with adopted children and for counseling such families.

*ADOPTION AND AFTER. Louise Raymond. Harper and Row. 1955. $3.95.
     Over 200 pages of helpful information on how to adopt a child and care for him.

COUNSELING THE UNWED MOTHER. Helen E. Terkelsen. Prentice-Hall. 1964. $2.95.
     While uniquely helpful to professional counselors and social workers, the book will supply guidance to anyone counseling with an unwed mother.

*CRISES IN MORALITY. C. W. Scudder, ed. Broadman. 1964. $3.50.
     A concise chapter on the unwed mother and how to help her.

LAW OF ADOPTION. Morton L. Leavy. Oceana. 1954. $3.00.
     A brief (96 pp.) presentation of the main legal factors related to adoption.

OUT OF WEDLOCK. Leontine Young. McGraw-Hill. 1954. $1.95 paper.
     Written out of experience with hundreds of unwed parents, a help-

ful, factual presentation of causes of pregnancy out of wedlock and approaches to help unwed parents.

UNMARRIED MOTHERS. Clark Vincent. The Free Press of Glencoe. 1961. $6.50.

Study of unmarried mothers from all social strata. Examines the problems of illegitimacy and premarital sex relations.

*UNWED MOTHER. Robert W. Roberts, ed. Harper. 1966. $3.25 paper.

An examination of some of the social forces which contribute to a critical attitude toward the unwed mother. Includes a psychological and sociological look at the unwed mother. A well-documented study.

ORGANIZATIONS AND SOURCES

CHILD WELFARE LEAGUE OF AMERICA, INC. Works with National Council on Illegitimacy to improve services for unmarried parents and their children. A number of helpful materials available.

44 E. 23rd St., New York, N. Y. 10010.

*CHILDREN'S BUREAU, DEPT. OF HEALTH, EDUCATION, AND WELFARE. Pamphlets and materials available on request.

Washington, D. C. 20201.

FAMILY LIFE BUREAU, U.S. CATHOLIC CONFERENCE. A number of pamphlets available on unwed parents and adoption.

1312 Mass. Ave., N. W., Washington, D. C. 20005.

NATIONAL ASSOCIATION ON SERVICE TO UNMARRIED PARENTS. Information on care of mothers and babies and help for fathers. List of sources and institutions.

171 W. 12th St., New York, N. Y. 10011.

*NATIONAL COUNCIL ON ILLEGITIMACY. Publications list available of a number of helpful materials. Most items $.35 each. NCI-Newsletter to members quarterly, subscription available to libraries for all materials at $9.00 per year. Individual membership $10.00 a year.

44 E. 23rd St., New York, N. Y. 10010.

List of maternity homes available from:

FLORENCE CRITTENTON ASSOCIATION OF AMERICA.

608 S. Dearborn St., Chicago, Ill. 60605.

NATIONAL CONFERENCE OF CATHOLIC CHARITIES.

1346 Conn. Ave., N. W., Washington, D. C. 20036.

NATIONAL COUNCIL ON ILLEGITIMACY.

44 E. 23rd St., New York, N. Y. 10010.

SALVATION ARMY NATIONAL HEADQUARTERS.
120 W. 14th St., New York, N. Y. 10011.

VOLUNTEERS OF AMERICA.
204 Throckmorton Blvd., Fort Worth, Tex. 76102.

State and local departments of public health and child welfare agencies.

PERIODICALS AND JOURNALS

FIELD REPORTER. BM $5.00. Articles, information and news about services to unmarried parents that will interest social and welfare agencies, and concerned individuals.
Florence Crittenton Association of America, 608 S. Dearborn, Chicago, Ill. 60605.

NATIONAL ASSOCIATION ON SERVICE TO UNMARRIED PARENTS NEWSLETTER. 3 times a year. Information on the association and on care and institutions for unwed parents.
171 W. 12th St., New York, N. Y. 10011.

*NATIONAL COUNCIL ON ILLEGITIMACY NEWSLETTER. Available with membership to council. $10. a yr.
44 E. 23rd St., New York, N. Y. 10010.

OURS. Q Mailed on request. Provides insight into the operation and service of a home for unwed mothers. A newsletter of the:
Edna Gladney Home, 2110 Hemphill, Fort Worth, Tex. 76110.

PRINTED MATERIALS

THE CHRONIC REVOLUTION: BIRTHS OUT OF WED-LOCK. A reprint furnishing statistical information.
Children's Bureau, U. S. Dept. of Health, Education, and Welfare, Washington, D. C. 20201.

*DIRECTORY OF MATERNITY HOMES AND RESIDENTIAL FACILITIES FOR UNMARRIED MOTHERS. Listing of approved facilities in U.S.A. $4.50.
National Council on Illegitimacy, 44 E. 23rd St., New York, N. Y. 10010.

HALFWAY TO HEARTBREAK: OUR UNWED TEEN FATHERS. One of the few materials available on unwed fathers. $.50.
Florence Crittenton Assoc., 608 S. Dearborn St., Chicago, Ill. 60605.

ILLEGITIMACY. Annotation of 34 key documents.
National Conference on Social Welfare, 22 W. Gay St., Columbus, Ohio 43215.

SO YOU ARE ADOPTED? A clearly-written pamphlet to aid in the understanding of adoption. $.35.

> Child Study Assoc. of America, 9 E. 89th St., New York, N. Y. 10028.

*SO YOU WANT TO ADOPT A BABY? A step-by-step guide to adoption with an analysis of the pros and cons of adoption. $.25.

*THE UNMARRIED MOTHER. A concise, helpful booklet from secular viewpoint. $.25.

YOU AND YOUR ADOPTED CHILD. A booklet to help answer questions and give encouragement to adopting parents. $.25.

> Public Affairs Pamphlets, 381 Park Ave., S., New York, N. Y. 10016.

*UNMARRIED PARENTS. Inexpensive booklet published by the U. S. Dept. of Health, Education, and Welfare giving statistics, causes of problem, and suggested responses. $.30. See also Health Services for Unmarried Mothers, $.25.

> Supt. of Documents, U. S. Government Printing Office, Washington, D. C. 20402.

*UNWED MOTHER, ADOPTION. Two pamphlets in a series on counseling. Especially valuable for ministers in counseling. $.02 each.

> Christian Life Commission, 206 Baptist Bldg., Dallas, Tex. 75201.

AUDIO VISUALS

*THE CHOSEN CHILD. 2 reels. Sound. B&W 52 min. $9.40 rental. Explores the process of child adoption and follows a young couple as they decide to adopt a baby. Pictures their experiences, from the contact with the welfare agency, to interviews at the agency and at home, to the climax of receiving the baby and taking it home. Comments by the narrator about problems and practices in adopting a child.

> Audio Visual Center, Indiana University, Bloomington, Ind. 47405.

THE EDNA GLADNEY HOME. 16 mm. Color. Sound. 15 min. No charge. Depicts the complete story of a home for unwed mothers, showing a resident's stay on campus, through the process of placement and adoption.

> The Edna Gladney Home, 2110 Hemphill, Fort Worth, Tex. 76110.

*FARE THEE WELL. 16 mm. B&W 20 min. $10.00 rental. Print from the Mr. Novak television series. It is the story of an appealing, well-adjusted 17-year old girl from a fine family who finds herself pregnant just a few months short of high school graduation.

*UNWED MOTHERS. 16 mm. B&W 30 min. $10.00 rental. Analysis

of the social and moral breakdown responsible for the more than 11,000 illegitimate pregnancies in Chicago each year.

Florence Crittenton Association of America, Inc., 608 S. Dearborn St., Chicago, Ill. 60605.

A FIRST INTERVIEW WITH MR. AND MRS. X, AN ADOPTION APPLICANT COUPLE. Tape. 50 min. $4.50. Helps couples seeking to adopt to understand the nature of their relation to the adoption agency.

Child Welfare League of America, 44 E. 23rd St., New York, N. Y. 10010.

A MIXED-UP LIFE. 16 mm. Color Sound. No charge. Presents graphic illustration of the work of the Volunteers of America Maternity Home, Hospital, and Child Placement Agency.

Volunteers of America, 204 Throckmorton Bldg., Fort Worth, Tex. 76102.

PHOEBE. 16 mm. B&W 29 min. $3.50 rental. Presents some of the realities and emotional aspects of premarital pregnancy, particularly as they affect the girl. Open-ended. Helpful discussion starter.

McGraw-Hill Audiovisual Institution, Coliseum 131, Corvallis, Ore. 97331.

URBANIZATION

(See also Crime, Juvenile Delinquency, Population Explosion)

BOOKS

CHURCH AND METROPOLIS. Perry L. Norton. Seabury. 1964. $2.95.

A professional city planner helps the church interpret its role in the processes of rapid change and explosive growth in the metropolis. Suggests there may be a need for a massive change in the institutional setup of the church to facilitate its effectiveness. Small, concise book.

THE CHURCH AND URBAN POWER STRUCTURE. George D. Younger. Westminster. 1963. $1.25 paper.

Focuses upon the context of power in the metropolis. The conclusion is that the church "abounding in hope" can and must share in the continuing reconstruction of metropolitan life.

*THE CHURCH RECLAIMS THE CITY. Paul Moore. Seabury. 1964. $4.95.

The focus is on a biblical, theological, historic church in the modern world ministering in a practical way to the city. Intended as a "how-to-do-it" handbook.

CITIES AND CHURCHES: READINGS ON THE URBAN CHURCH. Robert Lee, ed. Westminster. 1962. $3.50.

Presents 36 studies on the problems of the inner city churches. Helpful suggestions.

MISSION IN METROPOLIS. Jesse Jai McNeil. Eerdmans. 1965. $3.50.

A thoughtful analysis of the forces at work in our society that hamper the desire of faith to fulfill its mission for Christ. The sensitive Christian is to answer the challenge of this urbanized world with involved concern. A brief but significant book.

*THE NEW CREATION AS METROPOLIS. Gibson Winter. Macmillan. 1963. $.95 paper.

The new world of metropolis calls for new forms of the Church if there is to be a mission to the metropolitan world. The nature and form of such a mission is considered in this book.

NEW WORLD OF URBAN MAN. Constantinos A. Doxiadis and T. B. Douglass. United Church Press. 1965. $1.60 paper.

A look at modern man in his dilemma struggling for existence in the new order. Presented as a series of lectures at the University of Pennsylvania.

THE SECULAR CITY. Harvey Cox. Macmillan. 1965. $1.45 paper.

The effect of urbanization and secularization upon the traditional values and morals of religion. Suggests some rather "unorthodox" responses by Christians and churches.

SHOWDOWN IN THE CITY. Kenneth Chafin. Word. 1967. $3.50.

Analysis of the city in relation to the church. Offers positive suggestions on churches ministering in the city. Contends that the city will not be the death of the church but the occasion of rebirth.

THE SUBURBAN CAPTIVITY OF THE CHURCHES: AN ANALYSIS OF PROTESTANT RESPONSIBILITY IN THE EXPANDING METROPOLIS. Gibson Winter. Doubleday. 1961. $3.50. Macmillan, 1962, $1.45 paper.

Assesses the role of the churches in the metropolis as one of responsible participation and decries the fact that the churches are not playing a significant role in metropolitan planning. A solid book that challenges the church to rethink its ministry of renewal in the city.

*THESE CITIES GLORIOUS. Lawrence H. Janssen. Friendship. 1963. $1.75 paper.

Description of the church in North America's changing cities. Gives principles by which the church must act if it is to serve God in an urban society.

THE URBAN PROCESS: CITIES IN INDUSTRIAL SO-CIETIES. Leonard Reissman. Free Press. 1964. $6.50.

Affords a basic understanding of the dynamics of urban society and a basis for the proper steps in constructing a theory of urbanization and developing urban societies. Written by a professor of sociology at Tulane.

ORGANIZATIONS AND SOURCES

BOARD OF MISSIONS OF THE METHODIST CHURCH. Information on strategy of Christian ministry to the city.

Room 1301, 475 Riverside Dr., New York, N. Y. 10027.

*DEPT. OF HOUSING AND URBAN DEVELOPMENT. Booklet of their programs is available for $.20 from Supt. of Documents, U. S. Government Printing Office, Washington, D. C. 20402.

Washington, D. C. 20410.

*DEPT. OF CHURCH RENEWAL, DIVISION OF CHRISTIAN LIFE AND MISSIONS, NATIONAL COUNCIL OF CHURCHES. Conferences and publications of concern to the urban minister.

475 Riverside Dr., New York, N. Y. 10027.

HOME MISSION BOARD, SOUTHERN BAPTIST CONVENTION. Information on strategy of Christian ministry to the city.

161 Spring St., N. W., Atlanta, Ga. 30303.

HOUSING AND HOME FINANCE AGENCY, URBAN RENEWAL ADMINISTRATION. Publishes *Urban Renewal Notes* and has material on needed changes in the inner city and how they can be brought about.

Washington, D. C. 20410.

INSTITUTE FOR URBAN STUDIES, UNIVERSITY OF PENNSYLVANIA. Its purpose is to engage in basic research in urban problems. One of a number of such institutes created to meet the problems of growing cities.

Philadelphia, Pa. 19104.

JOINT URBAN PROGRAM, EXECUTIVE COUNCIL, EPIS-COPAL CHURCH.
> 815—2nd Ave., New York, N. Y. 10017.

UNITED STATES CONFERENCE OF MAYORS. Publishes an annual report on the problems of the cities, *City Problems*. $3.00.
> 1707 H St., N. W., Washington, D. C. 20006.

URBAN TRAINING CENTER FOR CHRISTIAN MISSION. Its purpose is to train clergy and laity for ministry and mission in the metropolis. Write for details of program.
> 40 N. Ashland Ave., Chicago, Ill. 60607.

PRINTED MATERIALS

CAN WE SAVE OUR CITIES? Primarily a discussion of the pros and cons of urban renewal as a way to help save cities. $.25.
> Public Affairs Pamphlets, 381 Park Ave., S., New York, N. Y. 10016.

*THE CHURCH AND URBANIZATION. A booklet analyzing the effects of urban culture on churches and the role of churches in such a culture. $.25.
> Council for Christian Social Action, United Church of Christ, 289 Park Ave., S., New York, N. Y. 10010.

*THE CHURCH IN AN URBANIZED WORLD. Effects of the U. S. population growth and urbanization on the church. $.25.
> Concordia Publishing House, 3558 S. Jefferson Ave., St. Louis, Mo. 63118.

DOES THE CITY HAVE A FUTURE? Background readings, bibliography, discussion questions, action suggestions. $.50.
> Distribution Center, Unitarian Universalist Assoc., 25 Beacon St., Boston, Mass. 02108.

ECONOMICS, ESTHETICS, AND ETHICS IN MODERN UR-BANIZATION. A pamphlet by Jean Gottmann on the world-wide problems of urbanization. 1962. Free.
> Twentieth Century Fund, 41 E. 70th St., New York, N. Y. 10021.

*URBAN REVIVAL: GOALS AND STANDARDS. Issue of the *Annals* related to city problems. $2.50.
> American Academy of Political and Social Science, 3937 Chestnut St., Philadelphia, Pa. 19104.

AUDIO VISUALS

*THE CHANGING CITY. 16 mm. Color. Study guides. 1962. 16 min. $5.65 rental. With photographs and animated maps, this film shows the complex character of urban and suburban life as towns grow into cities and then into metropolises. It describes the advantages of the city and reasons for its existence and importance. And it points out problems caused by city life—such as slums, minority group concentrations, overlapping governmental agencies, etc. Highly recommended.

Visual Aids Service, University of Illinois, Champaign, Ill. 61820.

THE CHANGING CITY CHALLENGES THE CHURCH. 35 mm. filmstrip in 5 sections. Guide. Color. $2.00 purchase. Sections present a factual account of physical changes that occur in a city, show groups of people caught up in these changes, show effect of the changes upon people, present the needs and problems of the people, show the services performed by the church and suggest what the individual can do about the city's problems.

Cokesbury.

*THE CITY OF NECESSITY. 16 mm. Color. Guide. 25 min. $12.00 rental. Describes urban society with particular attention to those forces distinctive to the inner city. Shows the needs and frustrations of the city in such a way that the viewer recognizes that the church's traditional ministry is no longer adequate for communicating the redemptive Gospel in an urbanized culture.

THE CLIFF DWELLERS. 35 mm. filmstrip. Color. Script. 70 frames. $2.50 rental. $7.00 purchase. Shows life in high-rise apartments and the challenge to the Church.

THE DETACHED AMERICANS. 16 mm. B&W 33 min. $6.50 rental. An "I-don't-want-to-get-involved attitude" is sweeping our country. The deep concern over this growing apathy is examined in this film.

Office for Audio Visuals, United Church of Christ, 1720 Chouteau Ave., St. Louis, Mo. 63103.

CITY SERIES. 16 mm. Six films produced in 1963 with views by one of the world's leading authorities on the city. $8.00 rental each. Based on Lewis Mumford's book *The City in History*, these films take a searching look at metropolitan growth and what it means. Filmed in many cities of the world, the series is, in fact, a master-view of all the achievements, failures and promises of urban culture.

THE CITY AND ITS REGION. B&W 27 min.
THE CITY AND THE FUTURE. B&W 28 min.
THE CITY AS MAN'S HOME. B&W 27 min.
THE CITY—CARS OR PEOPLE? B&W 27 min.
THE HEART OF THE CITY. B&W 27 min.
THE CITY—HEAVEN AND HELL. B&W 27 min.

Contemporary Films, Inc., 267 W. 25th St., New York, N. Y. 10001.

*CITY STORY. 16 mm. B&W 44 min. $12.00 rental. Produced by the National Council of Churches (Broadcasting and Film Commission) 1954. The new pastor of an inner city church is caught up in the changing community's problems. Families moving out of the area use the church for Sunday services only, yet refuse to provide week-long activity for the new members of the community. Highly recommended.

> Cokesbury.

PROFILE OF A PROBLEM. 16 mm. B&W 32 min. $8.00 rental (Free to UP-USA groups.) Produced by Board of National Missions, United Presbyterian Church, U.S.A., 1963. Through interviews and scenes of living conditions, viewers learn of the situation of three families who have been forced to leave their homes and move into run-down urban areas where churches once alive and vital in the surrounding community, have been completely or partially abandoned.

> Presbyterian Distribution Service, 200 W. Adams St., Chicago, Ill. 60606.

*URBANIZATION. 16 mm. B&W 30 min. Free. Explains problems of cities caused by continued accelerated growth, shows extent of many problem areas, and discusses "urban sprawl."

> Librarian, United States Bureau of the Census, Dept. of Commerce, Washington, D. C. 20233.

OTHER HELPS

BIBLIOGRAPHY ON POPULATION. Contains section on urbanization. Single copy free.

> Population Reference Bureau, Inc., 1755 Mass. Ave., N. W., Washington, D. C. 20036.

INTERNATIONAL BIBLIOGRAPHY AND REFERENCE GUIDE ON URBAN AFFAIRS. Rosemary H. Wallace. Ramsey. 1966. $5.00.

VENEREAL DISEASE

(See also Prostitution, Sex)

BOOKS

EDUCATIONAL APPROACH TO VENEREAL DISEASE CONTROL. Florence Benell. National Press. 1965. $1.50 paper.
> Suggestions on the control of venereal disease through education: approaches, facts, programs.

SYPHILIS: MODERN DIAGNOSIS AND MANAGEMENT. U. S. Dept. of Health, Education, and Welfare. 1960. $2.00 from U. S. Government Printing Office, Washington, D. C. 20402.
> A medical book indicating the seriousness of the disease in text and picture. Shows effect of syphilis. Helpful to shock people into concern.

VD MANUAL FOR TEACHERS. Samuel D. Allison, M.D., and June Johnson. Emerson. N.D. $2.50.
> A factual presentation of the technical side of venereal disease. Useful in teaching courses on venereal disease.

VENEREAL DISEASES. R. S. Morton. Penguin. $.95 paper.
> A popular discussion of the various types of venereal disease.

ORGANIZATIONS AND SOURCES

AMERICAN MEDICAL ASSOCIATION. Information on extent and treatment. Much valuable medical information.
> 535 N. Dearborn St., Chicago, Ill. 60610.

AMERICAN SOCIAL HEALTH ASSOCIATION. Research, public information and education dealing with venereal disease and commercialized prostitution. Excellent material available on venereal disease. Some free pamphlets; others for sale. Write for publications list.
> 1790 Broadway, New York, N. Y. 10019.

AMERICAN VENEREAL DISEASE ASSOCIATION. Professional and lay persons interested in diagnosis, treatment, and public health control of venereal disease.
> 47 Trinity Ave., S. W., Atlanta, Ga. 30334.

V. D. BRANCH, UNITED STATES PUBLIC HEALTH HOSPITAL. Specialty in treatment and information.
> 1600 Clifton Rd., N. E., Atlanta, Ga. 30333.

VENEREAL DISEASE BRANCH, PUBLIC HEALTH SERVICE, U. S. DEPT. OF HEALTH, EDUCATION, AND WELFARE. Pamphlets and statistics available.
> Washington, D. C. 20201.

PERIODICALS AND JOURNALS

*ABSTRACTS OF CURRENT LITERATURE ON VENEREAL
   DISEASE. Published 3 or 4 times a year. Up-to-date information on material available on venereal disease. Distribution at
   no charge to medical and other interested persons.
   > Public Health Service, Dept. of Health, Education, and Welfare,
   > Washington, D. C. 20201. or CDC, VD Program, Atlanta, Ga.
   > 30333.

SOCIAL HEALTH NEWS. M (except July, Aug.) $5.00. Free to
   persons with interest and activity in various fields of ASHA's
   program. Highlights ASHA program activities in field of venereal
   disease. Includes reviews of important literature in the field
   and surveys other activities of importance.
   > American Social Health Assoc., 1790 Broadway, New York, N. Y.
   > 10019.

PRINTED MATERIALS

CORKY THE KILLER. The story of the progress of syphilis in the
   human body. Presented by cartoon drawings and text. $.25.

*SOME QUESTIONS AND ANSWERS ABOUT V.D. A brief
   pamphlet giving essential facts. $.05.

TEEN-AGERS AND VENEREAL DISEASE. Helpful insight into
   attitudes and practices of young peoplt who contract venereal
   disease. Single copies free.

*TODAY'S VD CONTROL PROBLEM. A book published annually
   giving up-to-date information on the problem. Approximately
   100 pp. $1.00.

VENEREAL DISEASE. An excellent summary of past and present
   efforts to control VD. Single copies free.
   > American Social Health Assoc., 1790 Broadway, New York, N. Y.
   > 10019.

FACTS ABOUT SYPHILIS AND GONORRHEA. A 1965 publication of reliable facts and information. $1.00.

*HANDBOOK FOR VENEREAL DISEASE EDUCATION. A 1965
   publication of information and teaching suggestions. $2.00.
   > American Assoc. for Health, Physical Education, and Recreation
   > 1201—16th St., N. W., Washington, D. C. 20036.

JOHNNY GETS THE WORD. A comic book presentation of the
   facts about venereal disease. Very good for young people. $9.00
   per 100.
   > Information Materials Press, 25 W. 45th St., New York, N. Y.
   > 10036.

*VD FACT SHEET. Basic statistics on the venereal disease problem in the U.S. Published yearly. No charge.
    U. S. Dept. of Health, Education, and Welfare, Public Health Service, Communicable Disease Center, Atlanta, Ga. 30333.

VENEREAL DISEASE—A RENEWED CHALLENGE. Discussion of the current increase in VD and what steps must be taken in response. $.25.
    Public Affairs Pamphlets, 381 Park Ave., S., New York, N. Y. 10016.

WHAT THE PASTOR SHOULD KNOW ABOUT VENEREAL DISEASE. Appeared in Nov. 1965 issue of *Pastoral Psychology*. Free with self-addressed, stamped envelope.
    Family Life Publications, Inc., Box 6725, Durham, N. C. 27708.

AUDIO VISUALS

ABOUT VENEREAL DISEASE. 35 mm. filmstrip. Color. 12″ lp record. Illustrated manual. $16.50 purchase complete. Simple artwork and a lucid narration cover, in easy-to-understand fashion, the causes, effects, and treatment of the two most prevalent venereal diseases, syphilis and gonorrhea. Emphasis is placed on the early detection of the diseases, the fact that they are curable, the need to report them to responsible public health authorities, and that "quack-type" cures should be avoided.
    Bailey Films, Inc., 6509 De Longpre Ave., Hollywood, Cal. 90028.

*DANCE LITTLE CHILDREN. 16 mm. Color. Sound. 25 min. Free loan. This thought-provoking film for parents centers around a syphilis outbreak among teenagers in a typical American city. It illustrates the responsibility of the parents and gives information on the occurrence of the outbreak. Recommended by U. S. Public Health Service. 1961.
    Most state departments of public health or
    Calvin Productions, Inc., 1105 Truman Rd., Kansas City, Mo. 64106.

*THE INNOCENT PARTY. 16 mm. Color. Sound. 18 min. $1.75 rental. (Plus 30% for out of state bookings.) Presents a dramatic case history of a teenager who contracts syphilis from a casual contact and transmits it to his girl friend. Shows the emotional effects that both experience and stresses the necessity for prompt medical attention. The consequences of promiscuity and of unchecked syphilis are graphically explained by the boy's family doctor.
    The University of Arizona, Bureau of Audiovisual Services, Tucson, Arizona 85721.

THE INVADER. 16 mm. B&W Sound. 43 min. Free loan. An absorbing story of the history of syphilis beginning when it was first introduced to Europe from the Americas by the first explorers and ending with an explanation of the latest developments in venereal disease control. Along the way—with the aid of ancient woodcuts and short dramatizations—the film describes the changing attitudes toward the disease. An exceptional film for a large range of audiences.

LOOK AT A STRANGER. 16 mm. Color. Sound. 14 min. Free loan. In dramatic form, portrays an episode in the life of a young man. The film, suitable for showing to mixed groups, presents the facts about syphilis. A positive educational approach, together with the manner in which the film concludes, should encourage post-showing questions and discussion.

MESSAGE TO WOMEN. 16 mm. Color. Sound. 20 min. Free loan. Story of a young girl who contracted gonorrhea. Provides facts concerning gonorrhea and emphasizes roles played by family physician, women of the community, and the girl herself in prevention and control of venereal diseases. Designed especially for women's groups. It is not suitable for mixed audience. 1944.

From many state departments of health.

*A QUARTER MILLION TEENAGERS. 16 mm. Color. Sound. 16 min. Free loan. Shows the physiological aspects of venereal disease. The film concludes with a number of questions designed to stimulate discussion. Recommended by U.S. Public Health Service.

From many state departments of health or
Churchill Films, 667 Sunset Blvd., Los Angeles, Cal. 90012. or American Medical Assoc., Motion Picture Library, 535 N. Dearborn St., Chicago, Ill. 61610.

SIXTEEN TO TWENTY-SIX. 16 mm. Color. Sound. $5.65 rental. Designed for female audiences, this film presents the facts about the extent, transmission, course of infection, symptoms, and treatment of gonorrhea and syphilis. Is set against the background of informal discussion by a physician, and explains how these diseases can jeopardize future health and happiness.

VERY DANGEROUS. 16 mm. Color. Sound. 18 min. $5.65 rental. Discusses syphilis and gonorrhea, including the extent, transmission, course of infection, symptoms, and the treatments used. Designed for the male audience.

Audio Visual Center, Indiana University, Bloomington, Ind. 47405.

VENEREAL DISEASE AND YOUR HEALTH. 35 mm. Color filmstrip with record and guide. 40 frames. 14 min. $9.50 purchase. Frankly, realistically discusses syphilis and gonorrhea. Emphasizes need for diagnosis, treatment.

> Society for Visual Education, Inc., 1345 Diversey Parkway, Chicago, Ill. 60614.

WAR—PEACE

(See also Citizenship and Political Action, International Relations, Pacifism—Conscientious Objectors, United Nations)

BOOKS

*CHRISTIAN ATTITUDES TOWARD WAR AND PEACE. Roland H. Bainton. Abingdon. 1960. $2.25 paper.

> A history of war and peace in the West with an emphasis on Christian attitudes and action. From a pacifist slant, but bias does not dull the historian's objectivity.

*CHRISTIANITY AND WORLD ISSUES. T. B. Maston. Macmillan. 1957. $5.95.

> Two heavily documented chapters on war. Includes biblical teachings, historical survey, current Christian opinions, and a discussion of war and the Christian conscience.

NUCLEAR WEAPONS AND THE CONFLICT OF CONSCIENCE. John C. Bennett, ed. Charles Scribner's Sons. 1961. $3.95.

> A symposium by leading thinkers exploring the practical, moral, and religious aspects of nuclear war.

PEACE AND MODERN WAR IN THE JUDGMENT OF THE CHURCH. Karl Hormann. Newman. 1966. $3.50.

> A brief but thorough compendium of opinions of Popes and important theologians (451 footnotes in 101 pages) as exponents for peace in the warring world. Written by a German Catholic.

PEACE IS POSSIBLE. Elizabeth J. Hollins, ed. Grossman. 1966. $2.50 paper.

A non-technical discussion of approaches to eliminate war by persons from varying fields. Order book and complimentary study guide from World Law Fund, 11 W. 42nd St., New York, N. Y. 10036.

*PEACE! PEACE! Foy Valentine, ed. Word. 1967. $3.50.

A collection of chapters on peace from a biblical, historical, and current point of view.

THE STRATEGY OF WORLD ORDER. 4 vols. Richard A. Falk and Saul H. Mendlovitz, eds. World Law Fund. 1966. $14.00, $10.00 paper.

These semi-technical books are to be used in conjunction with *Toward a Theory of War Prevention,* also published by The World Law Fund. The titles are: INTERNATIONAL LAW, THE UNITED NATIONS, DISARMAMENT AND ECONOMIC DEVELOPMENT, WORLD PEACE THROUGH WORLD LAW.

*A STUDY OF WAR. 2 vols. Quincy Wright. University of Chicago Press. 1942. $2.95 abridged paper.

A definitive analysis of war: its history, causes, and control.

THINKING ABOUT THE UNTHINKABLE. Herman Kahn. Aron. 1964. $.95 paper.

Sets forth horrors of modern war and offers suggestions on practical responses. By a foremost academic authority on war and weapons.

WAR AND THE CHRISTIAN CONSCIENCE: HOW TO WAGE WAR JUSTLY. Paul Ramsey. Duke University Press. 1961. $6.00.

An examination of the just war theory in light of modern circumstances.

THE WAR SYSTEM AND YOU. Jok Lasley. Institute for International Studies. 1965. $1.95.

A plea for individuals to buck the warfare establishment of America and work for peace.

ORGANIZATIONS AND SOURCES

AMERICAN PAX ASSOCIATION. Association of Catholics and others who seek to promote peace and to encourage the practical application of Christian principles to the question of war.

Box 139, Murray Hill Post Office, New York, N. Y. 10016.

AMERICAN PEACE SOCIETY. Established in 1828, the society publicizes the evils of war and works for its abolishment. Distributes information on world affairs.

1307 New Hampshire Ave., N. W., Washington, D. C. 20036.

CARNEGIE ENDOWMENT FOR INTERNATIONAL PEACE. Catalog of publications available. They publish *International*

Conciliation five times a year. Their purpose is to study the causes of international war and practical paths to peace.

United Nations Plaza at 46th St., New York, N. Y. 10017.

*CENTER FOR THE STUDY OF DEMOCRATIC INSTITU-TIONS. Study papers, tapes, books on international affairs and war-peace issues.

Box 4068, Santa Barbara, Cal. 93103.

*COUNCIL ON RELIGION AND INTERNATIONAL AFFAIRS. Their work is implemented primarily through seminars, consultations and publications—the monthly *Worldview* and occasional pamphlets in a series "Ethics and Foreign Policy." List of materials available.

170 E. 64th St., New York, N. Y. 10021.

*DEPARTMENT OF STATE, U.S.A. Statements, reprints, pamphlets, etc. on war, peace, disarmament, nuclear test ban treaties, and related issues. Publications are available from Supt. of Documents, Government Printing Office, Washington, D. C. 20402.

Washington, D. C. 20520.

GENERAL COMMISSION ON CHAPLAINS AND ARMED FORCES PERSONNEL. Booklets and other material to aid chaplains and other Christians in the armed forces. Publishes monthly magazine, *The Link,* for general distribution and *The Chaplain* for chaplains.

122 Maryland Ave., N. E., Washington, D. C. 20002.

NATIONAL RESEARCH COUNCIL ON PEACE STRATEGY. Reports of scholars on issues related to world peace. Not a pacifist organization.

241 W. 12th St., New York, N. Y. 10014.

WORLD LAW FUND. Bibliographies, books, pamphlets on war and peace. Dedicated to seeking peace through law.

11 W. 42nd St., New York, N. Y. 10036.

WORLD PEACE FOUNDATION. Promotes peace by making facts of international relations available. Publishes *International Organization.*

40 Mt. Vernon St., Boston, Mass. 02108.

The following church-related organizations also have rather extensive materials available:

AMERICAN FRIENDS SERVICE COMMITTEE. Distributes large quantities of material from an anti-war perspective.

160 N. 15th St., Philadelphia, Pa. 19102.

CHRISTIAN LIFE COMMISSION, SOUTHERN BAPTIST CONVENTION.
>460 James Robertson Parkway, Nashville, Tenn. 37219.

COMMISSION ON RESEARCH AND SOCIAL ACTION, AMERICAN LUTHERAN CHURCH.
>422 S. 5th St., Minneapolis, Minn. 55415.

COUNCIL FOR CHRISTIAN SOCIAL ACTION, UNITED CHURCH OF CHRIST, INTERNATIONAL RELATIONS OFFICE.
>277 United Nations Plaza, New York, N. Y. 10017.

*DEPT. OF INTERNATIONAL AFFAIRS, NATIONAL COUNCIL OF CHURCHES.
>475 Riverside Dr., New York, N. Y. 10027.

DEPT. ON PEACE AND SOCIAL CONCERNS, BOARD OF CHRISTIAN SERVICES, GENERAL CONFERENCE MENNONITE CHURCH.
>720 Main St., Newton, Kansas 67114.

*THE DIVISION OF PEACE AND WORLD ORDER OF THE GENERAL BOARD OF CHRISTIAN SOCIAL CONCERNS OF THE METHODIST CHURCH.
>100 Maryland Ave., N. E., Washington, D. C. 20002.

U.S. CATHOLIC CONFERENCE (CATHOLIC ASSOCIATION FOR INTERNATIONAL PEACE).
>1312 Mass. Ave., N. W., Washington, D. C. 20005.

See also pacifist organizations listed in section on Pacifism-Conscientious Objection.

PERIODICALS AND JOURNALS

*FELLOWSHIP. M $3.00, $.30 per copy. A religious pacifist publication, covering such subjects as nuclear weapons, disarmament, race issues, social problems, etc. Also contains editorials on current issues, book reviews.
>The Fellowship of Reconciliation, Box 271, Nyack, N. Y. 10960.

FOREIGN AFFAIRS. Q $8.00. Published by Council on Foreign Relations, Inc. Main emphasis on international relations, but also contains scholarly articles on war and peace.
>58 E. 68th St., New York, N. Y. 10021.

INTERNATIONAL CONCILIATION. 5 times a year. $2.25, $.50 per copy. Each issue contains one original article which analyzes an important problem dealing with world affairs. Written by specialists.

Carnegie Endowment for International Peace, United Nations Plaza at 46th St., New York, N. Y. 10017.

INTERNATIONAL ORGANIZATION. Q $6.00, $2.00 per copy. A scholarly journal. Articles by authorities in the field. Summaries of activities of international organizations and a selected bibliography—U.S. and foreign—on international affairs.

World Peace Foundation, 40 Mt. Vernon St., Boston, Mass. 02108.

*WORLD AFFAIRS. Q $3.00, $.75 per copy. Publication providing information on war and peace through articles, editorials, and book reviews.

American Peace Society, 1307 New Hampshire, N. W., Washington, D. C. 20036.

WORLDVIEW. M $4.00, $.40 per copy. Book reviews, articles, and notes regarding materials available on international affairs.

170 E. 64th St., New York, N. Y. 10021.

See also periodicals listed in appendix, particularly *Between the Lines, Christian Century, Christianity and Crisis, Christianity Today, Concern, Concerns for Christian Citizens, Current History, Social Action, Social Progress,* and news magazines and newspapers.

PRINTED MATERIALS

THE BIBLE SPEAKS ON WAR AND PEACE. Brief pamphlet setting forth passages which deal with war and peace. $.02.

Christian Life Commission, 206 Baptist Bldg., Dallas, Tex. 75201.

*THE CHRISTIAN'S ROLE IN WORLD PEACE. A booklet with study guide and suggested resources for adults. $.20.

Brotherhood Commission, Southern Baptist Convention, 1548 Poplar Ave., Memphis, Tenn. 38104.

CONSPIRACY OF SILENCE. A British report on the development of chemical and biological weapons. $.25.

DISARMAMENT: A WORLD VIEW. A booklet in which 15 world leaders discuss disarmament. $1.95.

MILITARISM AND INDUSTRY. A book which charges there is a controling military-industrial complex in America. $1.65.

*PEACE REQUIRES PEACEMAKERS. Explores the idea that peace is not possible if some do not work for it. $.40.

THE ROAD TO PEACE. Essays on the means for achieving peace. $.85.

Fellowship Publications, Box 271, Nyack, N. Y. 10970.

*JUST WAR AND VATICAN II: A CRITIQUE; THE LIMITS OF NUCLEAR WAR by Paul Ramsey; MORAL TENSIONS IN INTERNATIONAL AFFAIRS by John C. Bennett; MORALITY AND MODERN WAR by John Courtney Murray . . . all $.50 each; PEACE, THE CHURCHES, AND THE BOMB, $2.00. Booklets on war by experts from a religious view point.

> Council on Religion and International Affairs, 170 E. 64th St., New York, N. Y. 10021.

ORIENTATION KIT CONCERNING THE SELECTIVE SERVICE SYSTEM. History, operation, and laws pertaining to the Selective Service. Free. Not for general distribution but available to those working on the subject.

> Selective Service System, 1724 F St., N. W., Washington, D. C. 20435.

PEACE PACKET. Selection of materials on war, militarism, pacifism, conscientious objection, nonviolence, and civil defense. $3.00.

> Church of the Brethren, Elgin, Ill. 60120.

WHY DIDN'T SOMEBODY TELL ME? A booklet for use in preparing young people for military service. Suggests options and resources for further information.

> The General Commission on Chaplains, 122 Maryland Ave., N. E., Washington, D. C. 20002.

AUDIO VISUALS

*ONE WORLD OR NONE. 16 mm. B&W 10 min. $3.00 rental. A dramatic film combining animated drawings and newsreel shots of Hiroshima, Bikini, and the Nuremberg trials, to summarize the world atomic situation and show the need for world control of atomic energy. Jr. Hi to adult.

> Visual Education Service, Church of the Brethren, 1451 Dundee Ave., Elgin, Ill. 60120.

OPERATION CROSSROADS, OPERATION GREENHOUSE, OPERATION IVY AND OPERATION SANDSTONE. 16 mm. Color. Free. Pictures of explosion of atomic weapons indicating their destructive power.

> Audio-Visual Branch, U. S. Atomic Energy Commission, Washington, D. C. 20545.

SHADOW OF HIROSHIMA. 16 mm. B&W 22 min. $3.50 rental. Produced in Japan, 1955. This film, supplied with an English sound track, pictures the effect of radiation through a series of case histories of persons who were exposed to the atomic blast in Hiroshima.

American Friends Service Committee, A-V Dept., 160 N. 15th St., Philadelphia, Pa. 19102.

*WORLD WAR II—TOTAL WAR. 16 mm. B&W 25 min. 1965. $8.00 rental. A film record, edited for schools, of the war years of 1939 to 1945. It does not minimize the brutality of war but shows how this "total war" involved almost every individual of every nation.

Contemporary Films Inc., 267 W. 25th St., New York, N. Y. 10001.

*THE WEAPONS REVOLUTION. 16 mm. B&W 29 min. $5.40 rental. Explores the world of weapons with emphasis on the revolutionary changes since World War I. Uses film clips to show the destructive potential of air power, rocket and missile power, and nuclear fission. Discusses the problems of total war, no time for preparation, and defense brought about by the advent of new weapons of war. Offers suggestions as to what can be done in international affairs to solve the problems raised by the weapons revolution.

Audio Visual Center, Indiana University, Bloomington, Ind. 47405.

OTHER HELPS

CATALOGUE OF PUBLICATIONS. Annotated listing of books on peace and international affairs. Single copy free.

Carnegie Endowment for International Peace, United Nations Plaza at 46th St., New York, N. Y. 10017.

CLASSIFIED CATALOG OF LATE LITERATURE ON PEACE, NONVIOLENCE AND RECONCILIATION. Books, pamphlets, folders, periodicals and free materials listed and described. Pacifist position. Single copies free.

Fellowship Publications, Box 271, Nyack, New York 10960.

SELECTED RESOURCES ON PEACE AND WORLD ORDER. The Methodist Church. Annotated selection of books, pamphlets, and films. Single copy free.

Service Dept., Methodist Church, 100 Maryland Ave., N. E., Washington, D. C. 20002.

APPENDIX

RELIGIOUSLY-ORIENTED AGENCIES DEALING WITH SOCIAL ISSUES

(These are useful sources of information and of denominational pronouncements on various issues.)

Assemblies of God

Spiritual Life-Evangelism
Commission
1445 Boonville Ave.
Springfield, Mo. 65802

Baptist

Baptist Joint Committee on
Public Affairs
200 Maryland Ave., N. E.
Washington, D. C. 20002

Christian Life Commission of the
Baptist General Convention
of Texas
206 Baptist Bldg.
Dallas, Tex. 75201

Christian Life Commission of the
Southern Baptist Convention
460 James Robertson Parkway
Nashville, Tenn. 37219

Div. of Christian Social Concern
American Baptist Convention
Valley Forge, Pa. 19481

Brethren

Church of the Brethren
Brethren Service Commission
1451 Dundee Ave.
Elgin, Ill. 60120

Catholic

Catholic Council on Civil Liberties
Publications Committee
P.O. Box 335
Hamburg, N. Y. 14075
or
Main Office
P.O. Box 1091
Pittsburgh, Pa. 15230

Catholic Council on Working Life
21 W. Superior
Chicago, Ill. 60610

U.S. Catholic Conference
1312 Massachusetts Ave., N. W.
Washington, D. C. 20005

National Catholic Conference
for Interracial Justice
1307 S. Wabash Ave.
Chicago, Ill. 60605

St. Thomas More Society
c/o St. Francis Xavier Church
30 W. 16th St.
New York, N. Y. 10011

Congregational

Congregational Church
2 Stimson Ave.
Providence, R. I. 02906

Disciples of Christ

Dept. of Christian Action and
  Community Service
Disciples of Christ
222 S. Downey Ave.
Indianapolis, Ind. 46207

Episcopal

Episcopal League for
  Social Action
Tunkhannock, Pa. 18657

Episcopal Society for Cultural
  and Racial Unity
5 Forsyth St., N. W.
Atlanta, Ga. 30303

Executive Council of the
  Episcopal Church
Dept. of Christian Social Relations
815—2nd Ave.
New York, N. Y. 10017

Evangelical Convenant

Evangelical Covenant Church
  of America
Chairman of Commission of
  Christian Citizenship
3225 Foster Ave.
Chicago, Ill. 60625

Evangelical United Brethren

The Evangelical United
  Brethren Church
Commission on Christian
  Social Action
601 W. Riverview Ave.
Dayton, Ohio 45406

Friends

American Friends Service
  Committee
160 N. 15th St.
Philadelphia, Pa. 19102

Friends Committee on
  National Legislation
245—2nd St., N. E.
Washington, D. C. 20005

Friends Temperance Committee
Box 4034
Philadelphia, Pa. 19118

Friends United Meeting
Board on Christian Social Concern
Board on Christian Vocations
101 Quaker Hill Dr.
Richmond, Ind. 47374

Jewish

American Jewish Committee
Institute of Human Relations
165 E. 56th St.
New York, N. Y. 10022

American Jewish Congress
15 E. 84th St.
New York, N. Y. 10028

Anti-Defamation League of
  B'nai B'rith
315 Lexington Ave.
New York, N. Y. 10016

Commission on Social Action of
  Reform Judaism
838—5th Ave.
New York, N. Y. 10021

Commission on Social Action
United Synagogue of America
3080 Broadway
New York, N. Y. 10027

Religious Action Center of the
Union of American Hebrew
Congregations
2027 Massachusetts Ave., N. W.
Washington, D. C. 20036

Social Action Commission
Synagogue Council of America
235 Fifth Ave.
New York, N. Y. 10016

Lutheran

American Lutheran Publicity
Bureau
315 Park Ave., S.
New York, N. Y. 10010

Board for Social Welfare
Lutheran Church—Missouri Synod
210 N. Broadway
St. Louis, Mo. 63125

Board of Social Ministry
Lutheran Church in America
231 Madison Ave.
New York, N. Y. 10016

Commission on Research &
Social Action
American Lutheran Church
422 S. 5th St.
Minneapolis, Minn. 55415

Division of Welfare Services
Lutheran Council in the U. S. A.
315 Park Ave., S.
New York, N. Y. 10010

Lutheran Human Relations
Association of America
Valparaiso University
Valparaiso, Ind. 46283.

Mennonites

Board of Christian Service
422 Main St.
Newton, Kansas 67114

Methodist

General Board of Christian
Social Concerns of the
Methodist Church
Division of Peace and
World Order
Division of Alcohol Problems
and General Welfare
Division of Human Relations
and Economic Affairs
100 Maryland Ave., N. E.
Washington, D. C. 20002

Board of Education
The Methodist Church
National Conference of the
Methodist Student Movement
Dept. of College and University
Religious Life
Division of Higher Education
Dept. of the Christian Family
P.O. Box 871
Nashville, Tenn. 37202

Christian Methodist Episcopal
Church
Commission on Social Action
6524—16th St., N. W.
Washington, D. C. 20012

The Methodist Federation for
Social Action (Unofficial)
11 Forest Blvd.
Ardsley, N. Y. 10502

Primitive Methodist Temperance
Society
704 Veronica Dr.
Pittsburgh, Pa. 15235

Nazarene

Church of the Nazarene
Committee on Public Morals
6401 The Paseo
Kansas City, Mo. 64131

Presbyterian

Board of Christian Education
Presbyterian Church in the U. S.
Box 1176
Richmond, Va. 23209

Div. of Homes and Christian
Welfare of the Board of
Church Extension
Presbyterian Church in the U. S.
341 Ponce de Leon Ave., N. E.
Atlanta, Ga. 30308

Office of Church and Society
United Presbyterian Church in
the U.S.A.
Witherspoon Bldg.
Philadelphia, Pa. 19107

Presbyterian Interracial Council
235 W. 53rd St.
Chicago, Ill. 60609

Unitarian - Universalist

Unitarian Universalist Dept.
of Social Responsibility
25 Beacon St.
Boston, Mass. 02108

Unitarian Universalist
Fellowship for Social Justice
245—2nd St., N.E.
Washington, D. C. 20002

Unitarian Universalist Service
Committee, Inc.
78 Beacon St.
Boston, Mass. 02108

United Church of Christ

Central Distribution Service
United Church of Christ
1505 Race St.
Philadelphia, Pa. 19102

Committee for Racial Justice Now
United Church of Christ
289 Park Ave. S.
New York, N. Y. 10010

Council for Christian Social
Action
United Church of Christ
289 Park Ave., S.
New York, N. Y. 10010

Council for Lay Life and Work
United Church of Christ
297 Park Ave., S.
New York, N. Y. 10010

Without Specific Denominational Affilation

American Council of Christian
Churches
5 Park Row
New York, N. Y. 10038

Institute of Ethics & Society
San Francisco Theological
Seminary
San Anselmo, Cal. 94960

National Association of
Evangelicals
Social Action Commission
1405 G St., N. W.
Washington, D. C. 20005

National Conference of
Christians and Jews
3 W. 57th St.
New York, N. Y. 10019

World Council of Churches
Dept. on Church and Society
Secretariat on Racial and
Ethnic Relations
475 Riverside Dr.
New York, N. Y. 10027

Commission of the Churches on
International Affairs
297 Park Ave., S.
New York, N. Y. 10010

Young Men's Christian Association
(Y.M.C.A.)
291 Broadway
New York, N. Y. 10007

Young Women's Christian
Association (Y.W.C.A.)
600 Lexington Ave.
New York, N. Y. 10022

National Council of Churches (the following departments deal extensive▶
with social concerns:)

Division of Christian Life
  and Mission
  Church and Culture Dept.
  Church Renewal Dept.
  International Affairs Dept.
  Social Justice Dept.
    Church & Economic Life
    Religion & Race
    Social Welfare
    Religious & Civil Liberties
  475 Riverside Dr., New York, N.Y. 10027

Division of Christian Education
  Educational Development Dept.
  Marriage and Family
Division of Overseas Ministries
  Church World Service Dept.
  Specialized Ministries Dept.
    World Literacy and Christian
    Literature

Note: In many states there are state councils of churches with social actic
departments.

For addresses of all religious groups and agencies see YEARBOOK C
AMERICAN CHURCHES. Constant H. Jacquet, Jr., ed. Department
Publication Services, National Council of the Churches of Christ in the U.S.▴

SELECTED PERIODICALS AND JOURNALS ON
SOCIAL ISSUES

AMERICAN JOURNAL OF SOCIOLOGY. A professional journ▶
related to sociological analysis, research, and theory in all are
of human relations, social action, and social principles. Mak
available advanced thinking in the field of sociology. BM $6.
$1.75 per copy.
       University of Chicago Press, 5750 Ellis Ave., Chicago, Ill. 6063

THE AMERICAN SCHOLAR. Published by the United Chapt◀
of Phi Beta Kappa. Deals in scholarly way with subjects
current interest. Q $4.00.
       1811 Q St., N. W., Washington, D. C. 20009.

AMERICAN SOCIOLOGICAL REVIEW. A scholarly journ▶
Contains helpful information on current social issues. BM $6.◀
$1.75 per copy.

Executive Office, American Sociology Association, 1001 Conn. Ave., N. W., Washington, D. C. 20036.

THE ANNALS OF THE AMERICAN ACADEMY OF POLITICAL AND SOCIAL SCIENCE. Issued bimonthly by the American Academy of Political and Social Science. Deals with controversial issues by presenting reliable information on all sides to aid in decision making. Each issue contains information on a current social problem. $10.00, $2 each issue.

3937 Chestnut St., Philadelphia, Pa. 19104.

AT ISSUE. Designed to deal extensively in each issue with a current controversial subject. Usually contains background readings, bibliography, and study questions. M $.50 an issue.

Distribution Center, Unitarian-Universalist Association, 25 Beacon St., Boston, Mass. 02108.

BETWEEN THE LINES. A newsletter with interpretation of current events, generally from a strong anti-war stance. By Charles Wells. BM $2.50.

BTL Circulation Dept., Newtown, Pa. 18940.

CHRISTIAN CENTURY. A nondenominational journal. Editorials and articles on matters of religious, political and social concern. Book reviews and news of the Christian world. W $8.50, $.30 per copy.

Christian Century Foundation, 407 S. Dearborn St., Chicago, Ill. 60605.

CHRISTIAN FAITH IN ACTION. A mimeographed newsletter published monthly by the Christian Life Commission of the Baptist General Convention of Texas. Carries news items, quotes, and statistics related to current issues. Sent upon request.

206 Baptist Bldg., Dallas, Tex. 75201.

CHRISTIAN LIVING. Designed to help answer the question, "What does it mean to be a Christian in a world like ours?" Emphasis on family and community. M $4.00. $.35 per copy.

Mennonite Publishing House, 610 Walnut Ave., Scottdale, Pa. 15683.

CHRISTIAN SOCIAL RELATIONS. Deals with current social issues such as race, peace, poverty. Published by the Dept. of Social Relations, Executive Council, Episcopal Church. M $2.00.

815 2nd Ave., New York, N. Y. 10017.

CHRISTIAN STATESMAN. Social problems viewed in the light of Christian teaching. Material on peace, gambling, race, liquor, smoking, education, and crime. BM $1.50. $.25 per copy.

109 Monitor Ave., Pittsburgh, Pa. 15202.

CHRISTIANITY AND CRISIS. Published by Christianity and
Crisis, Inc. An intellectual Protestant publication devoted to the
role of the Christian in today's world. Articles by ministers,
educators, scientists, and statesmen. BW 5.00. $.25 per copy.
537 W. 121st St., New York, N. Y. 10027.

CHRISTIANITY TODAY. Articles, editorials, and news features
discuss contemporary events of interest to religious leaders in
relation to the underlying theological issues. For clergymen
and laymen. BW $5.00. $.25 per copy.
1014 Washington Bldg., Washington, D. C. 20005.

COMMENTARY. Jewish publication with public affairs information. M $7.00.
165 E. 56th St., New York, N. Y. 10022.

COMMONWEAL. Catholic lay journal with some public affairs
information. M $8.00.
232 Madison Ave., New York, N. Y. 10016.

CONCERN. Carries articles on current social problems. Often an
entire issue is devoted to one problem. SM $4.00.
General Board of Christian Social Concerns of the Methodist Church,
100 Maryland Ave., N. E., Washington, D. C. 20002.

CONCERNS FOR CHRISTIAN CITIZENS. Published 8 times
yearly. Carries information on current issues. $1.00 per year.
Div. of Christian Social Concerns, American Baptist Convention,
Valley Forge, Pa. 19481.

CONTEMPORARY ISSUES. Forum for public discussion of contemporary social and political events. Frequently non-conformist
in views. Q $1.80. $.50 per copy.
Contemporary Press, P. O. Box 2357, Church St. Station, New
York, N. Y. 10008.

CRISIS. Information on issues related to social concern and action.
M $1.50.
20 W. 40th St., New York, N. Y. 10018.

CROSS CURRENTS. Explores the implications of the Christian
faith for our times. Q $3.50. $1.00 per copy.
103 Van Houten Fields, West Nyack, N. Y. 10994.

CURRENT. Abstracts from various sources and different points of
view on current issues. Economic, political, international relations main emphasis. M $8.00.
905 Madison Ave., New York, N. Y. 10021.

CURRENT HISTORY. Scholarly articles on world affairs. Helpful
bibliography. M $7.50.
1822 Ludlow St., Philadelphia, Pa. 19103.

DAEDALUS. Journal of the American Academy of Arts and Sciences. Excellent materials on current issues from reliable sources. Q $5.00.
280 Newton St., Brookline Sta., Boston, Mass. 02416.

DECISION. Deals mainly with evangelism and personal spiritual growth but also contains articles on social issues. M $2.00.
The Billy Graham Evangelistic Assn., 1300 Harmon Pl., Minneapolis, Minn. 55403.

ENCOUNTER. Journal of theological scholarship. Discusses vital issues among Christians throughout the world. Each issue is designed to cover a specific area of religious thought. Q $3.00. $1.00 per copy.
Christian Theological Seminary, Box 88267, Indianapolis, Ind. 46208.

ETERNITY. Protestant journal of theological and social thought. M $4.00. $.35 per copy.
Evangelical Foundation, 1716 Spruce St., Philadelphia, Pa. 19103.

ETHICAL OUTLOOK. Official organ of the Ethical Societies. Discussion of religious and ethical problems. SM $2.00. $.35 per copy.
American Ethical Union, 2 W. 64th St., New York, N. Y. 10023.

ETHICS. Social, political, and legal philosophy. Q $6.00. $2.25 per copy.
University of Chicago Press, 5750 Ellis Ave., Chicago, Ill. 60637.

FAITH AT WORK. Discusses application of Christian Faith to life. 8 times a yr. $3.50.
295 Madison Ave., New York, N. Y. 10017.

FOCUS. A publication of analysis and comment on public affairs. 20 issues a yr. $2.00.
Office of Public Relations, Lutheran Council in the U.S.A., 2633 16th St., N. W., Washington, D. C. 20009.

GUIDEPOSTS MAGAZINE. Stories of how people have applied religious principles to their lives. Seldom discusses in depth specific issues but helpful in general in human relations. M $2.00. $.20 per copy.
Guideposts Associates, Inc., 3 W. 29th St., New York, N. Y. 10001.

I. F. STONE'S WEEKLY. Newsletter with current news, commentary, and interpretation. W $5.00.
5618 Nebraska Ave., N. W., Washington, D. C. 20015.

INSIDER'S NEWSLETTER. News items not reported in the mass circulation periodicals. W $18.00.
Look Magazine, 488 Madison Ave., New York, N. Y. 10017.

JOURNAL OF SOCIAL ISSUES. Seeks to communicate scientific findings in the area of social-psychology in a non-technical manner. Deals with the psychological aspects of a social problem. Q $5.50. $1.50 per copy.

> Society for the Study of Psychological Social Issues, Box 1248, Ann Arbor, Mich., 48106.

JOURNAL OF SOCIAL PSYCHOLOGY. Deals with national, group, cultural, racial, and differential psychology. BM $30.00. $7.50 per copy.

> The Journal Press, 2 Commercial St., Provincetown, Mass. 02657.

KATALLAGETE. Covers religious, economic, political and social problems in the South as related to race relations. Published four times each year. $2.00.

> 1207—18th Ave., S., Nashville, Tenn. 37212.

LAW AND CONTEMPORARY PROBLEMS. Discusses issues of current legal importance giving detailed attention to their sociological, economic and political aspects. Q $7.50. $2.50 per copy.

> Duke Station, Duke Univ., School of Law, Durham, N. C. 27706.

LIGHT. Published several times a year by the Southern Baptist Christian Life Commission dealing with current ethical problems. Sent upon request.

> 460 James Robertson Parkway, Nashville, Tenn. 37219.

MEMO. Newsnotes of particular interest to concerned churchmen. $2.00.

> National Council of Churches of Christ, Washington Office, 110 Maryland Ave., N. E., Washington, D. C. 20002.

MOTIVE. Subjects of current concern in politics, culture, theology, and the arts are discussed. M (Oct. to May) $3.00. $.50 per copy.

> P. O. Box 871, Nashville, Tenn. 37202.

THE NATION. Articles, book reviews, and editorials on issues of national concern. Secular, liberal perspective in general. W $10.00.

> 333—6th Ave., New York, N. Y. 10014.

NATIONAL COUNCIL OF THE CHURCHES OF CHRIST INFORMATION SERVICE. Current information on significant social issues; often bibliographical information. BW (except July, Aug.) $3.50.

> 475 Riverside Dr., New York, N. Y. 10027.

NATIONAL OBSERVER. National and international news. Features about science, religion, medicine, education, and social issues. W $10.00. $.25 per copy.

Dow Jones & Co., Inc., 11501 Columbia Pike, Silver Spring, Md. 20904.

THE NEW REPUBLIC. Articles and book reviews on national and international issues from a secular liberal perspective. W $9.00.

1244—19th St., Washington, D. C. 20036.

OUR TIMES. A Catholic publication of general interest covering social issues, community problems, and religious news. W $5.00. $.10 per copy.

308 N. 2nd St., Yakima, Wash. 98901.

PASTORAL PSYCHOLOGY. For workers in the field of human behavior. Helps in gaining a psychological understanding of human behavior based on the scientific findings of psychiatry and psychology integrated with religious and ethical values. M (except July and Aug.) $5.00. $.50 per copy.

400 Community Dr., Manhasset, N. Y. 11030.

THE PROGRESSIVE. Public affairs information from a liberal perspective. M $5.00.

408 W. Gorham St., Madison, Wis. 53703.

PUBLIC OPINION QUARTERLY. Contains articles relating to role of public opinion, mass media, pressure groups, advertising, and public relations. Q $6.00.

Box 231, Princeton, N. J. 08540.

RELIGION IN LIFE. Directed primarly to the more scholarly minister, to university and seminary professors and students. Articles on theology, biblical studies, Christian social concerns, and related fields. Q $5.00. $1.50 per copy.

Abingdon Press, 201—8th Ave., S., Nashville, Tenn. 37203.

THE REPORTER. Public affairs information and articles on domestic and foreign events related to a wide range of interests. BW $7.00.

660 Madison Ave., New York, N. Y. 10021.

SOCIAL ACTION. Material on current social issues from a church-related and general point of view. M $2.00.

Council for Christian Social Action, United Church of Christ, 289 Park Ave., S., New York, N. Y. 10010.

SOCIAL ACTION FOR PRIESTS. Of special interest to priests but also helpful for others in gaining insight into the Catholic concept of social action. 10 times a year. Voluntary contributions.

United States Catholic Conference, 1312 Mass. Ave., N. W., Washington, D. C. 20005.

SOCIAL FORCES. Helpful sociological insight into current social issues. Q $6.00.
> University of North Carolina, Chapel Hill, N. C. 27514.

SOCIAL PROBLEMS. Official journal of the Society for the Study of Social Problems. Articles, thorough and scholarly, on current social problems. Book reviews. Very helpful for keeping up with latest information on specific problems. Q $5.00.
> P. O. Box 190, Kalamazoo, Mich. 49005.

SOCIAL PROGRESS. Deals with many areas of social concern. Race relations, international relations, economic life, and community affairs are frequently treated. BM $2.00. $.25 per copy.
> United Presbyterian Bd. of Christian Education, Witherspoon Bldg., Philadelphia, Pa. 19107.

SOCIAL QUESTIONS BULLETIN. Helpful insights and information on current affairs. M $2.00.
> Methodist Federation for Social Action, Oak Park, Ill. 60300.

SOCIAL RESEARCH. Social science publication. Articles by economists, political scientists, sociologists, social and political philosophers and psychologists. Q $7.50. $2.00 per copy.
> The Graduate Faculty of Political and Social Science of the New School of Social Research, 66 W. 12th St., New York, N. Y. 10011.

TRANS-ACTION. A national magazine for social science and modern society. Research reports and articles from the social sciences in popular language. 10 issues a year. $6.00.
> Box 1043 A, Washington Univ., St. Louis, Mo. 63130.

WASHINGTON NEWSLETTER. Public affairs newsletter with emphasis on American situation and legislation. M (except Aug.) $3.00.
> Friends Committee on National Legislation, 245—2nd St., N. E. Washington, D. C. 20002.

In addition, the national news magazines—NEWSWEEK, TIME, U.S. NEWS AND WORLD REPORT—and many popular magazines contain helpful articles on current issues.

The following newspapers are highly recommended for news of current events and social issues: NEW YORK TIMES, WASHINGTON POST, CHICAGO DAILY NEWS, CHRISTIAN SCIENCE MONITOR, ATLANTA CONSTITUTION.

AUDIO-VISUAL SOURCES WITH MATERIALS ON SOCIAL ISSUES

The following lists provide information on sources for audio-visual materials on social issues and concerns. Where more than one address is listed, write the one nearest you. The listings are made alphabetically by states followed by foreign and territorial listings.

A List of Selected Denominational Audio-Visual Libraries

(Write for catalog of available materials):

American Baptist Convention (American Baptist Films)
2855 Telegraph Ave., Berkeley, Cal. 94705.
Valley Forge, Pa. 19481.

The American Lutheran Church (Augsburg Publishing House)
3224 Beverly Blvd., Los Angeles, Cal. 90057.
426 S. 5th St., Minneapolis, Minn. 55415.
124 S. 24th St., Omaha, Neb. 68102.
57 E. Main St., Columbus, Ohio 43215.
219 W. 6th St., Austin, Tex. 78761.
2001—3rd Ave., Seattle, Wash. 98121.
806—3rd St., N. E., Calgary, Alberta, Can.

Church of the Brethren (Visual Education Service)
1451 Dundee Ave., Elgin, Ill. 60120.

Church of God (Warner Press, Inc., Dept. A-V)
P. O. Box 2499, Anderson, Ind. 46011.

Disciples of Christ (Christian Board of Publication)
Box 179, St. Louis, Mo. 63166.

Luthern Church in America (Lutheran Church Supply Stores)
3103 W. 6th St., Los Angeles, Cal. 90005.
355 N. Orange Ave., Orlando, Fla. 32801.
22 W. Madison St., Chicago, Ill. 60602.
639—38th St., Rock Island, Ill. 61201
5400 York Rd., Baltimore, Md. 21212.
122 W. Franklin Ave., Minneapolis, Minn. 55404.
17 Park Place, New York, N. Y. 10007.
32 N. 2nd St., Harrisburg, Pa. 17105.
2900 Queen Lane, Philadelphia, Pa. 19129.
818 Liberty Ave., Pittsburgh, Pa. 15222.
1233 Hampton St., Columbia, S. C. 29202.
1933 W. Wisconsin Ave., Milwaukee, Wis. 53233.
54 Robles St., Rio Piedras, P. R. 00928.
346 King St., W., Kitchener, Ont., Can.

Lutheran Church, Missouri Synod (Concordia Films)
3558 S. Jefferson Ave., St. Louis, Mo. 63118.

The Methodist Church (Cokesbury Regional Service Centers)
85 McAlister St., San Francisco, Cal. 94102.
1661 N. Northwest Hwy., Park Ridge, Ill. 60068.

1600 Queen Anne Rd., Teaneck, N. J. 07666.
201—8th Ave., S., Nashville, Tenn. 37203.
1910 Main St., Dallas, Tex. 75221.
5th and Grace Sts., Richmond, Va. 23216.

Presbyterian Church in the U.S. (TV, Radio, and Audio-Visuals)
341 Ponce de Leon Ave., N. E., Atlanta, Ga. 30308.

Protestant Episcopal Church (A-V Materials)
2451 Ridge Rd., Berkeley, Cal. 94709.
815—2nd Ave., New York, N. Y. 10017.

Southern Baptist Convention (Baptist Film Centers: 16 mm. films)
2020—8th Ave., S., Birmingham, Ala. 35233.
680 E. Shaw Ave., Fresno, Cal. 93716.
283 Peachtree St., N. E., Atlanta, Ga. 30303.
317 Guthrie St., Louisville, Ky. 40202.
125 N. President St., Jackson, Miss. 39201.
1017 Grand Ave., Kansas City, Mo. 64106.
315 N. College St., Charlotte, N. C. 28202.
208 N.W. 11th St., Oklahoma City, Okla. 73103.
2115 N. Akard, Dallas, Tex. 75201.
115 E. Grace St., Richmond, Va. 23219.
See also Baptist Book Stores for filmstrips and A-V equipment.

United Church of Christ (Office for Audio-Visuals)
1501 Race St., Philadelphia, Pa. 10102.

United Presbyterian Church in the U. S. A. (United Presbyterian Film Distribution Center)
475 Riverside Dr., New York, N. Y. 10027.

A List of Selected Producers and Distributors of Audio Visuals

(Write for catalog of available materials):

Anti-Defamation League (A-V Depts.)
315 Lexington Ave., New York, N. Y. 10016.
Regional Offices:
1715 City Federal Bldg., Birmingham, Ala. 35203.
590 N. Vermont Ave., Suite 217, Los Angeles, Cal. 90004.
40 First St., 3rd Fl., San Francisco, Cal. 94105.
623 Empire Bldg., Denver, Colo. 80202.
1184 Chapel St., New Haven, Conn. 06511.
330 Seybold Bldg., Miami, Fla. 33132.
41 Exchange Pl., S. E., Atlanta, Ga. 30303.
343 S. Dearborn St., Chicago, Ill. 60604.
222 W. Adams St., Chicago, Ill. 60606.
801-A Myers Bldg., Springfield, Ill. 62701.
108 E. Washington St., Indianapolis, Ind. 46204.
535 Gravier St., Suite 806, New Orleans, La. 70130.
72 Franklin St., Suite 504, Boston, Mass. 02110.
163 Madison Ave., Suite 120, Detroit, Mich. 48226.
635—2nd Ave., N., 303 Gorham Bldg., Minneapolis, Minn. 55403.
721 Olive St., Room 1525, St. Louis, Mo. 63101.
537 Securities Bldg., Omaha, Neb. 68102.
291 Delaware Ave., Room 201, Buffalo, N. Y. 14202.
24 Commerce St., Newark, N. J. 07102.
199 Main St., White Plains, N. Y. 10106.

82 N. High St., Suite 610, Columbus, Ohio 43215.
225 S. 15th St., Philadelphia, Pa. 19102.
908 Praetorium Bldg., Dallas, Tex. 75201.
421 Melrose Bldg., Houston, Tex. 77002.
Suite 1637, Central Natl. Bank Bldg., Richmond, Va. 23219.
1718 Smith Tower, Seattle, Wash. 98104.
1640 Rhode Island Ave., N. W., Washington, D. C. 20036.

Association Films

600 Madison Ave., New York, N. Y. 10022 (national office).
    (Branch Offices)
25358 Cypress Ave., Hayward, Cal. 94544.
561 Hillgrove Ave., La Grange, Ill. 60525.
600 Grand Ave., Ridgefield, N. J. 07657.
324 Delaware Ave., Oakmont, Pa. 15139.
1621 Dragon St., Dallas, Tex. 75207.
135 Peter St., Toronto 2B, Ont. Can.

Carousel Films

1501 Broadway, New York, N. Y. 10036.

Cathedral Films

2921 W. Alameda Ave., Burbank, Cal. 91505.

Churchill Films

662 N. Robertson Blvd., Los Angeles, Cal. 90069.

Contemporary Films

1211 Polk St., San Francisco, Cal. 94109.
614 Davis St., Evanston, Ill. 60201.
267 W. 25th St., New York, N. Y. 10001.

Coronet Films

65 E. South Water St., Chicago, Ill. 60601.

Encyclopedia Britannica Films

425 N. Chicigan Ave., Chicago, Ill. 60611 (National Office).
    Regional Offices:
5625 Hollywood Blvd., Hollywood, Cal. 90028.
277 Pharr Rd., N. E., Atlanta, Ga. 30305.
4420 Oakton St., Skokie, Ill. 60076.
26539 Grand River Rd., Detroit, Mich. 48240.
38 W. 32nd St., New York, N. Y. 10001.

Family Films

5823 Santa Monica Blvd., Hollywood, Cal. 90038.

Fellowship of Reconciliation

Nyack, N. Y. 10960.

Film Distributors International

2223 S. Olive St., Los Angeles, Cal. 90007.

Guidance Associates

23 Washington Ave., Pleasantville, N. Y. 10570.

Indiana University (A-V Center)

Bloomington, Ind. 47401.

McGraw-Hill Book Co. (Text-film Dept.)
330 W. 42nd St., New York, N. Y. 10036.

NET: National Educational TV Film Service
A-V Center, Indiana University, Bloomington, Ind. 47401.

Religious Film Libraries
2221 S. Olive St., Los Angeles, Cal. 90007.
1457 S. Broadway, Denver, Colo. 80210.
341 Ponce de Leon Ave., Atlanta, Ga. 30308.
22 W. Madison St., Chicago, Ill. 60602.
222 S. Downey Ave., Indianapolis, Ind. 46207.
426 S. 5th St., Minneapolis, Minn. 55415.
122 W. Franklin Ave., Minneapolis, Minn. 55404.
Beaumont & Pine Blvd., St. Louis, Mo. 63103.
17 Park Place, New York, N. Y. 10007.
57 E. Main St., Columbus, Ohio 43215.
240 W. 5th St., Dayton, Ohio 45402.
220 Grant St., Pittsburgh, Pa. 15219.
4006 Live Oak St., Dallas, Tex. 75204.
8 N. 6th St., Richmond, Va. 23219.
1205 N. 45th St., Seattle, Wash. 98103.

University of Michigan (A-V Center)
Ann Arbor, Mich. 48104.

University of Minnesota (A-V Education Service)
Westbrook Hall, Minneapolis, Minn. 55455.

University of Nebraska (Bureau of A-V Instruction)
Lincoln, Neb. 68508.

University of Oklahoma (Educational Materials Service)
Norman, Okla. 73069.

University of Southern California (Film Distribution Div.)
University Park, Los Angeles, Cal. 90007.

University of Texas (Bureau of Visual Instruction)
Austin, Tex. 78712.

University of Wisconsin (Bureau of A-V Instruction)
1312 W. Johnson St., Madison, Wis. 53706.

Word Records
4800 W. Waco Dr., Waco, Tex. 76703.

Check the yellow pages of telephone directories of cities near you
for information on local distributors of audio visuals.

GUIDE FOR FURTHER RESEARCH

This section is intended for those who want to go beyond the scope of this book in gathering information on a subject. Here is guidance in locating a complete list of resources and vast amounts of information on most topics.

I. *Books*

1. *Library Card Catalog.* (1) In determining what books are available in the library that you are using, check the card catalog. Begin by looking for books listed under the subject that you are researching. Often the catalog will suggest cross references for you to examine. Make a list of the call numbers (the number the library has assigned the book) of the books under your subject and check out the books to see if they meet your need. (2) If you have a list of books on a subject that you want to examine, look up the books in the card catalog using either the title of the book or the name of the author. Note the call numbers of the books and check them out.

2. *Books in Print.* Most libraries and book stores have copies of *Subject Guide to Books in Print, U.S.A.* (R. R. Bowker Co., 1180 Ave. of the Americas, New York, N. Y. 10036). This volume, published each year, contains a list of books in print by most publishers in the United States. It is organized according to subject and is therefore especially valuable in locating books on current issues. Title, author, publisher, date of publication, and price are included for each listing.

3. *Other Books.* For a listing of books by subject more complete than those found in *Books in Print,* see: (1) *Library of Congress Catalog, Books: Subjects, a Cumulative List of Works Represented by Library of Congress Printed Cards,* 3 vols., 1965, and (2) *Cumulative Book Index, World List of Books in the English Language* (published every two years). These two sources list (a) books published both in and outside of the United States and (b) recent books both in and out of print.

4. *Book Reviews.* Often a book review will help determine whether a book you have located in *Books in Print* or another source is worth purchasing. The following publications will help locate reviews of specific books: *Book Review Digest* (selected book reviews from about 75 American and English periodicals with brief excerpts) and *Book Review Index* (a guide to book reviews appearing in all media of general circuation—monthly with quarterly cumulations).

5. *Encyclopedias*. Encyclopedias seldom provide exhaustive information on a subject, but they often serve as an excellent introduction to information on a subject. Consult leading encyclopedias on the topic you are researching.

II. *Organizations*

The most complete guide to organizations in the United States is the *Encyclopedia of Associations:* Vol. I *National Organizations of the United States,* Vol. II *Geographic and Executive Index,* Vol. III *New Associations* (Gale Research Co., Book Tower, Detroit, Michigan). It will be found in most large libraries. Volume I contains a list of organizations according to general and specific interest. The address, membership, function, and publications of each organization, plus other information, are listed. In addition, the volume carries an alphabetical index of all organizations so that an address can be found quickly. Volume II lists the information of Volume I according to geograhic areas. Volume III is a loose-leaf binder to store supplements which keep the material up to date.

Also helpful is *Directory of Centers for the Study of Society* (1965) available from Towne House Publishers, 1942 Shattuck Ave., Berkeley, Cal. for $5.00. Lists and describes over 165 organizations.

These volumes should be consulted when you are doing depth research. List pertinent organizations with their addresses and write them to secure up-to-date information.

III. *Periodicals and Journals*

Using the two following approaches, list periodicals and articles related to the subject of your research. Then secure these materials from the serials section of the library.

1. *Publications on the Subject.*

For an extensive listing of American periodicals and journals according to subject and interest, the most complete source is *The Standard Periodical Directory* (Oxbridge Publishing Co., Inc., 420 Lexington Ave., New York, N. Y. 10017). This volume lists over 39,000 periodicals published in the United States and Canada and contains an introduction on how to discover periodicals covering a specific subject. Address, cost, and frequency of publication are listed for each periodical.

2. *Articles and Stories on the Subject.*

A number of reference books are useful in discovering articles and stories on a specific subject. Two of the most helpful are: *Readers' Guide to Periodical Literature* (an author, subject, and title index to about 130 leading magazines since 1900) and *International Index to Periodicals* (an index of about 170 titles in the humanities and social sciences according to subject and author).

IV. *Printed Materials*

The pamphlets, booklets, and tracts on many subjects are too numerous for a list to be practical. The best source of printed materials will usually be organizations which deal with the subject in which you are interested. (See Organizations.)

In addition, the United States government, which produces more printed materials than any other source, should be consulted. Write to the Dept. of Public Documents, U.S. Government Printing Office, Washington, D. C. 20402, and request a list of available materials on the subject you are researching. Consult also the following from the U.S. Government Printing Office: (1) the monthly and annual subject index to *United States Government Publications: Monthly Catalog,* (2) *Price Lists,* arranged by subjects with prices for individual publications, (3) *Selected U.S. Govt. Publications,* free BW publication listing samples of available materials.

Most large libraries have extensive holdings of booklets, pamphlets, and tracts. These are often stored by subject and indexed. Ask the librarian to show you the pamphlet index, usually called the Vertical File, or to help you locate materials.

V. *Audio Visuals*

Thousands of audio-visual aids are available. The following publications will help you locate those which deal with specific subjects:

(1) *Audio-Visual Resource Guide.* Published biennially by the Department of Educational Development of the National Council of Churches. Contains more than 3,000 classified evaluations of films, filmstrips and price information are supplied for each listing. Contains subject index and list of rental and purchase sources for audio visuals.

(2) *Educational Film Guide.* Wilson. Annual. Catalog of current 16 mm. educational films. Lists and describes more than 6,000 films. Includes subject index and directory of film sources.

(3) *Library of Congress Catalog: Motion Pictures and Filmstrips.* Catalog of films and filmstrips cataloged by the Library of

Congress with a subject index. Printed in three quarterly issues with annual cumulations. Lacks prices or rental information.

In addition, consult the Audio-Visual Appendix for a list of rental and purchase centers for audio visuals. Most of the agencies listed will supply catalogs on request. The following audio-visual centers have catalogs which are especially extensive and helpful.

Audio-Visual Center, Indiana University, Bloomington, Indiana 47401.

Visual Aids Service, University of Illinois, Champaign, Illinois 61820.

Visual Instruction Bureau, University of Texas, Austin, Texas 78712.

The Cokesbury Projector, Cokesbury, 201 Eighth Avenue South, Nashville, Tennessee 37203.

Film Log, Baptist Film Centers, Book Store Division, Sunday School Board, 127 Ninth Avenue North, Nashville, Tennessee 37203.

Reigner Recording Library, Audio-Visual Center, Union Theological Seminary, Richmond, Va. 23227.

VI. *Other Helps*

1. *Books on Research.* Consult books on library use and research for more extensive guides on depth research. The following are very helpful: *How to Do Library Research.* Robert B. Downs. University of Illinois Press. 1966. $1.45 paper.
   Research Manual: For College Studies and Papers. Cecil B. Williams and Allan H. Stevenson. 3rd ed. Harper. 1963. $2.50 paper.

2. *Librarians.* A skilled, trained librarian can be of great help in research. In large libraries, consult the librarian in charge of reference and research. The librarian will not do the research for you. He will, however, direct you to sources of information and save you a great deal of time.

3. *Interviews and Correspondence.* Persons who are experts or leading authorities on the subject that you are investigating can supply valuable insights and information. If possible, arrange for an interview. Otherwise, write a letter requesting information.

   Always state concisely and clearly what you want to know. Be specific. You may want to request suggestions on sources for excellent study or ask for facts and information. Be brief in interviews or in correspondence.